#61,849

D1124345

CP 17

Bitter Legacy

Bitter Legacy

POLISH-AMERICAN RELATIONS IN THE WAKE OF WORLD WAR II

Richard C. Lukas

THE UNIVERSITY PRESS OF KENTUCKY

Library of Congress Cataloging in Publication Data

Lukas, Richard C., 1937–
 Bitter legacy.

  Bibliography: p.
  Includes index.
   1. United States—Foreign relations—Poland. 2. Poland—Foreign
relations—United States. 3. Poland—Politics and government—1945-
4. United States—Foreign relations—1945-1953.
I. Title.
E183.8.P7L84   327.730438   82-1972
 ISBN 0-8131-1460-8   AACR2

Contents

To My Father, Franciszek

Preface

For a long time there has been a need for a detailed account of United States-Polish relations in the years immediately following World War II, the crucial period during which Poland became a Soviet satellite. This book not only deals with the political and economic relations between the United States and Poland but also explores the impact of these relations on such postwar issues as relief, repatriation, Polish American opinion, and most importantly the origins of the Cold War.

Many people have helped with this book, and it is a pleasure for me to thank them here for their assistance. To B.F. Jones, Richard Fraser, Wallace Prescott, and Arliss Roaden—all at Tennessee Technological University—I am indebted for the reduction in my teaching load and for some of the funds that enabled me to travel to the depositories where most of the research material for this book is located.

I owe a special debt to Tim Callahan, Pat Eggleston, Betty Huehls, Andrew Sorokowski, and Steve Williams for helping me with some of the research that has gone into this study.

Daniel Buczek was especially kind in providing me with material from the files of the Rev. A.A. Skoniecki. James Bochan, Waclaw Jedrejewicz, B.B. Kopecki, Stefan Korbonski, Pelagia Lukaszewska, Wanda Rozmarek, and Paul Zaleski shared their knowledge and personal experiences with me, greatly enriching my understanding of important aspects of the subject.

I am indebted to the librarians and archivists of the many institutions I visited to gather material for this study. Without exception they were efficient and unfailingly kind to me.

Linda Ogletree, who acquired material through interlibrary loan services for me, was most helpful. My thanks to Lois Richardson, who typed the rough draft of the manuscript, and Linda McDearman, who did the final copy. I am grateful to Nolan Fowler for helping me read proof, and also to Harry Lane for drawing the map.

Without the financial aid of the Kosciuszko Foundation, the American Council of Learned Societies, and the Social Science Research Council, this book would not have been a reality. To be sure, the findings and conclusions presented here do not necessarily represent the view of these donors.

My gratitude to my wife, Marita, can not be adequately expressed in words.

I The Road to Potsdam

Recent events in Poland have reawakened considerable American interest in that country. One of the questions often raised today is how did Poland become a communist state. This study, which focuses on Poland from the Potsdam Conference through the elections of 1947, is an attempt to fill a major gap in the historical literature by offering a detailed account of why United States policy was unable to reverse the process begun at the Yalta Conference that transformed Poland into a Soviet satellite.

American policy toward postwar Poland was based upon the unrealistic belief that the United States would be able to exert some political influence in an area that had been written off as a Soviet sphere of influence by the Roosevelt administration. Largely through economic diplomacy, the United States expected to maintain a presence in Poland and to insure that the Polish Peasant party of Stanislaw Mikolajczyk, the former premier of the Polish government-in-exile who took a seat in the provisional government in Warsaw, would have a place in the political life of Poland. On their part, Mikolajczyk and his supporters were just as unrealistic as the Americans in insisting upon free elections which the communists could not allow because an open expression of opinion by the Polish people would have expelled them from power. The failure of the communist-dominated block and Mikolajczyk's party to reach a modus vivendi doomed the hopes and expectations of the American and Polish people and underscored the limitations of American policy in an area where the Soviets were dominant and were determined to exclude American influence.

The Polish question, which had dominated so many of the discussions of the leaders of the Big Three during the war, continued to occupy a major place at Potsdam, the last meeting of the leaders of the victorious anti-German coalition. Although Poland's eastern frontier had already been decided and the Allied powers had supervised the establishment of a communist-dominated Polish provisional government of national unity, two major questions remained to be settled —the implementation of the Yalta Conference pledge that the Warsaw regime conduct "free and unfettered elections" to establish a permanent government in Poland and the settlement of Poland's boundary with Germany.

The long and tortuous road to Potsdam was not an easy one. After
the ill-fated September campaign of 1939, the Polish government fled
into exile and eventually found its permanent wartime home in London, from which it maintained contact with underground political
and military authorities in Poland. The London Poles, as they were
called, were recognized by the United States, by Great Britain, and
—after Hitler unleashed Operation Barbarossa in June 1941—by the
Soviet Union as the legal political representatives of the Polish state.
Preoccupied with its own survival during the early months of the
Russo-German conflict, the Kremlin could not afford to alienate its
western Allies over issues which had not been satisfactorily resolved
by the Polish-Soviet Treaty of July 1941. But as Soviet military fortunes improved, the Kremlin established a position of strength that
enabled it to deal more independently, and even arbitrarily, with
Polish authorities in resolving such questions as the supply and re-
cruitment of a Polish army on Soviet soil, the relief and evacuation
of Polish refugees, and most importantly the postwar boundary between the two nations.

One of the most divisive issues between Poland and the Soviet
Union was the controversial question of what should be their future
boundary. The London Poles insisted that the Riga Line be reestab-
lished. This line had been drawn by the Treaty of Riga after the
Russo-Polish War of 1920 and constituted the boundary between
Poland and the Soviet Union during most of the interwar years. The
Soviets favored the Curzon Line which came close to the line agreed
upon by the Kremlin and Berlin when they partitioned Poland by the
Molotov-Ribbentrop Pact in 1939.

Polish-Soviet relations deteriorated to the point that by the spring
of 1943 almost anything could have triggered a final break. In April
the Germans discovered the mass graves of thousands of missing
Polish officers in the forest of Katyn and charged the Soviets with the
atrocity. The Polish government in London headed by General Wladyslaw Sikorski, long suspecting Soviet culpability, asked the Red
Cross to investigate the German allegations. That was enough for
Stalin to cut off diplomatic relations with the London Poles.

Western sympathy for the Poles, and there was a great deal of it
especially during the early years of the war, never was translated into
strong political support because the United States and Great Britain
believed that their alliance with the Soviet Union was absolutely
essential to win the war against Germany and Japan. This preoccupation with military matters, coupled with the growing awareness that
Soviet armies would eventually be in a position to determine the

political future of Poland, placed the United States and Great Britain in the role of mediators between Poland and the Soviet Union rather than partisans for Polish interests. At no time during the war did London or Washington want to jeopardize its alliance with the Soviet Union over Polish issues.

Even though Washington was reluctant to take initiatives on Poland's behalf and possibly risk the Kremlin's displeasure, President Franklin D. Roosevelt encouraged the London Poles to believe that the United States would give greater support to Poland when the balance of power in Europe improved in the West's favor. Yet at the Tehran Conference late in 1943 Roosevelt joined Prime Minister Winston Churchill in agreeing to the Curzon Line without asking anything in return from Stalin. Roosevelt's agreement was kept secret for domestic political reasons until Soviet Foreign Minister Vyacheslav Molotov blurted it out to Premier Stanislaw Mikolajczyk, head of the Polish government-in-exile, a year later.

Roosevelt's lack of candor with the Poles and his buoyant optimism that satisfactory solutions to Polish issues would somehow be found eventually undermined the efforts of Churchill, who failed to convince the London Poles to compromise with the Soviets on the frontier question. Churchill hoped that such a compromise might pave the way for a solution, favorable to the London Poles, to the even thornier problem of what kind of government the Soviets would tolerate in Warsaw after the war.

The West had genuine cause for concern when the Kremlin announced in July 1944 the creation of the Polish committee of national liberation, or Lublin committee as it was popularly known. This group of Polish communists and socialists had been selected by Moscow to administer Polish lands liberated by Soviet armies. Although the Lublinites were not yet considered a government by the Kremlin, the fear that the group would soon receive such recognition was not an idle one.

Soviet political intentions in Poland were made clear at the time of the Warsaw Uprising in August and September of 1944. The Polish Home Army (*Armia Krajowa*), led by General Tadeusz Bor-Komorowski, rose up against German occupation forces in anticipation of a Soviet entry into the Polish capital. The Polish action was a bold political statement; the Polish government-in-exile through its military and political representatives on Polish soil hoped to assert its political control over the capital and confront the Kremlin with a fait accompli.

Stalin chose to make a political statement of his own. Soviet forces

brought their successful drive against the Germans to an abrupt halt
on the eastern bank of the Vistula River, claiming unconvincingly for
the next six weeks that they were unable to assist the beleaguered
Poles. The Kremlin even refused to permit aircraft of the United
States Army Air Forces to use Soviet air bases in shuttle operations
from England to Warsaw to aid the Poles. After substantial American
and British pressure, Stalin relented and gave his permission when
Polish capitulation to the Nazis was a virtual certainty. By the time
the Home Army surrendered on October 1, 1944, much of the prowestern Polish intelligentsia in the underground had been killed,
wounded, or taken prisoner. The Soviets now had an ideal opportunity to establish the Lublinites as the new political authorites in
Poland. Stalin lost little time; he extended recognition to the Lublin
committee as the provisional Polish government on the eve of the
Yalta Conference, confronting the West with a fait accompli of far-
reaching significance.

   In dealing with Stalin on the Polish question, Roosevelt had shied
away from balance of power politics with the result that the Kremlin
was able to impose the kind of settlement it wanted concerning the
controversial boundary matter and the complexion of the future government in Warsaw. When the Big Three met at the Yalta Conference
in February 1945 the United States and Great Britain confirmed their
earlier agreement to the Curzon Line for which Poland was to receive
compensation at German expense in the North and West and endorsed an imprecise political understanding which called for the Lublin regime to "be reorganized on a broader democratic basis with the
inclusion of democratic leaders from Poland itself and from Poles
abroad." Once reorganized, the current Polish government would be
called the Polish provisional government of national unity and would
be recognized as the legal government of Poland by the United States
and Great Britain. The reorganized government would "be pledged
to the holding of free and unfettered elections as soon as possible on
the basis of universal suffrage and secret ballot." Although Roosevelt
exuded an optimistic sense of achievement over the settlement,
Churchill was closer to the mark when he told the House of Commons
upon his return to England that whether Poland was to be free or a
projection of the Soviet Union depended upon Soviet good faith.

   Western hopes concerning the Polish settlement did not last long.
The differences in the interpretation of the Yalta agreement reflected
the huge gulf between the perception of the Soviet Union on the one
hand and the United States and Great Britain on the other concerning
the political future of Poland. The stalemate provoked by the Krem-

lin's interpretation of the agreement dragged on so long that when it finally ended in May 1945 it appeared that a genuine breakthrough had been made in East-West relations over Poland. But as Churchill observed, it was nothing more than an advance on the deadlock over the implementation of the Yalta agreement.[1]

During the discussions held in Moscow among various Polish factions in June 1945, which finally led to the establishment of the provisional government of national unity, Stalin made it clear to the Poles and to the western powers who controlled events in Poland. He staged the trial of sixteen Polish leaders who had been arrested by the Soviets after they had been enticed under false pretenses from the safety of the underground. Stalin dubbed the Poles "violators of the law for safeguarding the rear of the Red Army." Fifteen men (one was not tried because of illness) received sentences of from four months to ten years. Of those tried, only one did not break down and sign a prefabricated confession. Several of the prisoners died in prison and many of those released were arrested again in Poland. A few managed to flee to the West.[2]

As originally constituted, the Polish provisional government of national unity consisted of twenty-one seats, of which sixteen were occupied by the Lublinites, a communist-dominated coalition. The non-Lublinites got only five seats and one of those declined his portfolio. The new government was no less friendly to the Soviet Union and was considerably stronger than its predecessor.[3] The major parties included the Polish Workers party (*Polska Partia Robotnicza* or PPR), the Polish Socialist party (*Polska Partia Socjalistyczna* or PPS), and the Polish Peasant party (*Polskie Stronnictwo Ludowe* or PSL). There were three smaller parties—the Peasant party *Stronnictwo Ludowe* or SL), the Labor party (*Stronnictwo Pracy* or SP), and the Democratic party (*Stronnictwo Demokratyczne* or SD).

The leadership and direction of the new Polish government was in the hands of a capable group of Polish communists, a large number of whom were Jews who had spent years in political training in the Soviet Union. Boleslaw Bierut, the president of Poland, was a friend of Stalin, who regarded him highly. Born in Lublin and a printer by profession, Bierut became a communist shortly after Poland regained its independence following World War I and worked for the Polish section of the Communist International in Moscow. On his last prewar trip to Poland from the Soviet Union he was arrested by Polish authorities on charges of conspiracy but was later handed over to the Soviets. Bierut played a role in the organization of the *Krajowa Rada Narodowa* (KRN), a communist-sponsored parliament, which became the source of authority of the Polish committee of national liberation. Soft-spoken and undistinguished in appearance, Bierut was essentially a titular leader. In order to persuade Mikolajczyk to join the communist-dominated government in Warsaw, Bierut told him, "We are not Soviet agents, we do not want to Sovietize Poland." Arthur Bliss Lane, the first American ambassador to postwar Poland, described the Polish president in unflattering terms: "He impressed me as a shifty and opportunistic individual who was not master in his own house."[4]

Even communist sources acknowledge that Jakob Berman was the éminence grise who, though he occupied only lesser positions in the government, had greater power than Bierut. Berman had close ties with Moscow, where he had received his political training. Like Bierut, Berman was arrested on charges of conspiracy against the Polish state and spent some time in prison before World War II. After his release from prison, he returned to the Soviet Union and sat out the war there with other Polish communists. Ambassador Lane soon learned that if he wanted to cut through the red tape of Polish officialdom, he had to seek out the highly intelligent and dignified Berman to get results.

Hilary Minc was reputed to be Poland's economic genius. Like Berman, Minc was a Jew who spent most of World War II in the Soviet Union. Specializing in law and economics, Minc served as minister of industry and chairman of the economic committee of the cabinet, which in effect made him the tsar over the Polish economy. Fluent in French, Minc impressed American officials with the range and depth of his knowledge of financial and economic matters.

Universally hated was Stanislaw Radkiewicz, a Polish Jew who headed the ministry of public security, an agency which controlled by 1947 over 200,000 members of the security police. In close contact with Lavrenti Beria, his counterpart in the Soviet Union, Radkiewicz became a communist at an early age, went to Moscow in the 1930s and became an NKVD officer. He returned to Poland with the Lublin committee in 1944 as chief of the agency that eventually helped turn Poland into a communist-dominated country.[5]

In contrast to so many of the Moscow-trained communists, Wladyslaw Gomulka, who served as secretary of the central committee of the PPR, first deputy premier, and minister of western territories, was not a Jew and spent most of his life in Poland. Raised as a socialist from early youth, Gomulka first joined *Sila,* the youth organization of the PPS. Only later did he join the Polish Communist party, serving as a trade union organizer and political writer in the 1920s and 1930s.

Gomulka was both a communist and a patriot. "He saw no reason why he should choose between country and ideology," one biographer wrote. As subsequent events bore out, however, he would be forced by his own party to resolve the dilemma of a man who as a Marxist respected the Soviet Union and as a nationalist loved his country. Gomulka was an extremely intense man and fiery orator, convincing some of his opponents that he was a deranged fanatic.[6]

Like President Bierut, Poland's premier, Edward Osobka-Morawski, was not an impressive individual. Had it not been for the figurehead role the communists wanted him to play, Osobka-Morawski would have remained a rather diffident, good-natured petty agitator in the Polish Socialist party. Morawski came from Konski, where he worked as a bookkeeper. He joined the PPS and had advanced only to the district committee of the party in Radom when, with Moscow's help, he was catapulted to the presidency of the central committee of the PPS. In July 1944 Moscow named this modest man who loved to attend political meetings, where he said he heard "the voice of the people," to head the Polish committee of national liberation.[7]

Marshal Michal Rola-Zymierski vel Lyzwinski, ostensibly with no party affiliations, headed Poland's defense ministry. After his brother murdered the manager of a bookstore, and the bad publicity following the incident, Lyzwinski changed his name to Zymierski. He trained officers for Polish regiments in Austria and later served with the Polish legionnaires in World War I. He advanced to the rank of general after Poland's war with the Soviet Union in 1920. Zymierski became involved in a bribery scandal when he was chief of administration in the ministry of military affairs, was dismissed from the army, and was sentenced to prison. After his release, he lived in France and came into contact with communists during the Spanish Civil War. When the Polish Home Army spurned his offer to serve with it during World War II, Zymierski joined the communists and became head of the People's Army (*AL*) as "Rola," his nom de guerre. After the war, Rola-Zymierski had obvious value to the new Polish government as an experienced army officer, and because of his questionable past he was not very likely to pose a political threat to the regime. In any case, effective political control of the army remained in the hands of General Marian Spychalski, a gifted old-line communist whose background was in architecture, not the military. But this did not prevent his advancement to the rank of general and "guardian angel," as one observer described him, to Rola-Zymierski.[8]

One of the weakest members of the Lublinite coalition was Wincenty Rzymowski, who served as foreign minister. A leftist writer who

was expelled from the Polish academy of literature before the outbreak of World War II, Rzymowski was not very highly regarded
even in Polish government circles. Lane commented that it was
"never possible for any foreign diplomat, with the possible exception
of the Russian, to see him alone." Invariably, Rzymowski, who Mikolajczyk claimed was a Soviet citizen, was shadowed by his nervous but
able deputy, Zygmunt Modzelewski.[9]

The best-known non-Lublinite in the Polish provisional government of national unity was Stanislaw Mikolajczyk, who served as
vice-premier and minister of agriculture. Unsophisticated but shrewd,
Mikolajczyk came from peasant stock in western Poland. In some
ways his career was as meteroric as Osobka-Morawski's. Mikolajczyk
was not very well known before the war; his political constituency was
in Poznan, where he represented the conservative wing of the Polish
Peasant party. He became vice-premier and minister of interior in
Sikorski's government-in-exile and, after the general's death in July
1943, succeeded him as premier. In time Mikolajczyk saw that he
presided over a doomed government, despised by Stalin and inade-
quately supported by Roosevelt and Churchill. The longer the Polish
government-in-exile refused to compromise on the controversial
boundary with the Soviets and to change its political complexion
enough to satisfy the suspicious leader in the Kremlin, the more it
became isolated from the Big Three who openly and privately criticized the London Poles for their stubbornness. Convinced that acceptance of the Curzon Line was the sine qua non of an agreement with
Stalin, Mikolajczyk failed to win the support of any political party
except his own in the London government. He resigned in November
1944. With Mikolajczyk's departure, the London Poles became increasingly Russophobic and irrelevant.[10]

The months Mikolajczyk was out of the political limelight must
have been difficult for this ambitious man who enjoyed politics and
hobnobbing with Allied leaders. He was also a patriot who believed
that the only way to deal with the communist threat was, in his words,
"by pitting oneself against the task on the spot, in Poland, notwithstanding the enormous risks and hazards."[11] His decision to join the
Polish provisional government of national unity was hailed by his
prowestern countrymen but was widely condemned in émigré circles
in Great Britain and the United States.

When President Harry S. Truman and his secretary of state, the
able and ambitious James F. Byrnes, came to the Postdam Conference, they had no intention of pursuing goals which could be inter-

preted as a challenge to Soviet hegemony in Poland. Byrnes, to whom Truman gave more latitude than Roosevelt had given to Hull and Stettinius, was more interested in the resolution of the German question than that of Poland.[12]

When the subject of future elections in Poland was raised, Truman and Byrnes were no more inclined to press for international supervision than Churchill and his foreign minister, Anthony Eden, had been. Byrnes thought the "best observers" were the "gentlemen of the press" and rejected the advice of the Department of State which had recommended that it was necessary to work out some arrangements for the supervision of the Polish elections by representatives of the Big Three.

"Unsupervised elections might give [a] free hand to the growth of Soviet influence," the State Department warned. It was aware that Washington would not oppose a political scenario which gave the Soviets hegemony in Poland but, it reasoned, "neither would it desire to see Poland become a Soviet satellite and have American influence there completely eliminated."[13]

Neither did the appeals of thirty-four distinguished American leaders—including John Dewey, Alfred Landon, A. Phillip Randolph, and Herbert Hoover, who urged Truman to secure "concrete guarantees of truly free elections" from the Soviets—influence the president or the secretary of state. To these men, the Warsaw government was essentially composed of holdovers from the Lublin regime, and therefore "by no stretch of the imagination can this be called an honest fulfillment even of the Yalta agreement." They recommended that Soviet troops be withdrawn before the Polish elections, and if the Kremlin was unwilling to remove its forces, then American and British troops should join the Soviets in Poland during the electoral period.[14]

Appeals of Polish Americans fell on deaf ears too. Charles Rozmarek, head of the Polish American Congress, the spokesman for most Americans of Polish descent, had been one of the earliest and most vocal critics of the Yalta agreement.[15] Early in July 1945, before Truman went to Potsdam, Rozmarek warned that free elections in Poland could not be held "under the rule of Soviet bayonets, Soviet police and Soviet puppets." The Polish American leader, who also headed the Polish National Alliance, the largest Polish American fraternal organization, seemed to echo the opinion of most Americans of Polish descent when he scored Washington for following a policy of appeasement toward the Kremlin.[16]

During the fifth plenary meeting of the Big Three on July 21, 1945, at the Cecilienhof Palace, Truman casually raised the question of the Polish elections. He referred to his six million Polish American constituents, indicating that a free election in Poland "would make it easier to deal with these Polish people." In other words, Truman, like Roosevelt before him, made it appear to Stalin that the Americans considered the election issue in terms of its impact on American politics, not as a serious matter related to the independence of Poland.

Stalin was more concerned with a statement in a proposed draft on Poland that referred to the freedom the Allied press should enjoy in order to report on developments in Poland before and during the elections. Stalin pointed out that press correspondents were already in Poland and had freedom to report. "There is no use repeating," he said. "The Poles are very touchy and will be hurt." But Stalin saw that Truman and Churchill were united on the question of a free press reporting on the future Polish elections. Although Stalin failed to have the reference to the press deleted from the text that eventually was approved on Poland, he did succeed in getting Truman and Churchill to accept an amendment which watered down the force of the statement.[17]

The election issue was not entirely resolved before Churchill's government was swept out of power while he and Eden were at Potsdam. Clement Attlee, dour head of the Labor party, replaced Churchill as prime minister, while Ernest Bevin became the new foreign minister. Bevin tried to do something that Mikolajczyk had urged the United States to do, namely, to link western agreement on Poland's western frontier with guarantees that the Polish elections would indeed be free.[18] But this was not the linkage that interested Byrnes or Truman. Bevin's efforts simply garnered verbal assurances from Bierut and the Polish delegation that the elections would be held as soon as possible, it was hoped not later than early 1946, and that the foreign press would be free to monitor them. In his conversations with Bevin, the Polish president tried to make the timing of the elections contingent upon the repatriation of Polish citizens from abroad. After Bevin received Bierut's assurances concerning the elections, he agreed to go along with Poland's claims for its western frontier.[19]

Predictably, the Soviets were more interested in the activities and assets of the London Poles, no longer recognized as the legal representatives of Poland by the Big Three, than they were in the implementation of the Yalta pledge concerning free elections in Poland.[20] When Stalin complained about the continued activities of the London group, Churchill gave him a short course in English civil liberties: "You cannot prevent—in England—individuals from going on talking," the prime minister snapped.[21] As for Polish gold in England, Churchill assured him that the Warsaw regime would get it. It was during this exchange that Stalin affirmed that the Polish armed forces under British operational command during the war should be subordinated to the Polish government of national unity. Britain would try to persuade the men to return home, said Churchill, but it would not force them to do so.[22]

The Polish boundary with Germany proved to be the most difficult issue to resolve, revealing just how far apart the Big Three were on this sensitive and potentially explosive matter. Warsaw's claims for German territory to the Oder-western Neisse River were strongly supported by the Soviets, who had turned over administration of the area to Polish authorities when they occupied it. The United States and Great Britain criticized the Soviets for thus unilaterally creating what amounted to another occupation zone. Although the United States and Great Britain agreed that Poland should receive territorial compensation at the expense of Germany, they opposed what they considered to be exaggerated Polish claims. Churchill believed that the success of the conference hinged upon an agreement on this issue. In the end, Byrnes came up with a compromise, an arrangement that tied the frontier question with two other issues—German reparations and admission of Italy into the United Nations. The Byrnes proposals were accepted and the divisive Polish boundary question was resolved —at least until September 1946, when the permanency of the Polish-German boundary was questioned by the same man who had offered the compromise at Potsdam to settle it.

The Poles based their claims to the Oder-western Neisse frontier upon impressive historical, political, economic, demographic, and ethnic arguments. They declared that the lands between the Oder and Vistula "may be considered as the primordial territories of the Polish state." If Poland acquired the new frontier with Germany, the Polish government felt that the country would be a natural and geographical unit just as it had been when the Piast dynasty controlled the Oder and Vistula river systems. In order for Poland to be strong and independent, a goal the Big Three had consistently endorsed during the war, the country needed adequate territory, especially in view of the fact that it had given up a major chunk to the Soviets in the east. If all Polish claims to German lands were granted, Poland would still be 22 percent smaller than it had been in 1939; yet Germany, the defeated aggressor, would be only 18 percent smaller. The density and natural growth of population demanded that the country acquire the western lands, Warsaw argued. The Poles imitated the Czechs by

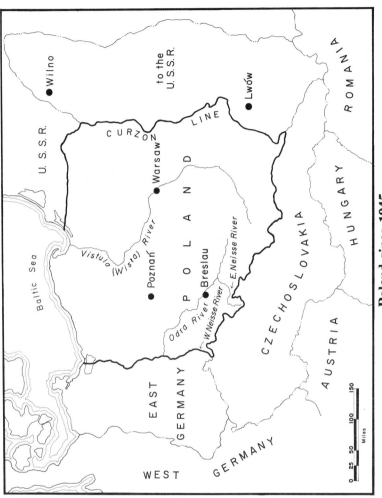

Poland since 1945

suggesting that from a geographical point of view, the Polish position on the Oder-western Neisse would help it to play the role of an intermediary between East and West. Not the least of the justifications for the coveted land was the need to improve Poland's economic recovery by increasing agricultural yields and industrial output. And with the additional land along the Baltic, including the ports of Stettin, Gdansk, and Elbing, German hegemony on the Baltic would end and the Polish connection between these coastal areas and the hinterland would be strengthened. Warsaw suggested that Polish control of the Oder, the area that historically constituted the place d'armes from whence Germans had invaded Poland, would end the threat of German aggression in the future and thus be of obvious interest to all peace-loving nations. To communist and noncommunist Poles the frontier they claimed with the Germans was especially significant because it weakened Germany. Mikolajczyk echoed the views of most Poles when he told leaders of his party, "The Germans should be controlled forever. They will always be a danger to peace."[23]

The United States and Great Britain once had held views which came close to endorsing Polish claims to German territory. In February 1944 Churchill asked Stalin to join him to see that Poland incorporated not only Gdansk, Silesia, and East Prussia but also "as much territory up to the Oder as the Polish government sees fit to accept."[24] On November 2, 1944, in the so-called Cadogan Letter, the British told the Mikolajczyk government that they supported Polish acquisitions to the Oder, including the port of Stettin, though to which Neisse River—there were two of them—was not made entirely clear. Churchill told the House of Commons that "the Poles are free so far as Russia and Great Britain are concerned to extend their territory at the expense of Germany to the West." And he was not sensitive at that time about the total expulsion of Germans from the area acquired by Poland.[25] Roosevelt, who played a low-key role on the question, told Mikolajczyk at this time that the United States would go along with Great Britain, the Soviet Union, and Poland on any agreement regarding Poland's frontiers, including territorial acquisitions from Germany. Mikolajczyk, unable to get the endorsement of his government for what amounted to a quid pro quo—acceptance of the Curzon Line in the east for substantial acquisitions in the west— left office, his place taken by one of the grand old men of Polish socialism, Tomasz Arciszewski, whose strongly Russophobic government stubbornly refused to accept the Curzon Line and made only very modest claims to German lands.[26]

When the Big Three met at Yalta in February 1945 the position of

the London Poles on the boundary question had become an academic
point because Stalin now recognized the Lublin Poles as the government of Poland, which endorsed the Curzon Line with the Soviet
Union and wanted the Oder-western Neisse line in the West. But now
the American and British positions had changed, doubtless because
of communist hegemony in Poland. Churchill himself admitted, "We
need not make the same concessions to the Lublin Poles which we
were prepared to make to M. Mikolajczyk in order to obtain a solution
of the Polish problem." Roosevelt joined Churchill in agreeing to
Polish territorial compensation to the Oder River but not to the
western Neisse River. Now the president and prime minister expressed their concern about the large number of Germans who would
be forced out of the area claimed by Poland. Roosevelt wanted the
transfer of population to be gradual, and Churchill wondered if the
Poles had the capability to absorb the frontier even to the Oder River,
remarking that "it would be a great pity to stuff the Polish goose so
full of German food that it died of indigestion." Since maps of the area
involved were not even used in these discussions and, as Churchill
admitted, "The distinction between the Eastern and Western Neisse
did not emerge as clearly as it should have," there is little wonder that
this vital issue became so beclouded and confusing.[27] In the end,
Roosevelt, Churchill, and Stalin at Yalta pinned down the Curzon
Line which, with minor rectifications, would constitute the Soviet-
Polish boundary. But they failed to delineate the German-Polish
boundary, simply stating "that Poland must receive substantial acces-
sions of territory in the North and West."[28]

By the time the Big Three met at the Potsdam Conference, the
Warsaw government had inherited the administration of Germany's
eastern lands from the Soviets and promptly divided them into four
voivodeships—Upper Silesia, Lower Silesia, West Pomerania, and
East Prussia.[29] This action greatly disturbed the president and the
prime minister. Truman's anger came through in a notation he made
in his diary: "At the Conference Poland and the Bolsheviki land grab
came up. Russia helped herself to a slice of Poland and gave Poland
a nice slice of Germany. . . . Just a unilateral arrangement without so
much [as] a by your leave. I don't like it."[30]

During the fifth plenary meeting on July 21, 1945, Truman took the
initiative on the issue and questioned Stalin's right to assign the Poles
what amounted to an occupation zone without consulting him or
Churchill. Stalin justified his action on the grounds that since the
Germans had fled from the advancing Russians, some friendly administration in the area was necessary to ensure stable conditions to the

rear of the Soviet armies. Besides, Stalin argued, the Kremlin saw no harm in allowing Poles to administer an area where allegedly only Poles remained and which was likely to be ceded to them anyway. Truman countered that he could not accept the separation of eastern Germany when the matter was, after all, related to such vital questions as German reparations and food supplies.[31]

Churchill was concerned that the area claimed by the Poles had been a major food and coal producing area for Germany. He erroneously claimed that the Poles were taking more from the Germans than they had lost to the Soviets, and he fretted over the expulsion of millions of Germans who would become a burden on the remainder of Germany. "We should not have a mass of people dumped upon us, while the Poles acquire food which the Germans need," Churchill said. With his propensity for hyperbole, the prime minister intoned that the Allies might be confronted with a situation similar to the starvation which afflicted the victims in German concentration camps.[32]

"No single German remained in the territory to be given Poland," Stalin declared, apparently with a straight face. Even Polish communists admitted that there were 1–1.5 million Germans left in the area.[33] As one scholar has aptly observed, Churchill's concern over the transfer of Germans from Polish-controlled territory contrasted sharply with his earlier views on the matter, for only one year before he had invited Stalin to join him in supporting "the removal from Poland including the German territories to be incorporated in Poland of the German population."[34]

The leaders had reached an impasse, and in an effort to break it they agreed to invite representatives of the Polish government to Potsdam to hear their views on the question. The Poles were ready. Although the Polish government was asked to send only two or three representatives to Potsdam, Bierut appointed three members—Osobka-Morawski, Mikolajczyk, Rzymowski—and because of the importance of the issue involved, he himself decided to attend. Before the Polish question was resolved, several other Polish leaders had made their way from Warsaw to Potsdam. It was no accident that the Warsaw government included the Polish leader the United States and Great Britain most admired—namely, Mikolajczyk, who was in complete agreement with his colleagues on territorial acquisitions to the Oder-western Neisse. It was significant, too, that other prowestern Poles were included in the expanded Polish delegation—Professor Stanislaw Grabski, one of the vice-presidents of Poland who prepared a brief submitted by Warsaw to the Allies, and Jan Stanczyk, a prominent left-wing socialist with close ties to Bevin and the British Labor party.[35]

The Poles, obviously well prepared to argue their case, had several opportunities to present their views to representatives of the Big Three. Most of the arguments were esentially a restatement of Polish views presented to the United States and Great Britain before the Potsdam Conference convened. Mikolajczyk cogently argued that the western lands were needed as a reservoir to absorb the Polish population east of the Curzon Line, Poles who returned from the West, and Polish people who lived in the overcrowded central districts of Poland. Linking the frontier question with the pledge of the Warsaw regime to hold free elections, he showed that if a decision on Poland's western frontiers were delayed, "then there would be no possibility either of transfer of population from the east or the west, or of holding elections there." He convincingly argued that without the settlement of the western frontier, Poland could only conduct partial elections while the Soviets stood "as hosts" in the western lands claimed by Warsaw. Emphasizing the fact that the Poles already administered the area they claimed, Bierut bluntly told Churchill: "Recognize the fact which already exists. We want to live and not to die slowly."[36]

Polish arguments did not change Churchill's view that the Poles were simply asking for too much land, which would force Germans into the American and British zones of occupation to be fed. Truman agreed and reiterated his position that the Polish frontier should be settled at a peace conference. Meanwhile, if the Poles were to have an occupation zone, which the United States and Great Britain opposed, "they were responsible to the Soviet Union for it."[37]

But the deadlock did not last much longer. On July 26 Averell Harriman, who served as American ambassador to the Soviet Union, met with Mikolajczyk and other members of the Polish delegation and revealed that the United States was moving in the direction of separating the question of the Polish-German boundary from the more immediate issue of Polish administration in order to enable the Poles to secure the harvest and organize the industrial production of the occupied area. "The Russians cannot do it," Harriman said, "it has to be done by the Poles."[38]

A few days later, July 29, Molotov met Truman and Byrnes—Stalin was ill—and was handed an American proposal to resolve the boundary question. The United States agreed to accept Polish administration of land to the Oder-eastern Neisse until a final peace conference determined the boundary. Byrnes made it clear that the American offer was part of a quid pro quo by which the Soviets would accept

American proposals regarding German reparations that allowed each of the occupation powers to take its share of reparations from its own zone and provided for the admission of Italy into the United Nations. Molotov indicated that Stalin would not be pleased with the offer because it denied Polish administration of the area between the two Neisse rivers. Moreover, he also had reservations about the American reparations offer which did not mention specific figures.[39] Truman did not exaggerate when he told the Soviet foreign minister that the American offer "represented a very large concession on our part;" the State Department had strongly advised him that he should agree "only with reluctance" to the Oder-eastern Neisse frontier.[40]

Meanwhile there was a flurry of activity among the Poles and Russians. On July 29, Stalin met with Bierut and asked whether the Poles would not agree to make some concessions in view of the fact that the United States had gone so far. After consultations with experts the Poles bent a little, agreeing to the establishment of the boundary somewhere between the western Neisse and the Queiss (Kwisa). But later the same day the Poles reconsidered their position; Bierut, accompanied by Rola-Zymierski, returned to Stalin and argued against any compromise with the Americans. Stalin told his Polish protégés that he would defend their position at the conference.[41]

But Stalin's pledge to the Poles did not have to be tested, for on July 30, without further pressure from the Poles and Soviets, Byrnes offered a "package deal," apparently suggested to him by Joseph Davies, one of the American advisers at Potsdam, which linked a settlement of the Polish question with reparations from Germany and the admission of Italy into the United Nations.[42] The package was a quid pro quo—United States acceptance of the Polish-Soviet position on the boundary in return for Soviet acceptance of American terms on German reparations and the admission of Italy into the United Nations. Byrnes, working closely with Truman, was anxious for an accord. He emphasized to Molotov that the three issues had to be considered as a unit and that the United States would accept "all three or none." To dramatize this "last" American offer to resolve the impasse, Byrnes told Molotov that he and the president intended to leave for the United States on August 1.[43] Byrnes's offer produced results. On July 31, at the eleventh plenary meeting of the Big Three and their advisers, agreement was reached, though only after considerable Soviet haggling over the amount of German reparations they would receive from the western zones of occupied Germany.[44]

The Byrnes initiative had produced a compromise that appeared to be satisfactory to all parties. The Poles obviously considered Potsdam a major success for them.[45] The Untied States, though long opposing a Polish-German arrangement that inevitably made Warsaw more dependent upon Moscow, could not continue its opposition on an issue which ran the risk of jeopardizing whatever influence Washington still expected to exert in postwar Poland. After all, Mikolajczyk, the man the West hoped could prevent Poland from becoming completely communist, had joined his communist colleagues in eloquently presenting the Polish case. Byrnes and Truman could not be totally oblivious to that fact. Besides, as Brynes himself wrote later, neither the United States nor Great Britain "knew of any way to force the Soviets to oust the Poles and to take back the administration of the territory concerned, short of resorting to force."[46] In the final analysis a resolution of the reparations issue was probably more important to Truman and Byrnes anyway, and if they had to give in on the Polish issue to secure a satisfactory settlement on German reparations, it was worth it to them.

As has been seen, British acceptance of the Polish position on the western frontier was made after Bevin had been assured by Bierut that there would indeed be free elections in Poland. If Churchill's government had not been defeated in the summer of 1945, there is some reason to doubt whether Truman and Byrnes would have been so successful at Potsdam. Churchill claimed later that he never would have agreed to the Oder-western Neisse and was ready for a "showdown" and "if necessary, to have a public break rather than allow anything beyond the Oder and the eastern Neisse to be ceded to Poland."[47]

Even though the Potsdam communiqué stated that a permanent boundary between Germany and Poland had to await a future peace conference, what the Allied leaders did at Potsdam constituted a de facto territorial settlement.[48] The manner in which the agreement was achieved, based on Byrnes's three-point package, made it clear that this was not considered a provisional arrangement. It would have been absurd, not to mention inhumane, for the Big Three to agree to Polish administration of an area that involved the transfer of millions of people only to cast doubt on the validity of their decisions at some future peace conference. As Bevin told Stanczyk, one of the Polish representatives, "To return the western land to you means to return this land forever."[49] Joseph Davies said the same thing: "It was taken as a matter of course that the three powers would support the Polish claims as to those frontiers at the final Peace Conference, which had to ratify all territorial changes."[50] The Soviets had no doubt about what transpired at Potsdam. Scarcely two weeks after the conference, they signed a treaty with the Poles, fixing the Oder-western Neisse as Poland's postwar boundary with Germany.[51]

At Potsdam the Untied States lost an opportunity to concert measures with the British and link the Polish election and frontier issues. To have done so would have been a major departure from Roosevelt's policy of postwar accommodation with the Soviet Union. Truman and Byrnes, along with Attlee and Bevin, displayed no inclination to challenge the Soviets on the election issue and risk a break. Perhaps, too, they were reminded of Stalin's admission that freely elected governments in eastern Europe "would be anti-Soviet and that we cannot allow."[52] Besides, Poland no longer had the same priority it once had to American policy makers. Truman and Byrnes were far more concerned now with the political and economic recovery of those areas in Europe not under Soviet influence.

II Postwar Poland

Polish politics were far more fluid before the controversial elections of January 1947 than is often realized. Although the dominant group in the government was the PPR, the Polish communists were in no position to establish their domination over the entire country. During this dynamic period in the political life of postwar Poland, the PPR ruled in a coalition with the PPS and a few smaller political parties and regarded the PSL, which they identified with reaction, as its major threat.[1]

Ever since the creation of the Polish provisional government of national unity, the communists had held the vital portfolios in the regime—police, army, industry. Although Premier Osobka-Morawski was a socialist, Vice-Premier Gomulka, who served as administrator of the western territories, was much more powerful. The same was true of the courts; the jurisdiction of the socialist minister of justice, Henryk Swiatkowski, only applied to lesser offenses, while major cases, including political ones, were tried before military courts. One of the few PSL members in the government, Wladyslaw Kiernik, served as minister of public administration, but control of the police was left to Radkiewicz, a communist. Mikolajczyk's power as minister of agriculture was curtailed not only by Gomulka's ministry but also by the PPR-controlled ministries of food and forests. The PPS filled almost every other major post not held by the PPR. But every noncommunist minister had a communist vice-minister to supervise the affairs of his department. Thus communists like Berman ran the premier's office while Modzelewski was the de facto foreign minister. Instead of cabinet mettings being limited to ministers, communist supernumeraries also attended, puffing up the number of people at these sessions to more than a hundred.[2]

The commanding political position of the PPR was not a reflection of its popular support and leaders of the party knew it. Estimates of communist strength vary from a low of fewer than 200,000 in 1945 to an inflated claim of almost 600,000 in 1946.[3] But in candid conversations most informed communists seldom claimed the allegiance of more than 12 percent of the Polish people. Even communist sources admit the poor quality of the active members of the party; fewer than 20 percent of them in 1945 had a higher education.[4] Most of the specialists and experts, which the government depended upon to rehabilitate the ravaged country, were not communist.

The PPR was far from being a monolithic party. The major dichotomy was between the "Nativists" and the "Muscovites." The former were a homegrown variety of communist whose perspectives were strongly colored by domestic influences and realities. Gomulka was a representative of this group, a devoted communist who reserved his most scathing attacks for Mikolajczyk and the PSL. Yet Gomulka never seriously believed that Polish socialism should be a mirror image of Soviet experience. Although not an original intellect, Gomulka had the courage to challenge not only the "Muscovite" wing of the party but also the Soviets themselves. The Soviet army was notorious for its looting in the western provinces, making it difficult for Gomulka as minister of these lands to rehabilitate the area. Gomulka ordered Polish troops to fire on Soviet soldiers who were caught looting and communicated his order to Soviet military authorities.[5] Gomulka's assets in 1945 proved to be liabilities in 1948 when he lost his position as secretary general of the PPR.

The "Muscovites" had spent a long time in the Soviet Union and had become indoctrinated in the Soviet Marxist experience. These Sovietized Poles, represented by the Bierut wing of the party, were less enthusiastic about the spontaneous policy lines followed by the party during the early postwar period and tended to rely more on the Kremlin. Bierut was so devoted to Moscow that he once suggested that the Polish national anthem, *Jeszcze Polska Nie Zginela* ("Poland Is Not Yet Lost"), be replaced by one that was not so nationalistic. Stalin restrained his protégé, saying, "It's a good song. Leave it for a while."[6]

The PPR had a major liability in the large number of Jews who were top leaders of the party, something which even the Zionist leader, Emil Sommerstein, regretted. As one scholar has pointed out, "Given the numerical weakness of the party and the traditionally high percentage of Jews in the leadership of the Polish communist movement, it is not surprising that they became highly visible."[7] Since Polish Jews were part of the Muscovite wing of the party and linked with the more repressive aspects of the regime, little wonder that anti-Semitism became an issue in postwar Polish politics.

Stalin, who distrusted all Poles, including those who collaborated with him, shared the views of the Gomulka wing of the PPR that intimidation and terror alone would not achieve communist goals in Poland. In order to win over a people who were historically anti-Russian and anticommunist, communism had to be made acceptable to the Polish people.[8] What better way was there than to show the nation that Polish communists were really patriots who were anxious to rebuild their devastated country? This approach was more likely to win over noncommunist Poles—including the skilled technicians and experts, the Poles who lived abroad, and the people whose political views had not crystallized yet—to help the PPR-dominated coalition rebuild the country. Such a strategy was necessary too in order to assure the United States and Great Britain that the Warsaw government intended to fulfill the Yalta and Potsdam political pledges. This emphasis on Poland's own road to socialism obviously worked to mitigate Polish resistance to communism and helped to undermine the efforts of the PSL to challenge the regime effectively.

Even with Soviet backing the PPR had every reason to be apprehensive about its ability to control the uncertain political situation in the country at a time when the communists suffered a decline in membership and the PPS had the loyalties of most of the urban proletariat.[9] But most Polish socialists recognized that it was necessary to forge a united front with the PPR and to work for close cooperation with the Soviet Union. They realized that their country was irrevocably in the Soviet sphere of influence and that Poland's future lay in its ability to accommodate itself to Soviet economic and foreign policy. This did not prevent the PPS from demonstrating its independence from the PPR from time to time; in the fall of 1945, for example, the PPS even admitted anticommunists into its party.[10]

The left wing of the party, led by Jozef Cyrankiewicz, an intellectually gifted opportunist, was prepared to go much farther in sacrificing the independence of the PPS than many moderates and the right wing believed was either necessary or prudent. Cyrankiewicz, who had served as secretary of the Krakow district committee of the PPS in the 1930s, fought in the resistance against the Germans and was arrested. He was sent to a concentration camp where he became converted to the idea of close collaboration between the socialists and communists.[11] Cyrankiewicz's belief was reinforced when he visited London, sized up the Polish political situation there, and returned to Poland with the conviction that his future—always a major preoccupation with this ambitious politician—and that of the PPS were tied to the PPR.[12] He told Liston Oak, the managing editor of the *New Leader,* "I do not want to be an emigre or to be isolated and powerless. Neither do I want to be merely an agent of Moscow. . . . Believe me, I am still a Socialist and not a Communist. If I am compelled to capitulate to the Communists it is because of 'realpolitik' and not because I want to do so. I hope for a change in international relations which will enable me and my party to reassert our independence.[13] Kazimierz Rusinek, another leader in the PPS, felt much the same way. Rusinek, who headed the Seamen's and Cokers' Union of Gdynia before the war, also spent time in a Nazi concentration camp, and it was there that he too became convinced that the future of the PPS lay in collaboration with the PPR after the war. Rusinek was a major figure in postwar Poland, heading the powerful central committee of Polish trade unions.[14]

The PPS was convinced that it should collaborate with the PPR or risk losing political power to the PSL, which enjoyed the greatest popularity and support among the Polish people. A PSL victory, the PPS believed, would trigger a Soviet occupation, which no Pole, not even the PPR, wanted. PPS collaboration with the PPR appeared to make sense to party members in view of the large number of prewar reactionaries, with no legal party of their own in postwar Poland, who rallied around an embarrassed Mikolajczyk.[15]

The right wing of the PPS was led by Zygmunt Zulawski, a tall aristocratic-looking man whose socialist roots went back to the prewar period. Zulawski recognized the political realism of cooperating with the Kremlin but tried unsuccessfully to maintain the integrity and independence of the PPS. In October 1945 Zulawski failed to establish a separate Social Democratic party. A few months later, as a sop to his group, Zulawski and his followers were given eleven seats on the executive council of the PPS. But Zulawski soon discovered that the left wing of the party had no intention of allowing him and his colleagues to have any influence in the party, and he resigned his affiliation within a year.[16]

The PSL was a large, though not a unified, party which had come into existence after the PPR had created a communist-front group to draw people away from the large and popular prewar party of Wincenty Witos and Stanislaw Mikolajczyk. Upon his return to Poland, Mikolajczyk's party took the name PSL in order not to confuse it with the SL, the original name of the Polish Peasant party now appropriated by the protégés of the communists. Mikolajczyk's shrewd maneuever greatly disturbed the PPR, which claimed that the Moscow discussions that led to the establishment of the Polish provisional government of national unity did not provide for Mikolajczyk and his followers to be associated with a party other than the SL. To the anger of the PPR, Mikolajczyk returned to Poland like a conquering hero and presided over the most popular political party in Poland, which numbered at least 600,000 members by January 1946.[17]

As has been seen, Mikolajczyk chose to return to Poland and work within the political framework imposed upon Poland by the Big Three at the Yalta Conference. His views were no different from those of other members of his party who spent the war years in the homeland; he shared with them the view that it was foolish, if not suicidal, to adopt the position of the London Poles and fight the Soviets. Mikolajczyk's aims were to encourage the peasants to cooperate in the reconstruction of the country, to bolster the morale of a people physically and emotionally exhausted by the war, to avoid further bloodshed, to fight for social change, independence, and democracy by legal means, to develop friendly relations between Poland and the Soviet Union and Poland and the West, and to execute the Yalta decisions concerning Poland.[18]

Mikolajczyk was able and courageous, but his judgment was often faulty. He gave little thought to developing a political strategy that had any chance of genuine success other than the unrealistic one of refusing to join an electoral bloc, except on the most exaggerated terms, and urging that the Polish elections, promised at Yalta and Potsdam, be held as early as possible. He believed the sooner the elections were held, the better the chances would be for a PSL victory. Even when the weakness of his strategy became increasingly apparent, he did not display sufficient flexibility to modify it.

Mikolajczyk did not return to Poland with the belief that he would receive strong support from the United States and Great Britain in his domestic battles with the communists. On the basis of his wartime relationships with Roosevelt and Churchill that led to Tehran and Yalta, Mikolajczyk was under no illusions about receiving firm support from the West. On his departure from London for the Moscow talks in June 1945, Churchill conveyed to him his pessimism about the Polish situation and did not hold out the offer of assistance from the democracies, which Churchill predicted would return "to bed and rest" after the war. Mikolajczyk's personal assessment of the likelihood of his party's getting any kind of effective help from the West was equally pessimistic.[19] Yet when he returned to Poland he did not disabuse his followers of the notion that he had returned home with an Anglo-American guarantee of support. He believed that he could not tell his followers the truth because he wanted not only to win and hold the support of the overwhelming majority of Poles but also to impress his political opponents with the belief that if the PSL were pushed too far it would indeed receive the support of the West.

Even Mikolajczyk's closest associates believed that their leader had some secret agreement from the United States and Britain concerning Poland's future. One of Mikolajczyk's colleagues, Stefan Korbonski, a distinguished attorney who served as chief of the civil resistance during World War II, assumed that Mikolajczyk had returned with some assurances from the West. "Surely Mikolajczyk wouldn't be so stupid as to come on his own with nothing at all," Korbonski wrote in his diary at the time.[20] Even when Mikolajczyk finally revealed the truth to his followers, Korbonski and others assumed that their leader demurred in order to safeguard the secret of future American and British aid.[21] The leaders of the PSL were no different from the mass of Polish people who convinced themselves that Mikolajczyk had brought with him a plan to save Poland. There were high hopes among the Polish people, especially in late 1945, that the United States and Britain would indeed free Poland. The most common question American correspondents were asked by the Poles was, "When is the American army coming to liberate us from the Russians?" There was also a widespread belief among Poles at home and abroad that a war between the United States and the Soviet Union was imminent. One Pole told an American correspondent that the United States intended to use the atomic bomb on the Soviet Union because Mrs. Truman was Polish![22]

If Mikolajczyk's strategy did not depend upon American and British support but only on the illusion of it, how did he expect to maintain the PSL as a viable force in Polish political life? Mikolajczyk possessed a strong conviction of the power of Polish nationalism and the ability of the Poles to defend their independence. He believed that traditional Polish hostility toward the Russians and communism could work to the advantage of his party. He reasoned that Moscow understood the Polish national character and was unlikely to risk satellization of a people who could and would resist it.[23] Besides, there was ample evidence in other countries in eastern Europe that the Kremlin allowed peasant parties to participate in the government and, in the case of Hungary in 1945, even to win a political victory.[24] Mikolajczyk believed that if he could convince Stalin that the PSL wanted friendly relations with the Soviet Union, the Soviet chief would then allow reasonably free elections in Poland, and Mikolajczyk expected to win. Like Benes and Masaryk, Mikolajczyk mistakenly assumed that Stalin would allow Poland and Czechoslovakia to be a bridge between the Soviet Union and the West. But, as one scholar has aptly put it, "Moscow regarded them merely as a bridgehead."[25]

Mikolajczyk, who came from western Poland and never really understood the Russians, had misjudged Soviet intentions concerning Poland. To him the party that had survived Pilsudski could survive

Stalin; it proved to be a fatal miscalculation. The irony is that Mikolajczyk transferred the illusions he once had about western support for an independent Poland to the Soviet Union. As late as the fall of 1946 Mikolajczyk told a British journalist about the rightness of his policy of legal peaceful opposition,[26] even though by then the intimidation, harassment, and murder of members of the PSL should have jolted him into the realization that the communists would not allow his party to win power. By then, the PSL's strategy against the communist-dominated regime was appropriately described as "a struggle between bare buttocks and a whip."[27]

After Mikolajczyk fled to the West in 1947, he told an interviewer that had he remained in England and refused to go to Poland in the summer of 1945, "It could have been said that no Pole could be found who was willing to cooperate, to compromise." Paul Zaleski, Mikolajczyk's former aide and confidant, added: "Without Mikolajczyk there, the United States and Britain would have blamed him for making no effort to prevent Poland from becoming Communist."[28] As one astute observer pointed out at the time, Mikolajczyk's return to Poland emerged as part of "a horrifying indictment of the sacrifices which had been demanded of Poland to appease not simply Russia, but the Allies in their appeasement of Russia."[29]

The reform program of the PSL was close but not identical to that of the PPR and PPS. Like the other two parties the PSL supported the nationalization of large industry, but it wanted to preserve private ownership of smaller and medium-sized industry. The PSL supported land reforms that would go farther than those favored by the PPR in creating strong independent farmers. To do this it urged dividing up church and state lands and consolidating small and inefficient holdings. The PSL also urged what most Poles wanted—namely, an end to the ministry of internal security. As one of Mikolajczyk's lieutenants said, the major difference between the government's economic reform program and that of the PSL was, "we believe in civil liberties."[30] The party also stood for friendly relations with the Soviet Union and the West, but it had a serious problem countering the PPR, which placed itself in the position of claiming a monopoly on the intentions of Poles who wanted close relations with the Soviet Union.[31] As Mikolajczyk soon discovered, the PSL's view of Polish foreign relations did not coincide with the Kremlin's concept of what constituted a dependable pro-Soviet regime in Warsaw.

According to the agreement that resulted in the establishment of the Polish provisional government of national unity, Mikolajczyk's party was supposed to receive one-third of the seats in the temporary parliament when it was called into session. But the PSL never received the seats because the regime insisted that members of the fellow-traveling SL also be included. Eventually, when the parliament convened between December 29, 1945, and January 3, 1946, the PSL was offered fifty-two seats, considerably fewer than the one-third that had been originally proffered. The PSL decided to accept the seats because important legislation concerning the nationalization of industry and the nation's electoral law were scheduled to come before the parliament.[32]

Shortly after the PSL took its place in parliament, the PPS took the initiative on behalf of the communist bloc and, repeating an earlier offer, invited the PSL to join an electoral bloc in which it would have 20 percent of the seats. In a candid but conciliatory reply to the PPS and PPR on February 22, 1946, the PSL indicated that it shared many of the aims of the PPR and PPS and recognized that whatever the results of the future elections the three major parties must be reflected in the composition of a future permanent government for Poland. But it rejected the offer of 20 percent of the seats, indicating that 75 percent of the parliamentary representation should go to the representatives of the peasants—the PSL and SL. As Mikolajczyk later explained, the PSL "wanted only 51–52 percent." In its reply, the PSL also called for the abolition of the ministries of supply and propaganda and information, and demanded that the regime cease its attacks linking leaders of the PSL with the underground.[33]

The demand for 75 percent of the seats was rejected by the PPR, which was willing to grant the PSL and SL approximately 200 out of 444 seats, substantially fewer than the majority Mikolajczyk wanted. Because the PPR and PPS claimed peasant groups of their own, Gomulka argued that the peasants would be represented in parliament according to their actual strength.[34]

The refusal of the PSL to accept the offer of the government bloc condemned it in the eyes of the opposition to the reactionary camp. In the months that followed, the opposition increased propaganda attacks against the PSL, intimidated, harassed, and even murdered members of the PSL and seriously curtailed the press activity of the party. By the spring of 1946 the regime became more brazen in its efforts to intimidate the PSL. On March 12, for the first time, the security police raided the party's headquarters. In April the regime legalized ORMO, a kind of citizen's militia which had the effect of expanding the system of terror associated with the security police. Stanislaw Banczyk, vice-chairman of the PSL, delivered a major speech in parliament condemning the use of terror:

There is so much falseness, hypocrisy, and injustice in Poland today that an honest person is overcome by fear. We are pushed by the Marxists along the path which leads to the dictatorship of the proletariat by the use of superior force and oppression of all other parties. It is claimed that the Polish Peasant Party is reactionary. The criterion is that anyone who is not in favor of dictatorship is reactionary. Even our Boy Scouts have been declared a reactionary force. What became of our sacrifices during the war? The ordinary citizen feels worse than he did when there was no hope of improvement. There is no legality or security. In order to maintain itself the government has to keep many thousands of police who do not ask the citizen what he does or how he does it, but only in what he believes.

On May 3, 1946, the conflict between the PSL and its supporters on the one hand and the regime on the other became so bitter that the police attacked crowds of people who had gathered in several cities to celebrate the constitution adopted by the Polish Diet in 1791, the anniversary of which was observed as a Polish national holiday. Political feelings reached such a fever pitch of intensity that there was talk of a Polish civil war.[35]

The PSL could not effectively respond to the growing use of terror by the government. Controls and censorship of the press prevented the party from communicating the extent of the persecution through its newspapers and periodicals. *Gazeta Ludowa,* the official organ of the PSL, could not be published before it was subjected to government censorship. Once censored—usually 30 percent of the political contents of the paper was affected—the newspaper could not appear with blank spaces. Censorship even affected some commercial advertisements. Since distribution of the newspapers was a state monopoly, the distributors were often threatened with arrest and the papers seized by the security police.[36] That is why the PSL, which theoretically still had the right to assemble, tried to communicate the extent of the regime's political persecution by meetings and demonstrations which grew more difficult.

The severe pressure began to take its toll on the PSL. During an executive council meeting of the PSL at the end of May 1946, it was apparent that some leaders of the party favored joining an electoral bloc on terms substantially lower than those Mikolajczyk was holding out for. They argued that to continue to remain in opposition isolated the PSL from the political process. "We are not the navel of the world," one member exclaimed. Mikolajczyk's critics believed that

the PSL should not hold out for the future elections but try instead
to develop a political orientation that had the stamp neither of the
London Poles nor of the Soviet Poles. Faced with the rising criticism
of his own associates, Mikolajczyk shot back: "I did not tell anyone
to count on any miracle or on the threat of the atomic bomb."[37]

While the regime escalated the level of violence against the PSL,
Mikolajczyk and his colleagues countered with demands that the
promised elections be held by July 28, 1946, one year after the Potsdam Conference. The KRN, however, called for a referendum instead. The referendum would approve or disapprove three major
questions—the incorporation of the western lands from Germany, the
land reform and nationalization of industry, and the abolition of the
Senate. The government bloc's decision was an obvious attempt not
only to blunt the repeated criticisms of the regime by the PSL for
delaying the elections but also to demonstrate to the United States and
Britain, with whom the government wanted to firm up economic
relations, that the communist-dominated coalition enjoyed the popular support of the nation. At first the PSL threatened not to take part
in the referendum which was scheduled for June 1946 but later decided to participate after the regime pledged itself to hold the promised elections in the fall of 1946.[38]

The American State Department opposed the efforts of the communists and their supporters to present the Polish electorate with a single
list of candidates which might relegate the PSL to a role of ineffectiveness. Yet it revealed the weakness of the American position when it
advised in a policy and information statement in May of 1946, "Care
should be taken, however, not to overplay our support of Mikolajczyk
and his followers to the point where it might have the reverse of the
desired effect."[39] Like Mikolajczyk and his followers, the Department
of State did not anticipate the implications of insisting on a political
course that could only result in fraudulent elections.

One of the persistent themes in the attacks leveled by the PPR
against the PSL was the alleged link between it and the reactionary
elements in Poland who wanted to topple the government and establish a capitalist regime. The fact that the PSL repudiated the support
of reactionary groups failed to impress the communists, who were
convinced that the Polish underground was tied to the PSL. In May
1946 Gomulka said that "the time had come to announce to PSL
leaders that according to the wishes and interests of the major part
of the Polish nation and in conformity with the resolutions of the
Yalta and Potsdam conferences only antifascist democratic organizations can act legally in Poland."[40] To the communists, the PSL

wanted it both ways—to function as a legal body and to operate in collusion with terrorists.

In response to charges that it supported underground bands, the PSL declared: "These are irresponsible accusations and harmful charges, poisoning public life, filling it with the greatest distrust, calculated to disturb agitated people and people who are impassioned against the serious and responsible People's Movement." Then it tried to put the opposition on the defensive: "The agitators of PPR on many occasions have tried to join PSL with these bands. And when we come out in defense of our party and our honor immediately there is raised the great cry that we are defending these bands. Gentlemen, please stop joining PSL with these bands and then we will not have to write such articles because there will be no need for them. PSL does not organize bands and has no need of this."[41] One of the ironies in postwar Poland was that the actions of the Warsaw government were largely responsible for creating a new underground which, by supporting the PSL, seriously compromised the PSL's position and made it easier for the PPR to undermine it.

The Polish underground consisted of a heterogeneous group of political and military organizations which shared a common hostility toward the communists and with few exceptions supported the PSL. Some members came from the wartime underground—former soldiers in the Home Army—while others were newcomers, including deserters from the Polish Army, who were driven to clandestine operations against the Warsaw regime. Depite the fact that thousands of men ended their association with the underground by the amnesty granted by the government in August 1945, there were still probably 50,000–100,000 people in Poland's underground in the period 1945–1947.[42]

Several underground political groups established the coordinating commission of political parties, known as "The Center," to which was later added a military organization called "Freedom and Independence," or WIN, after the Polish words *Wolnosc i Niezawislosc.* WIN assumed control over former Home Army units and other partisan units which operated in the forests. WIN's commander, Colonel Jan Rzepecki, was arrested on November 5, 1945, but his place was taken by Colonel Franciszek Niepokolczycki, who met the same fate a short time later.[43] Other important groups of the underground included the National Armed Forces, or NSZ, an active right-wing group, and the Ukrainian Liberation Army, known as the UPA.

The scale of the underground's operations is revealed by the government claim that 15,000 people were killed by the underground in the period 1945–1948—7,500 in 1945 alone—with the greatest activity concentrated in Bialystok, Lublin, Rzeszow, Warsaw, Krakow, and Kielce.[44] The security police, dubbed the "Red Gestapo," were quite efficient in discovering, infiltrating, and attacking underground units. The success of the government's campaign was obvious by the decline in the underground's attacks from 1,214 in October 1946 to 178 in April 1947.[45]

Korbonski offered a vivid portrait of the chaos that existed in some parts of southern Poland in early 1946:

> These southern districts of ours, formerly called the "Wild Fields," comparable to the American Wild West early in the nineteenth century, are a veritable no man's land, haunted by Ukrainian gangs, a few scattered Home Army guerrillas, Zymierski's troops, and Soviet troops. It has become difficult to say who fights whom, for as a final touch, gangs of Soviet deserters attack all others. Zymierski's troops liquidate the latter with special ruthlessness. They express all their hatred for the Soviets on those innocent deserters. In many cases they also battle with "the fraternal Soviet army."[46]

One of the best-known leaders of a partisan band was Jozef Kuras, a Polish mountaineer who was known by the name of Ogien. Famous throughout Galicia, Ogien operated freely and virtually paralyzed the government's administration of the area. Protected by the local populace, he managed to conduct operations until early 1947 when he and his men were surrounded by security troops. After a battle in which his men were killed, Ogien committed suicide rather than be taken prisoner.[47]

Early in March 1946 the American ambassador to Warsaw, Arthur Bliss Lane, and his British counterpart, Victor Cavendish-Bentinck, were concerned by the scale of underground activities at a time when several thousand Soviet troops had recently been moved to the vicinity of Otwock and Anim, only a few miles from Warsaw. Lane and Bentinck feared that the dissatisfaction of so many Poles, coupled with the escalation of underground attacks, might spark an uprising which would result in stern retaliatory measures by the Soviets. Lane and Bentinck contacted individuals who were connected with the underground and urged restraint to avoid a repression which, in Lane's words, "would give the people to the east the excuse of imposing a military dictatorship on a permanent basis."[48]

Although the underground continued activities after 1947, its leadership, organization, and morale were seriously weakened. As a result

of the amnesties granted by the government, the ministry of public
security reported on May 7, 1947, that 55,277 people had revealed
themselves to the authorities. Of these, 22,887 were members of WIN,
4,892 came from the NSZ, 8,432 were members of forest units, and
7,448 had deserted from the Polish army.[49]

Following the war, relations between the Roman Catholic church
and the provisional government were tense, but neither side made an
overt effort to disturb the delicate modus vivendi. The government
allowed the church a brief respite while it dealt with the reconstruction needs of the state and the opposition represented by the PSL. To
be sure, the government left no doubt about what its policy toward
the church would be. In 1945 it voided the concordat of February
1925, justifying its action by the alleged pro-German policies of the
Vatican during World War II. Once the concordat was abrogated, the
church operated in a kind of vacuum until a new agreement replaced
it. Even the "Little Constitution" of 1947 did not allude to the subject
of religion.[50]

Relations between church and state grew increasingly strained
when Cardinal Augustus Hlond criticized the government following
the Kielce pogrom in July 1946.[51] Later, he and other prelates openly
endorsed the PSL in the elections of January 1947. "We had no
choice," Hlond told one interviewer. "It was a matter of atheism or
Christianity; barbarism or civilization"[52] It was predictable that
sooner or later the church would become the major source of opposition to the regime after the PSL was eliminated as a political factor
in Polish politics, playing a role so familiar to it in Poland's history.
Government activity against the church escalated in succeeding years,
reaching a high point in the spring of 1950 when the state nationalized
church land.

World War II had devastated Poland. Over 6 million Poles, almost
20 percent of the nation's people had died, the highest percentage of
loss suffered by any country overrun by Nazi Germany. According to
the Polish war reparations office, Poland lost 6,028,000 citizens between 1939 and 1945. Approximately 10.7 percent of the people died
as a result of military operations, while 89.9 percent perished as a
result of the Nazi terror. Of the total number of victims of the terror,
3,577,000 died in death camps or as a result of pacifications and
executions, 1,286,000 died in concentration and labor camps and in
prisons, and 521,000 died from wounds, injuries, overwork, or physical exhaustion. Among those who perished—mostly as victims of the
mass extermination campaign—were 3,200,000 Polish Jews.[53]

Economically, the country was in ruins. The Poles sustained losses estimated at $50–$60 billion or approximately 40 percent of the country's total wealth.[54] Poland lost 60 percent of its industrial capacity, 40 percent of its farm buildings and machinery, 72 percent of its sheep,and 60 percent of its cattle. Polish cities were gutted—almost 85 percent of Warsaw was destroyed and 80 percent of Wroclaw suffered damages.[55] When Mikolajczyk returned to the Polish capital in June 1945 he commented on seeing a devastated city and the smell of corpses lying under the rubble "like an evil blanket on the ruins." Irving Brant, a correspondent for the *Chicago Sun* who visited Warsaw in October 1945, wrote: "An American enters Warsaw with the feeling that he has stepped out of the real world into something which could not possibly exist. These rows of roofless, doorless, windowless walls, reaching in parallel columns mile on mile, might have been dug out of the earth by an army of archaeologists."[56]

Since the Nazis placed a high priority on destroying Polish culture, little wonder that Poland's cultural losses were so devastating. The intelligentsia died by the thousands. Polish educators especially suffered a very high mortality—700 university professors, 1,000 high school teachers and 4,000 elementary school teachers were eliminated. The Germans destroyed historical monuments, library collections and works of art. What the Germans did not destroy, they looted. One postwar visitor to Poland noted that when she walked into any government ministry, the walls were lined with heavy but empty bookcases. "In all of Poland," she said, "there are not enough books to cover the walls of the ministries."[57]

The task of reconstruction facing Poland was enormous. During the period 1945–1947, the PPR-controlled government wisely chose to pursue the goal of recovery, not socialism. Like Lenin's Russia in the 1920s, Poland needed a commitment to reconstruction, not ideology. Besides, the regime expected that its moderate political and economic policies would lure the intelligentsia who had survived the war to help rebuild the nation and to facilitate getting credits from the United States and Great Britain. The policy of moderation in these years worked. Even Mikolajczyk commented upon "the initial period of unbelievable enthusiasm" which characterized the spirit of the Polish people during the early postwar years.[58]

The Poland that emerged after World War II was approximately 20 percent smaller than it had been before the war. The Poles lost territory east of the Curzon Line, including oil fields, timber, salt deposits, and the major cultural centers of Vilna and Lwow. Moscow claimed the area the Poles won from Germany was worth at least two-and-a-half times more than what they had lost to the Soviet Union. One authority has indicated that the acquisitions in the West were so significant that even when war damages are factored, by 1946 Poland had an industrial production capacity one-third greater than prewar Poland.[59]

There is no doubt that despite its losses to the Soviets, Poland was potentially a stronger nation from an economic point of view than it had been before the war. It had acquired coal mining centers in Silesia, the richest coal fields in Europe, which even surpassed the reserves of the Ruhr. Poland not only acquired the hard coal and chemical industry of Silesia but also picked up lignite mines, rich deposits of zinc and lead, and machine-making, rolling-stock, textile, and glass factories. These lands also substantially added to Poland's output of electricity. And even though the Poles lost more agricultural land to the Russians than they gained from the Germans, the quality of the new lands was better.

The geographical changes gave Poland 500 kilometers of coastline in contrast to the prewar 140 kilometers. Poland now had several ports—Gdynia, which it had before the war; Gdansk, which had been the free city of Danzig but tied by a customs union with Poland; and Szczecin (Stettin), which was a major new gain. The acquisition of Szczecin was especially important because it enabled the Poles to use the Oder River, economically a far more important waterway than the Vistula, to export coal to Sweden and to import Swedish iron ore to Silesia.[60]

Poland was a more homogeneous nation than it had ever been in the past. Almost one-third of the people of prewar Poland were not Polish. Some of its largest minorities included 5 million Ukrainians, over 3 million Jews and 750,000 Germans. This ethnic heterogeneity was reflected in the diversity of religions—75 percent of the people were Roman Catholic and 25 percent belonged to the Orthodox, Jewish, and Protestant faiths. But after World War II there were only 500,000 non-Poles in the country, and 98 percent of Poland's citizens were Roman Catholic.[61]

One of the immediate tasks facing the Warsaw government was to resettle the lands acquired from Germany. Stalin argued at the Potsdam Conference that all the Germans had fled the area before the arrival of Soviet troops. This, of course, was an exaggeration. There was a large German population there when the Poles began to administer the area. Moreover, many Germans who had fled out of fear of Soviet retribution returned to their homes, unable or unwilling to accept the fact that eastern Germany was now Polish. Even after most of the Germans were transferred from the region in 1946, many Germans assumed that Polish mismanagement would inevitably lead to the appointment of other administrators for the area—no doubt Germans.[62]

In view of the enormous devastation, the dismantling and looting of property by the Soviets, and the sheer magnitude of transferring Germans out of and Poles into the area, it is remarkable that the new provinces began to assume a Polish character as soon as they did. On November 20, 1945, the Allied Control Council approved a plan which provided for the transfer of 3.5 million Germans from western Poland—the Soviets agreed to accept 2 million and the British 1.5 million in their zones of occupation. The major expulsions of Germans from Poland were completed by 1946, though another 500,000 were transferred from Poland to the Soviet zone of Germany in 1947. By 1948 approximately 5.25 million Poles lived in the western territories while only 100,000 Germans remained there. Considering what the Poles had experienced at the hands of the Germans during the war, they were not overly sensitive to the conditions under which the expellees were transferred from the area. One recent critic has claimed that the transfer of Germans from Poland and Czechoslovakia was conducted in such a way as to constitute a crime against humanity.[63]

The Poles were so enthusiastic about acquiring the new lands that even a heavy tax, the proceeds of which were to be spent on the development of the region, was not unpopular. The Polish settlers in the "Recovered Territories," the term the Poles used to describe the lands which had once been part of medieval Poland, were very poor and came from the more densely populated areas of the nation. The inhabitants of the western lands were shocked by the poverty and the ignorance of intensive farming methods of the new immigrants. No doubt this was the basis of the German expectation that the Polish settlers would fail to develop the resources of the area. Belying all predictions of disaster, the Poles succeeded in rebuilding the region and in producing a bumper crop by 1949.[64]

Poland's early postwar economic policy was characterized by the nationalization of key industries and land reform. Before World War II a high percentage of Poland's industrial reserves had been foreign owned. In 1936, almost 90 percent of the oil industry, 60 percent of the chemical industry, more than 50 percent of the metal industry and more than 80 percent of the nation's electric power were in foreign hands. Out of 1,066 joint-stock companies, more than one-third had heavy foreign capitalization. What was not under foreign control fell under state ownership. The state owned the armament and commer-

cial air industries and controlled most of the iron, railway, merchant
marine, and salt industries. During the Nazi occupation, most factories and mines had come under German control and, in effect, their
owners had been dispossessed. Czeslaw Milosz, the Nobel laureate,
said: "We must remember that five and a half years of Nazi rule had
obliterated all respect for private property."[65]

Thus the substance of the nationalization law of January 3, 1946,
which allowed the government to take over enterprises employing fifty
people or more during a single shift, did not provoke much controversy in Poland. There was debate, however, over how the measure
would be administered. Except in the case of German-owned enterprises, the principle of compensation was recognized. This meant that
American investors, whose investments totaled $210 million in Po-
land before the Second World War, could expect to receive compensation. The State Department looked upon the nationalization of
industry in broader terms than simply the amount and method of
compensation to former owners. It viewed the nationalization program as a determined effort by the Polish communists to diminish
Poland's western orientation and to tie it more closely to the Soviet
Union. "Next to Catholicism and immigration," the State Department declared, one of Poland's most intimate ties with the West was
western involvement in key Polish industries. The department opined,
"One of the most interesting aspects of the political contest in the
months ahead is likely to be the endeavors of Polish traditionalism,
as typified in Mikolajczyk and his movement, to preserve these Western ties in economic as in other ways."[66]

Another law passed the same day protected private enterprise in
businesses not covered by the nationalization law. According to an
UNRRA report published in April 1947, 80 percent of the Polish
working class was employed in privately owned enterprises and only
20 percent worked in the nationalized sector of the economy.[67]

One of the major problems facing the Warsaw government was the
shortage of workers for all the nation's industries. Late in 1945, Minc
himself admitted that in order to meet the minimum needs of the
territories acquired from Germany, 300,000–400,000 additional Polish workers were required.[68] The shortage of workers emphasized the
pragmatic necessity for the Warsaw government to project an image
of moderation at home and abroad in order to induce the Polish
skilled workers and technicians to return to work and help rebuild the
nation. No doubt, too, this impelled the Poles to keep rather than to
repatriate the skilled German workers who lived in postwar Poland.

Predictably the poor wages paid to Polish workers was another problem facing the government. The rise of wages never did keep up with the rise in the cost of living. Although nominal wages doubled in 1946 and 1947, real wages increased only 29 percent. In March 1947 the index of real wages was still only 51.2 percent of the 1938 level. To make matters worse, wages were often paid in kind. In January 1946 less than half of the workers' salaries were paid in cash. It was not unusual for workers to be paid in bread. Worker dissatisfaction with the situation resulted in strikes among the employees of textile factories in Lodz who objected to what was called the 'Pstrowski' system, a Polish version of Stakhanovism.[69]

Throughout 1946 and much of 1947 the Polish government especially emphasized the private enterprise component of its hybrid economy in its dealings with the West. As will be seen in more detail later, this was a time during which the credit-hungry Polish government was most anxious to foster and develop closer economic ties with the United States, the country that was in the best possible position to meet Polish economic needs.

The agrarian reform of September 6, 1944, extended to all parts of the nation by the end of the war, was a major factor in neutralizing the peasantry at a time when the PPR was trying to isolate and eventually destroy the PSL as a force in Polish political life. The land reform, popular among the poor peasants who benefited most from it, provided that all estates exceeding 100 hectares in total area or 50 hectares of cultivable land in central Poland would be expropriated. In western Poland, only holdings in excess of 100 hectares, regardless of the amount of cultivable land, were broken up. The land made available by the reform was divided into 5-hectare farms. In the western territories, however, the regime permitted individual farms to be a little larger—7–15 hectares and up to 20 hectares for dairy farms.[70] The PSL, criticizing the small size of the holdings, hoped that a middle class of peasant farmers would be created in Poland. To Mikolajczyk and his followers, the PPR-inspired reform was a deliberate effort to sabotage the success of the newly created farms—they were considered too small to be productive—and to make it easier eventually to collectivize them. The PSL's criticism did not find a responsive audience among farm laborers and small peasants whose land hunger was appeased by what appeared to them to be a concerned government.[71]

The area most affected by the land reform was western Poland. It was there that more than two-thirds of the 6 million hectares which were available for private use was distributed to individual farmers. The state held back almost 4 million hectares and converted most of

the acreage into state farms.[72] A substantial amount of the arable land
in western Poland remained in Soviet hands, ostensibly to feed the
Soviet army there. As late as April 1947 the Poles and Soviets signed
an agreement which looked toward a reduction of Soviet land holdings from 340,000 to 180,000 hectares.[73]

In the period 1945–1947, the PPR-dominated government was in
no position to carry on a major political struggle with the PSL without
trying to mitigate the fear of the Polish peasants that collectivization
was just around the corner. There was at least no open talk of collectivization. Czeslaw Milosz remarked that "whoever dared to speak of
collectives at that time was punished as an enemy of the people for
spreading alarm and slandering the government."[74] One American
authority on Polish agriculture has suggested that before 1948 the
PPR was not even thinking in terms of collectivized agriculture. And
when it finally got around to doing so, the PPR announced the extremely modest target of collectivizing only 1 percent of Poland's
privately owned farms in 1949.[75]

Predictably, Poland's principal trade partner in 1945 was the Soviet
Union. Approximately 91 percent of the nation's imports and 93
percent of its exports were exchanged with the Soviets. Yet by 1946
the figures had dropped to 70 percent and 46 percent, respectively. In
1947, despite increased volume, the Soviet share of Poland's imports
and exports dropped to less than 30 percent. The same pattern was
true of Poland's foreign trade with other eastern European nations in
this period.[76] This decline stemmed largely from the fact that Polish
economic needs could not be met exclusively by the Soviet Union and
the other states of eastern Europe.

This does not mean that the Kremlin allowed Polish economic
interests to take priority over those of the Soviet Union. Despite
imaginative and resourceful efforts by Warsaw to diversify its commercial connections with the West, the Soviet Union subjected Poland
to a consistent pattern of economic exploitation. The Poles first got
a taste of it when the Soviets seized and dismantled property from
Poland's western lands. That was accompanied by robbing, looting,
and raping by soldiers of the Soviet army, a situation not limited to
the western territories alone.[77] Beginning in 1945, the price structures
in bilateral agreements between the two nations revealed the extent
to which Poland was exploited by the Soviets. Evidence suggests that
before 1948 Poland was required to pay 131 zloty for every dollar of
imports from the Soviet Union while the Soviets paid the equivalent
of 75 zloty for every dollar of Polish goods.[78]

The most notorious example of Soviet economic exploitation was contained in the Soviet-Polish Frontier and Reparations Agreement of August 16, 1945. In compensation for waiving its rights to former German mines in Poland's western territories and for the delivery to Poland of 15 percent of German reparations, the Soviet Union was to receive 8 million tons of coal from Poland in 1946 and 13 million each year thereafter until 1950 at which time deliveries were to level off to 12 million tons a year as long as Germany was occupied.[79]

During the discussions that led to this agreement, the Soviets had suggested an exchange of stock in the eastern Galician oil and potash deposits for Polish-owned concerns in the territory acquired from Germany. Since that inevitably meant Soviet control of much of Polish industry and little or no Polish influence in the oil and potash industries in eastern Galicia, the Poles turned down the offer. Thereupon the Soviets wanted the Poles to sell them coal for $1.00 a ton when the official export price was $8.00 a ton and some countries had offered Poland as much as $12.00 a ton. Premier Osobka-Morawski defended the deal on the grounds that Polish assistance to the Soviet Union "will be returned to us." As finally worked out, the Soviets ended up paying the Poles a few more cents—$1.25-$1.30 a ton. In Mikolajczyk's account of the background to this agreement he suggests that the Soviets originally were willing to pay the cost of mining the coal, which was $5.00 or $6.00 a ton, but that Minc was allegedly responsible for lowering the figure that was finally agreed upon. When Mikolajczyk characterized the deal as robbery, Minc rebuked him saying, "You seem to forget how much Soviet Russia has done for us; how it liberated us and helped us." Mikolajczyk was unimpressed. "If Hitler had not attacked them, they'd still be the enemy of Poland and all the Allies," he replied. Mikolajczyk was overruled. The agreement stood.[80] In March 1947 the amount of the so-called "reparation coal" was reduced by half, but an agreement of January 1948 determined Poland's coal export to the Soviet Union at 6.5 million tons. By then, the Soviets had agreed to pay a higher price for the coal—$2.25 a ton —but still considerably less than it cost the Poles to mine it.[81]

Despite the large amounts of coal that were exported to the Soviet Union at ridiculously low prices in the period 1945–1948, Polish coal production was so high—24 million tons in 1945, 47 million tons in 1946[82]—that Poland was able to sell large quantities to western Europe, which regarded it as a major factor in its postwar recovery. The French not only admitted their dependency upon Polish coal but also stressed the important role of Poland in the economic unity of Europe. In July 1947 French President Paul Ramadier said: "Indeed, it is indispensable that this unity should include Poland for it can be said that Europe extends as far as [the] Vistula. Beyond, things are different. To wish to have Europe stop this side of [the] Vistula would be equivalent to having [the] United States stop at [the] Mississippi."[83]

On July 2, 1947, the Sejm passed the Three Year Plan of Economic Reconstruction which was intended to raise the standard of living of the working people above the prewar level by concentrating on restoring existing plants to full capacity. Three sectors of the economy—state, cooperative, and private—would operate according to the guiding principles of the national economic plan.[84] One of the major aims of the plan was to unify the former German lands with central Poland. To that end, Gomulka's separate ministry for the administration of the former German areas was abolished and the new land was incorporated within the framework of the general administrative system of Poland.[85]

Neither the Poles nor the Czechs, both of whom expressed cautious interest in the American offer of the Marshall Plan, were permitted by the Kremlin to participate in a program that linked them economically with the West. With the advent of the Cold War, whatever economic autonomy the Poles had managed to establish within the Soviet sphere of influence between 1945 and 1948 gave way to new political and economic dynamics within the communist world which now emphasized long-range planning and development in order to strengthen and integrate the political and economic systems of the Soviet Union and the satellites.

III From Potsdam to Kielce

Washington recognized that Poland was in the Soviet sphere of influence, but it expected to exert some political and economic influence there after World War II. Whatever optimism Washington may have had about its ability to play a role in postwar Warsaw soon gave way to uncertainty, resulting in an ambivalence in American policy toward Poland. In the months following the Potsdam Conference, the United States believed that Polish reconstruction needs made Poland dependent upon American economic aid, which presumably would enable Washington to moderate communist rule in Poland and to safeguard the position of Mikolajczyk and the PSL, around which the hopes of the United States were based.

Despite the urging of its ambassador in Warsaw, the United States did not directly tie its economic aid to Poland to political conditions. Rather, Washington extended credits after receiving Polish assurances of an economic open door for the United States in Poland. Since Poland had enormous reconstruction needs and would require additional American aid, Washington expected to have a lever to influence the political situation in the country. Before and after the extension of economic aid to Poland, the communists steadily expanded their political grip over the country, intimidating, harassing, and terrorizing the PSL. By the summer of 1946, Washington policymakers no longer believed that genuinely free elections would ever be held in Poland, but they still had hope that the future of the PSL and American interests, which were closely tied to it, was not entirely grim.

Before the Potsdam Conference, the State Department had advised the president about the impact of American economic assistance to Poland: "Immediate action on our part to facilitate by credits and otherwise the supplying to Poland of urgently needed equipment and relief materials will promote in a far-reaching and enduring manner a healthy American influence in Poland, especially in regard to the holding of free elections, the final step in the Yalta program." In order to maximize the influence of economic aid, the State Department preferred that American efforts be on a national basis rather than through an international organization such as UNRRA. Betraying an obvious sensitivity to the relationship of the Polish issue to American domestic politics, the State Department urged that the sooner relations between the two countries were normalized the better it would be: "The rapid establishment of normal friendly relations and contacts between our two countries is particularly important, since the populations of Polish extraction in our country might otherwise seek to make a domestic American political issue of conditions inside Poland."[1]

Averell Harriman, the American ambassador to the Kremlin who kept a close eye on Polish developments prior to the time Lane took up his diplomatic post in Warsaw, had long been a proponent of American economic leverage in dealing with the Soviet Union.[2] And Poland was no exception. Harriman was convinced that "if we continue to take a sympathetic interest in Polish affairs and are reasonably generous in our economic relations there is a fair chance that things will work out satisfactorily from our standpoint."[3] Harriman advised Washington that "it is of inestimable importance from a political standpoint" to grant at least small credits to Poland to permit purchase and shipment of equipment needed for reconstruction. He saw these smaller credits being expanded later through the Export-Import Bank when Congress appropriated additional funds. To Harriman there was "no doubt" that prompt aid to Poland would "have a far-reaching and permanent effect on the influence of the US in the political scene in Poland." The ambassador felt that an immediate and dramatic gesture, such as sending several hundred used trucks from the United States army in Europe, would help to strengthen the prowestern elements in the Polish government. "In other words," Harriman declared, "I feel that a small gesture made quickly will be of even greater political as well as practical value than substantially larger transactions made at a later date."

By the time of the Potsdam meeting, the United States had drawn up a tentative program of economic assistance by which Poland would receive UNRRA supplies, surplus war materiel—including the army trucks—and eventually, after certain legal barriers were removed, loans from the Export-Import Bank. The United States looked to the early reestablishment of private trade and regarded the Treaty of Friendship, Commerce and Consular Rights, negotiated in 1931, as still effective, though welcomed an improved treaty with Poland. State Department officials urged the Poles to submit a list of their reconstruction needs, and at the Postdam Conference the Polish delegation presented its priority needs, which included ports and port equipment, the city of Warsaw, railways, cars, locomotives, bridges, highways, trucks, and road building machinery.[5] It was assumed that whatever credits the United States extended to the Polish government would be contingent on equality of trade opportunities and investments and access to sources of information for the United States.[6]

United States aid to Poland had been predicated on the assumption that the Polish need was so great that the Warsaw regime would not take actions to jeopardize it. That assumption was disproved after Arthur Bliss Lane took up his post in Warsaw as ambassador to Poland. Lane, born into a wealthy Brooklyn family, had graduated from Yale in 1916 and only a few years later served as second secretary of the American legation in Warsaw under minister Hugh Gibson. After that, he served with distinction in several diplomatic posts in Europe and Latin America.[7] Lane was conscientious and professional, though at times he could be too idealistic and unimaginative. He was tenacious in devoting himself to the fulfillment of America's commitment to see that free elections were held in Poland as provided in the Yalta and Potsdam declarations. When Lane saw early in his mission that Poland was unlikely to become independent, he believed that the Polish experience could serve as a valuable lesson to educate the American public in the failure of a policy based on accommodation with the communists, thereby forcing a reevaluation of American policies toward the communist world.[8] Having an abrasive diplomat like Lane in Warsaw during this crucial time in United States-Polish relations did not augur well for the future. What the United States needed in Poland was a more imaginative and flexible man who, by being sensitive to the political and economic nuances of postwar Poland, could exploit various opportunities to American advantage.

After Lane's arrival in Warsaw, the Poles made clear their eagerness to establish economic contacts with the United States. In return for the promise of economic aid, Bierut told Lane that Poland was prepared to permit American consulates to open in several cities— Gdansk, Krakow, Lodz, Poznan, Breslau—to allow planes of the United States Army Air Forces Air Transport Command to fly to Warsaw, to permit American newsmen to enter the country and report on developments there, and to welcome a congressional committee on a tour of the country.[9] It did not take Lane very long to establish contacts with antiregime leaders—Archbishop Stefan Sapieha, Stanislaw Grabski, Wincenty Witos, Zygmunt Zulawski— who convinced him that an American credit to Poland would be interpreted by the Polish people as acquiescence in the undemocratic and even brutal practices which existed in the country.[10] Lane himself had observed several actions of the regime which made him question the wisdom of extending credits.

In the political area, Lane complained about the lack of freedom of the press. Before Lane's intervention in the matter, Polish author-

ities wanted newsmen to submit copies of their stories to the Polish
foreign office before they were transmitted abroad. He criticized the
lack of political freedom, which included the terrorization of noncommunist parties and the arrests by the security police of many people
who claimed American citizenship. In order to bolster the position of
the PSL, Lane endorsed Mikolajczyk's plea that the United States
strongly press the Kremlin to withdraw the Soviet army from Poland.
Lane expressed concern about the prospect of Poland ever having free
elections when terror was used against the political opposition and
tied the entire matter to Poland's request for American credits.[11]
Bierut, who took a strong dislike to Lane, bluntly told him that
Poland would not accept American meddling in its internal affairs as
the price of economic aid, a position that the Warsaw government
steadfastly maintained throughout Lane's tenure in Poland.[12] On his
part, Lane did not share the optimism of the Polish people in 1945
about the prospect of free elections. He told Elbridge Durbrow, chief
of the division of Eastern European affairs of the State Department
on October 22, 1945: "Unfortunately, I feel that as both the Government and the Government to the east desire that the local crowd
here should remain in power, I do not see much hope of a free
expression of opinion."[13]

In the economic area, Lane was concerned that the proposed nationalization program might not adequately compensate former owners. He was especially disturbed by Warsaw's failure to establish a
reasonable rate of exchange. The official rate of 100 zloty for $1.00
was unrealistic, considering the rampant inflation in Poland. The
black market rate was 200 zloty for $1.00 in the summer of 1945, and
six months later it catapulted to 1,300 to 1. The impact of the official
exchange rate was such that Lane joined other ambassadors in Warsaw and exchanged their currencies for zloty on the black market.[14]

Lane urged Washington not to extend credits to Poland as long as
Warsaw engaged in political and economic policies opposed by the
United States. He recognized that American refusal to extend the
credits could make the Poles even more dependent upon the Kremlin.
But, Lane told Byrnes: "I feel that unless we speak clearly and em-
phatically to the Polish government at this moment, when the regime
here is requesting definite financial assistance, we will be losing an
opportunity to make felt our prestige and at the same time we may
be able, as has been shown on other occasions in Soviet-controlled
territory, to influence conditions for the better by taking a strong
determined stand against any movement to stifle democratic life in
Poland." In other words, as Lane wrote later, he was determined to

use American economic leverage to pressure the Poles to follow policies acceptable to the United States.[15]

The State Department saw matters more in economic than political
terms, though it did not reject attaching political conditions to credits
for Poland. Dean Acheson, who served as acting secretary of state
while Byrnes was preoccupied with the problem of the postwar peace
treaties, advised Lane that if Poland did not grant American business
treatment as favorable as that it granted other countries he saw no
hope for substantial American financial aid to Warsaw. Byrnes later
told Lane much the same thing, emphasizing the important point that
before the United States granted credits it would have to have economic data regarding commercial arrangements between Poland and
other countries. But Byrnes also indicated that political conditions
relating to freedom of the press and the promised elections had not
been ruled out.[16]

While the State Department tried to come to grips with a definite
policy concerning aid to Poland, the Poles made it clear that their
economic needs were both substantial and immediate. Ludwik Rajchman, a kind of Polish Talleyrand who once enjoyed the confidence of
premier Wladyslaw Sikorski and now was Poland's representative to
UNRRA, played a major role in promoting his government's economic needs in Washington. He told State Department officials in
October 1945 that his country needed an immediate loan of $380
million and looked toward a total figure of $700 million.[17] Durbrow
worried that the resourceful Rajchman might succeed in convincing
the right people in Washington to give the Poles the sought-after
credits. Durbrow confided to Lane: "While so far we have had success, I frankly do not feel that we can guarantee that things will
remain this way since Dr. Rajchman has many friends, some of whom
may be able to swing this way from the firm position we have all taken.
In any event, we shall keep up the good fight from our end."[18]

Lane, Durbrow, and others had indeed succeeded in convincing the
administration not to give large credits to Poland in 1945. The United
States had agreed to a three-year credit for the purchase of a thousand
army trucks which, considering the Polish need for vehicles, Poland
did not appear very eager to take advantage of. However, the United
States refused to grant credits to cover the equipping of the Polish
army with uniforms, boots and overcoats. Though Warsaw had been
included in the list of governments to receive a cotton credit through
the Export-Import Bank, the State Department recommended against
it.[19]

Late in 1945, however, the visit of Mikolajczyk, who stopped in Washington on his return from a United Nations food and agriculture meeting in Quebec, proved to be a turning point in American economic relations with Poland. Unlike so many of Lane's contacts in Poland, Mikolajczyk believed that United States credits were one of the best assurances of Poland regaining its independence and showing the Polish people that the West was still very much interested in them. In addition, American credits would offset the image of the Soviets, who had made more promises than they were able or willing to keep.[20] When Mikolajczyk saw Truman on November 9, 1945, the president was agreeable to assisting Poland to meet its immediate needs to buy trucks, rolling stock, tractors, and harbor and road repair machinery. Mikolajczyk did not ask for nor did Truman agree to an unlimited credit for Poland.[21] Based upon this understanding, the State Department planned to release surplus stocks of trucks and other equipment, to approve $25 million for projects approved by the American embassy in Warsaw and to provide an additional $25 million to fund one major reconstruction project, such as a port. Byrnes, after hearing Mikolajczyk's assessment of the Polish situation, believed that the stopgap credit policy would let the Polish people know that the United States had not abandoned them; yet, it would not necessarily contribute to the prestige of the Warsaw regime. Lane agreed to the limited credit policy, though he still opposed long-range loans to the Warsaw government, which, in his words, would make "political capital" out of it.[22]

By the end of 1945 Washington concluded that it could not procrastinate much longer in developing an economic policy that would give at least a token American presence in Poland. Byrnes, still optimistic about the situation for the United States in Poland, believed that it was not wise to politicize American aid to Warsaw at a time when he was anxious to secure Soviet agreement to peace treaties with the Balkan states and to a four-power pact which might induce the Soviets to loosen their grip over east central Europe. Byrnes was interested in finding common political ground with the Soviets, even though some of his rhetoric at times sounded abrasive. As one scholar has aptly put it, "Byrnes continued to seek an arrangement whereby Soviet control in East Europe would be dominant, but not exclusive."[23] Moreover, the State Department believed that it was easier for the United States to apply economic than political pressure in Warsaw. Economic issues were specific and obviously less likely to provoke charges of American interference in the internal affairs of Poland. Even though it was doubtful that the promised elections in

Poland would be free, "Washington could more easily object to what had already happened than to what might be expected to occur later."[24]

Besides, the political situation in Poland was not entirely grim. After all, the PSL flourished, despite communist harassment. The PSL was still represented in the government and the PPR and PPS courted Mikolajczyk's party to join the government bloc. Even Lane, usually so pessimistic about the situation in Poland, noted some improvement at this time concerning press freedom and commented on the effort of the government to come to terms on some of the issues dividing the United States and Poland.[25] Byrnes still thought the political experiment in Warsaw was sufficiently positive to use as a model to solve problems in Rumania in the fall of 1945.[26]

Byrnes's reluctance to protest every political transgression of the PPR-dominated government is revealed by his refusal to take a strong stand, urged upon him by Lane, when the communists limited political parties in Poland to six organizations. To be sure, the United States could not defend the anti-Semitic Endeks, one of the prewar right-wing groups excluded from the Polish political spectrum. Besides, Mikolajczyk feared that more than six political parties might draw away support from the PSL. Finally, just as the State Department had anticipated, even a relatively moderate protest by Lane to Bierut on the issue brought a tough rejoinder that the United States should mind its own business.[27]

But Byrnes could not ignore domestic and foreign sources which pressured him to speak out against the mounting repression that was taking place in Poland. Late in January 1946, while the American delegation to the United Nations met in London, foreign secretary Ernest Bevin in the House of Commons strongly condemned the political murders that had occurred in Poland and charged the Polish security police with the crimes. The American delegation felt the United States should take some position on the matter.[28] Senator Arthur Vandenberg of Michigan, one of the members of the delegation, felt very strongly about the issue. Vandenberg, sensitive to the opinion of the large number of Polish American voters in his state, had close ties with Frank Januszewski, publisher of the Detroit *Dziennik Polski (Polish Daily News)* and one of the founders of KNAPP —the *Komitet Narodowy Amerykanow Pochodzenia Polskiego* (National Committee of Americans of Polish Descent)—a nationalistic, anti-Soviet organization established in New York in June 1942. Januszewski, who also was prominent in the Polish American Congress, a huge federation of Polish American fraternal, church, and professional organizations which had been established in May 1944,[29] had urged Vandenberg for a long time to speak out strongly for the rights of Poland and to condemn the policies of the Soviet Union. Shortly before the Vandenberg mission to London, Januszewski wrote an emotional appeal to the senator:

> Make our people realize that Polish rights have been trampled under the boot of an aggressor—her courts robbed of their independence—her press of freedom of speech—her working class of freedom of assembly—all persons deprived of the right to choose their work and excluded from the possibility of right to the results their work may bring. Make them see that since Teheran, Yalta,and Potsdam each of us is responsible for thousands of executions of brave Polish patriots, tens of thousands of political arrests, hundreds of thousands of deportations.[30]

Vandenberg, regarded by Polish Americans as the major defender of the rights of the Polish nation in the United States Senate, believed that the United States should "defend whatever Polish equities may still remain" in Poland.[31] He met with members of the former Polish government in exile and threatened to make a statement about the political situation in Poland unless Byrnes made one himself. Senator Thomas Connally, chairman of the Senate foreign relations committee and also a member of the American United Nations delegation in London, told Byrnes how strongly Vandenberg felt about the matter: "We kind of thought that if you decided to make a statement, you could base it on Bevin's. I think that will satisfy him, but if you don't . . . I think he will go on his own and make a statement along the line of Bevin's. He said in conversation to me the other night 'My God! Why can't we do something like this!' And he has been bawling on this ever since."[32]

Byrnes was reluctant to make a statement as strong as the one made by the British foreign minister unless the facts justified it. He preferred to deal in general terms, avoiding, as he put it, "a general row." Byrnes's statement, far more restrained than Bevin's, noted that the Polish security police appeared to have been implicated "in a number" of the murders which hindered Poland's fulfillment of its election commitments. He called on the Polish government "to take necessary steps to assure the freedom and security which are essential to the successful holding of free elections."[33] While Vandenberg thought the statement too mild,[34] the Poles thought Byrnes had gone too far. Foreign minister Rzymowski charged that members of the Polish security police had been murdered by underground groups who allegedly took orders from General Wladyslaw Anders, a well-known Russophobe who had led Polish soldiers out of Russia in 1942 and commanded them in several gallant military operations in the West during World War II. Rzymowski further charged that the British had evidence of this activity but refused to stop it. The Pole also suggested that some of the leaders of the Polish terrorists were ensconced in the American occupation zone in Germany.[35]

Before the United States came up with a definite economic policy toward Poland, Lane, who had angered Polish officials by his candid observations concerning the growing repression in their country, became the victim of a crude attempt by the Warsaw regime to discredit him. After the nationalization decree of January 1946, the Polish government distorted Lane's remarks about the rights of former owners to inspect their properties slated for nationalization to suggest that he opposed the decree. The effort to discredit Lane was well orchestrated and involved Rajchman, whose mission in Washington played a major role in seeking loans for Poland, and Rzymowski, who flew to Paris to complain directly to Byrnes about Lane.[36] The misrepresentation of remarks made by Lane and statements of Byrnes concerning the exchange rate was too much for the harried secretary of state who wanted the Poles to know that their tactics "cannot fail to have an unfortunate effect upon our relations with the Pol[ish] Provisional Gov[ernment] and upon the current credit negotiations in particular."[37]

United States–Polish economic negotiations began to crystallize early in 1946. The decisive factor was western Europe's need for coal and Poland's ability to deliver it, provided the Poles had enough locomotives and gondolas to do so. As Byrnes cabled Lane, "If we should refuse credit [for] this purpose now we might be open [to the] accusation next winter that vitally needed Polish coal could not be moved to western Europe because [the] U.S. Gov[ernment] refused credits." Moreover, there were obvious benefits to help orient Polish trade toward the West,[38] a healthy development which Polish officials continually repeated would reduce Poland's dependence upon the Soviet Union.

The United States was prepared to grant Poland a $40 million credit from the Export-Import Bank, considerably less than the Polish request to buy 500 locomotives and 20,000 gondola cars at an estimated cost of $90 to $100 million. The credit was contingent upon Polish acceptance of six conditions, only one of which was political in nature. Poland was expected to affirm the principles of free trade, agree with American proposals for expansion of world trade and employment, extend most-favored nation treatment to the United States, agree to respect rights of American citizens and compensate them for the nationalization of their properties, provide full information on Polish economic relations with other countries, and reaffirm the Potsdam commitment concerning free elections. If the Poles accepted the conditions and concluded a bilateral air agreement with Washington, then the State Department was prepared to extend additional credit to Warsaw. If the Poles did not agree to the six conditions, the State Department was prepared, as a demonstration of friendship to the Polish people, to agree to a $25 million credit.[39]

In addition, Washington offered a $50 million credit to purchase surplus property, excluding munitions and other military supplies, from the Federal Liquidation Commission.[40] The credit for surplus goods, however, was not tied to the six conditions imposed on the Poles for the Export-Import Bank credit for the obvious reason that the United States wanted to get rid of the property it not longer needed.

Polish and American officials exchanged notes for the $40 million credit on April 24, 1946, and the Poles promised to publish the notes in the Polish press. Two days later Osobka-Morawski told the Polish parliament that the promised elections would be held in accordance with the Yalta and Potsdam pledges and that the upcoming referendum, scheduled for June, was to be "an initial step leading to these elections."[41]

Lane had consistently opposed American credits to Poland until political repression and violations of freedom of the press had stopped. To Lane, it simply made no sense to grant credits at a time when the Warsaw regime flouted its Yalta and Potsdam pledges. "Mikolajczyk's chances of winning the elections are virtually nil," he wrote in March 1946. He doubted there was much the United States could do in the next few years in Poland "except to show sympathy for the Polish people and to maintain our firm position regarding American rights." But there was an important educational value to the grim future for Poland and other eastern European countries. He told H. Freeman Matthews, director of the office of European affairs of the State Department,

> I feel that we should look at the situation in Poland from a long range viewpoint and in connection with similar situations in other countries within the Soviet orbit. I believe it essential for the Congress and for the American public to be informed regarding conditions in Poland, Yugoslavia, etc. Education of the

public cannot take place overnight. In my opinion, it will perhaps take a year or two. There will be attacks on us from the left-wing press and from some of the more radical labor elements to the effect that we are endeavoring to bring about hostilities with the Soviet Union. Our stand should, in my opinion, be based not on ideologies but on determination to protect American lives and property rights.[43]

When he learned that Washington intended to follow through with the credits, Lane pleaded with Byrnes not to do it: "With the greatest earnestness of which I am capable I beg the Department not to approve the extension of any credit facilities at this time." When the United States–Polish agreement was reached, Lane interpreted the State Department's action as a vote of no confidence in him as ambassador.[44] Lane attended the meeting of the Polish parliament on April 26 when Osobka-Morawski jubilantly announced to the delegates that Washington had granted the long-sought credits. The spectacle was too much for Lane; he became so enraged that his hands trembled and his speech became so incoherent that his interpreter, Lt. William Tonesk, thought he had suffered a stroke.[45]

The British position came close to that of Lane. Bevin was "dismayed" by Washington's decision to grant the credit because, in his judgment, all the United States received in return were "paper commitments." The British hoped that the United States would at least defer the credit until the Polish government set a definite date for the elections or until after the June referendum. Ideally, the British hoped the United States would not grant Warsaw any credits until after the promised elections actually took place.[46] Like Lane, the British government urged Washington to tell the Poles that no aid would be forthcoming until political conditions improved, especially an end to the activities of the security police against the PSL and a definite date had been set for the elections. The British foreign office wanted Britain and the United States to "make it clear that, until the elections have taken place, they meant to insist upon the full observance of the Moscow Agreement as the result of which recognition was granted to the present Polish Provisional Government."[47]

Shortly after the Poles and Americans exchanged notes on the credit agreement, the Polish government made an effort to appease the United States on two issues which had disturbed relations between the two countries—namely, the question of compensating Americans whose property had been nationalized and allowing American embassy officials to communicate with jailed individuals who claimed to be American citizens.[48] For months Lane had tried to protect American interests on both issues but without much success. When Lane approached Polish officials concerning arrested Poles who claimed American citizenship, he usually was told that the people had acquired Polish citizenship and had been jailed for being members of criminal and terrorist bands. As a gesture of conciliation, the Polish government granted exit visas to fifty-six American nationals at this time. It also proposed that the two governments establish a commission composed of representatives from both nations, to determine the citizenship of the arrested claimants. However, the first meeting was not held until June 1947.[49]

There were still additional snags to be untangled in the credit arrangements. Poland did not publish the exchange of notes of April 24 in the Polish press and did not provide its economic treaties with other nations to the United States, both of which the two governments had agreed upon during the negotiations. Lane flew to Paris to meet Byrnes and convinced him that the United States should stop aid to Poland until the Poles met all the conditions of the agreement. Byrnes wired Acheson that all but $3.7 million worth of surplus, which had already been delivered to the Poles under the surplus property arrangement, be stopped. Also, the United States did not intend to implement the credit authorization under the Export-Import Bank until the Poles met the conditions of the agreement.[50]

The Warsaw government eventually got around to publishing the conditions of the American credit in the Polish press and promised to provide the treaty information to the United States. On June 26, 1946, the State Department resumed deliveries under the surplus property agreement on the assurance of receiving the treaties but would not sign the Export-Import Bank credit until the treaties were actually received. It took until October 2 before the Export-Import Bank credit was finally signed.[51]

Polish failures to publish the notes and to provide the United States with the treaties appear to be more the result of bureaucratic bungling than a studied attempt to avoid commitments to the United States. The Poles were angry over the American freeze on the credits. Oscar Lange, who renounced his American citizenship to become postwar Poland's first ambassador to Washington, seriously questioned whether United States policy would make it possible for Poland to rely upon American assistance. President Bierut was so angry he refused to see Lane, who had made three attempts to see him in order to explain the American position on the controversial matter.[52] Lane's personal relations with Polish officials had deteriorated so badly that when he tried to board a plane in Warsaw for Paris, the security police tried to search his luggage on the grounds that he might be smuggling gold out of the country![53]

Even after the Polish government published the text of the credit notes, C. Burke Elbrick, assistant chief of the Department of State's division of Eastern European affairs and a close friend of Lane's, favored withholding all credit to Poland because of the deterioration in the political situation in Poland. By then, a serious question was raised concerning the press freedom for foreign correspondents in Poland. Larry Allen of the Associated Press filed a dispatch which included a denunciation of the security police by Stanislaw Banczyk, formerly a member of the SL who joined the PSL. The dispatch was not received in New York until after Washington suspended the credit deal.[54]

After the Poles met the conditions of the credit, Lane reluctantly reconciled himself to following through with the surplus property agreement but not the Export-Import Bank loan "until other commitments under the Yalta, Moscow and Potsdam agreements are fulfilled." He even thought the entire Polish issue should be aired before the United Nations.[55] The British, too, wanted to see the United States pursue a tougher policy. But Byrnes refused to agree to the imposition of new conditions and did not bend to the pressure.

Before the delicate credit issue had finally been laid to rest, General Tadeusz Bor-Komorowski visited the United States. Bor was the former commander of the *Armia Krajowa* which had launched the unsuccessful uprising against the Germans in Warsaw in August 1944. After the uprising, the London Poles appointed him commander-in-chief of the Polish armed forces. Even though there is some question about the wisdom of his decision to order the uprising against the Nazis before the Soviets had fully committed themselves to the liberation of Warsaw,[56] Bor was a courageous officer who in many ways symbolized the plight of the Polish people at a time when the Soviets refused to launch an offensive to liberate Poland's capital.

Bor's five-week visit in May and June of 1946 could not have been more poorly timed from the standpoint of United States–Polish relations. The presence in the United States of a representative of the London Poles, whom the communists linked with the terrorist underground in Poland, and the friendly reception he was given by American military and political officials was considered an unfriendly act by the Warsaw government. Coming at a time when there was some talk in the United States Congress of establishing a kind of foreign legion of Polish veterans who refused to return from the West to Poland,

Bor's visit gave Polish officials a bad case of the jitters. Ambassador Lange seriously inquired of the State Department whether Bor was to lead an army of Polish émigrés in a war against the Soviets.[57]

The general's visit, arranged by the Polish American Congress which was hostile to the PPR-dominated regime in Poland, was part of a general campaign launched by the organization against the communists. Bor spoke to many Polish American audiences in the United States, but none received him more enthusiastically or emotionally than the 200,000 people who gathered in Humboldt Park in Chicago on May 5 to commemorate the 155th anniversary of the Polish constitution. While in the United States, Bor urged America's Polonia to defend the independence and sovereignty of Poland, a charge that characterized the activities of the Polish American Congress for years. Bor repeated what most Polish Americans already knew: there could never be free elections as long as Soviet armed and police forces occupied Poland.[58] The political embarrassment that the Bor visit caused the State Department convinced Byrnes that in the future he did not want any London Poles to make visits to the United States and further complicate Washington's delicate relations with Warsaw.[59]

The Polish referendum of June 30, 1946, conducted just four days after the surplus property agreement had been approved by the United States, provided the communist-dominated government with several political advantages. In view of the constant pressures from the United States and Britain concerning when and under what conditions the promised elections would be held, the Warsaw government saw the referendum as an opportunity to placate the West and defer the elections. In Osobka-Morawski's words, the referendum would be "an initial step leading to these elections."[60] The referendum also was an effective method to ascertain the strength of the PSL and to test the efficiency of the government's electoral machine. In Mikolajczyk's opinion, the referendum gave the PPR more time to continue its intimidation of the population and to rig the future elections.[61] It was clear that as late as the summer of 1946 the PPR and the security police were still a long way from having sufficient control over the Polish nation; if they had, the regime would have conducted the elections instead of the referendum.

The three issues which were to be decided by the referendum— abolition of the senate, maintenance of the land and nationalization reforms, and establishment of Polish frontiers on the Baltic and the Oder-Neisse—posed some problems for the PSL. There was no doubt that the PSL approved of the acquistions of the new lands in the West and the land and nationalization reforms. But the first question—the abolition of the senate—presented the PSL with a quandary. Historically, the party had favored a unicameral legislature and in less difficult times would have abolished the senate. This was the dilemma facing the PSL—to approve the abolition of the senate meant that the party was not in conflict with the policies of the communist bloc; to disapprove the issue meant an open challenge to the regime and its reliance on the security police to stay in power. The PSL's political committee did not favor a challenge to the regime on the referendum, preferring to husband resources until the elections. Stefan Korbonski, one of the members of the committee, wrote in his diary two days before the referendum: "Let us keep all our trumps for the election. . . . Less damage will be done if we now vote 'three times yes' than if we stake everything on the referendum."[62]

Despite the fact that a majority of the PSL's supreme council also favored voting affirmatively on all three questions, Mikolajczyk intervened, arguing that it was necessary to oppose the PPR during the referendum and not to wait until the elections. Mikolajczyk presented his reasons in a Delphic way, alluding to the possibility of support from the West. The political committee changed its position and recommended to the party's supreme council to vote against the first question in the referendum.[63] But not all members of the party agreed with Mikolajczyk on the matter, and some of them chose to vote with the PPR. For their breach of party discipline, they were booted out of the PSL and called themselves the PSL-*Nowe Wyzwolenie (New Liberation)*.[64]

The referendum was conducted in an atmosphere of intimidation and even terror. The PSL was not allowed to publish the party's position on the matter in its own newspaper, *Gazeta Ludowa,* and even its posters could rarely be seen in the country in contrast to the widely publicized slogan of the PPR and PPS: "Three Times Yes." Lane reported that on polling day 3,000 members of the PSL were arrested in the Poznan area and were unable to vote.[65] Foreign newspaper correspondents also reported on glaring irregularities. Derek Selby, Warsaw correspondent for the *Sunday Times,* said that Mikolajczyk had exposed "one of the greatest scandals in the history of Polish politics." Christopher Buckley, Warsaw reporter for the *Daily Telegraph* and the *Scotsman,* declared that he saw enough to invalidate any figures that might be issued. H.W. Henderson, another journalist, personally witnessed "thuggery" and opined that if the future elections in Poland were not held under international supervision, the same results could be predicted.[66] The *New York Times,* revealing that even reporters favorably disposed toward leftist regimes regarded the referendum as a sham, said: "The Government cannot lose, unless the vote is so heavily against it that even fraud cannot offset it. Yet in the larger sense the Government has already lost, irrespective of the vote, for it has lost in the confidence of the Polish people and of the outside world."[67]

The government claimed that out of the 11,530,551 qualified ballots cast, 7,844,522, or approximately 68 percent, voted to abolish the senate.[68] Mikolajczyk, on the other hand, claimed that the referendum had been defeated by almost 84 percent of the voters. Mikolajczyk's claims were supported by the fact that in 2,805 districts where the ballot boxes had not been tampered with, almost 84 percent of the people voted against question one.[69] In Krakow, for example, where the electoral commission tabulated the votes before instructions had been received from the government to remove the ballot boxes for tabulation at the district commissioner's headquaters, the same figure emerged—84 percent were against abolition of the upper chamber.[70]

The United States reacted mildly to the results of the referendum, apparently preferring to concentrate on the conditions it wanted to see in the future elections.[71] The Warsaw government, no doubt impressed by the timidity of the American response, coupled with the extension of credits before the referendum, dismissed the American protest as an infringement on Poland's sovereignty. In the weeks that followed, the Polish government through its embassy in Washington tried to convince Americans that Polish people who ordinarily did not take an active part in politics endorsed the referendum and deplored that it had become a pawn of international interests.[72]

The Polish referendum quickly lost its prominence in the western press when the Warsaw government announced that a pogrom had occurred in the city of Kielce. In view of Nazi crimes against the Jews during the war, it was understandable that the incident at Kielce received special attention in the American press.

Anti-Semitism had existed in Poland between and during the war years. But there was a very great distinction between the anti-Semitism of the Third Reich and that which existed in Poland. Few Poles committed violent acts against Jews; that was usually the work of extreme rightist groups, such as the NSZ. During the Second World War, Poles joined Jews in the gas chambers. Although some Poles as well as Jews collaborated with the enemy, most came together as never before because they shared a common tragic fate.[73] As Polish and Jewish writers have pointed out, there would not have been any Jewish survivors in Poland, the only Nazi-occupied country where aiding a Jew was punishable by death, had it not been for the assistance of Polish people.[74] Understandably, most of the Jews who survived—estimates range from 40,000 to 120,000[75]—were interested in emigrating from the country.

The official policy of the government toward the Jews in the early postwar years was tolerant. Jews organized a network of central and local bodies in as many as 235 towns and villages. Major Jewish centers were located in Lodz, Warsaw, Krakow, Czestochowa, Katowice, Bialystok, and in Wroclaw and Szczecin in the lands acquired from the Germans. Polish Jewry developed its own cultural institutions and until 1947 was free to remain in contact with Jews abroad. After that, Jewish political and other activities came increasingly under government control.[76]

In the years immediately following World War II there were sporadic anti-Semitic outbreaks in Poland, most of which were the work of criminal elements associated with the nationalistic right wing of the Polish underground. The scope and effect of the attacks were exaggerated in the western press. Mikolajczyk, who was not an anti-Semite, pointed out that he was in Radom and Krakow at the time when the western press reported that pogroms had occurred in these cities. What he had witnessed, on the other hand, were political riots against the communists.[77]

In view of the large number of Jews who were members of the PPR, including the universally despised security police, it is little wonder that there was a revival of anti-Jewish feeling in postwar Poland. Since most Poles regarded the regime as an alien-imposed system, the obvious prominence of Jews within the government, along with those who returned to Poland from the Soviet Union after the war, created an extremely tense situation. The American chargé d'affaires in Warsaw, Gerald Keith, described it this way: "It is a paradox that after a period of six years when Jews were more mercilessly killed off than any other race, this country finds itself under a very marked Jewish governing and industrial influence." And he added, "I consider it difficult to estimate what proportion of the resentment towards the government may be attributed to the part played by the Jews in the government and government-controlled industry, but it is surely of considerable consequence."[78]

Polish officials were well aware that the anti-Jewish currents in postwar Poland represented an expression of hostility toward the Polish and Soviet regimes. Foreign minister Rzymowski himself ad-

mitted that the outbreaks were "aimed primarily against the present
regime in Poland and only in the second place against the Jews."[79]
After the pogrom in Kielce in July 1946, an American Jewish journalist visited the scene of the tragedy and conveyed his view that the
attack had been directed against Jews "as an easier way of showing
displeasure against the government than to attack the government
directly."[80]

On the morning of July 4, 1946, an attack against Jews occurred
in Kielce, a charming old city in southeastern Poland. Before the
outbreak vicious rumors had circulated about the Jews in the area,
including the libel of ritual murder of Gentile children which was so
characteristic of the Okhrana-organized pogroms in Russia. On July
1, one day after the controversial referendum, an eight-year-old boy
disappeared from his home, only to return two days later with a story
of his alleged confinement in a Jewish home where he claimed he had
seen the bodies of Christian children. His father took him to the police
on July 4 where the boy told his story. Not long afterward, an ugly
crowd assembled in the front of the house occupied by several Jewish
families and the pogrom began, lasting most of the day.[81]

Predictably, press coverage of the referendum gave way to the
pogromists of Kielce. As a result of the attack, forty-one Jews and
four Poles were killed. Twelve people were convicted; nine received
the death penalty and three received prison sentences.[82] Significantly,
the government brought charges against members of the militia and
the army, arresting the commander and deputy commander of the
Kielce militia and the chief of the security police of the province.[83]

Although there were many discrepancies in the accounts of the
tragedy, both communist and noncommunist sources, in Ambassador
Lane's words, "admitted that it was not spontaneous, but a carefully
organized plot."[84] The government blamed the underground and the
PSL with the crime because of their dissatisfaction with the results of
the referendum.[85] Anticommunist sources charged the regime deliberately orchestrated the grim scenario to divert the attention of the
United States and Britain from the fraudulent referendum and to
discredit the PSL.[86] The evidence strongly suggested complicity of
agencies of the regime, especially the security police, militia, and army
in the Kielce tragedy.[87] Though some controversial questions still
remain to be answered about the incident, one thing soon became
apparent: Kielce provided the government with an opportunity to
escalate its assault not only upon the underground but also on the PSL
and others who opposed the PPR. Equally clear was the understandable panic that gripped the surviving Jewish community in Poland.

Before the Kielce incident, Jews emigrated at the rate of about 70 per week. After Kielce, the figure jumped to 700 per day, creating a critical problem for authorities in the American zone of Austria where as many as 22,980 Jewish refugees arrived during the month of August 1946.[88]

The Polish government tried to offset the bad press it had received from these anti-Semitic incidents by featuring stories about the Jews and their rehabilitation within Polish society in *Poland of Today,* a magazine published in the United States by the Polish embassy.[89] Despite the efforts of the Polish government to offer a more balanced view of Jewish life in Poland, the Kielce incident seriously marred the Polish image in the United States. And as subsequent events revealed, political and economic issues divided the United States and Poland so much that it appeared almost impossible to bridge the growing gulf between the two countries.

IV Credits and Elections

By the middle of 1946 American relations with Poland were seriously affected by Washington's tougher policy toward the Kremlin. Soviet policies in Iran and Germany convinced American policymakers that it was necessary for the United States to take a firmer line toward the Soviet Union. Public confidence in Soviet willingness to cooperate with the United States continued to sag while Washington officials increasingly saw the primary motivation behind Soviet actions in terms of Marxist ideology.

Little wonder that developments in Poland and America's growing problems with the Soviet Union convinced Washington not to extend additional credits to Poland before the Polish elections in January 1947. The State Department made it clear to Polish officials that the manner in which the elections were conducted would have a significant impact on United States–Polish economic relations in the future. In a remarkable about-face, Ambassador Lane, nearing the end of his term of service in Warsaw, urged that economic aid to Poland not be tied to political conditions. Lane belatedly came to the conclusion that economic aid without the attachment of political strings would help to bolster the PPS faction in the government coalition and thus prevent a complete Polish slide into the Soviet orbit.

Whatever hope the Poles had in the United States was undermined by Secretary Byrnes's speech at Stuttgart, Germany, in September of 1946, when he challenged the permanency of the Oder-Neisse boundary between Poland and Germany. Although he probably did not give much thought to the impact his speech would have on the Poles, Byrnes's action played into the hands of the communists, who could point with authority to their oft-repeated claim that the Soviet Union, not the United States, was Poland's only true friend. The impact of the speech on the PSL, which had been linked with the United States and Britain, was devastating.

As many policymakers in the West had predicted, the Polish elections, conducted in a campaign of intimidation and harassment of the PSL, simply confirmed communist domination over the government and excluded the Polish Peasant party from cabinet positions. Significantly, the United States did not develop a political strategy prior to the fraudulent elections—other than saying it was unwilling to extend more loans to Poland until the vote had been taken—aimed at strengthening the PSL and weakening the communists.

In the summer of 1946 the Poles resumed efforts to get additional economic aid from the United States. Rajchman's delegation in Washington painted a grim picture to American officials concerning Poland's ability to finance imports of food and raw materials in 1947.[1] A little later the Poles applied for a $600 million credit—$200 million slated for expenditure in 1947—from the World Bank. The Poles also hoped to get credits for cotton and tobacco from the Export-Import Bank.[2] The Warsaw government, well aware of American desires to sign a bilateral aviation agreement with Poland, hoped to use the aviation matter as a lever to extract additional aid from Washington. In July 1946 Jozef Olszewski, director of the political department of the Polish ministry of foreign affairs, had implied to Lane that after the original Export-Import Bank credit had been finally implemented, the aviation agreement would probably be executed. But after that credit had been agreed upon, Lane's subsequent queries about the aviation agreement only brought evasive answers from the Poles.[3]

The United States did not respond favorably to Polish requests for more economic aid. By the early fall of 1946, Byrnes reassessed Washington's economic policies toward eastern Europe and urged a stiffer attitude. Byrnes told Will Clayton, assistant secretary of state for economic affairs, "The situation has so hardened that the time has now come, I am convinced, in the light of the attitude of the Soviet Govt and the neighboring states which it dominates in varying degrees, when the implementation of our general policies requires the closest coordination. In a word we must help our friends in every way and refrain from assisting those who either through helplessness or for other reasons are opposing the principles for which we stand.[4]" Byrnes's statement did not preclude financial assistance to Poland, provided the aid was tied to assurances that coal-poor western Europe received a share of Poland's coal exports. Byrnes told Acheson: "Certainly we should give no financial assistance to Poland without absolute guarantees that a reasonable proportion of coal exports will be allocated to countries west of the iron curtain." Accordingly, Acheson informed the secretary that when the Poles applied for a loan to develop their coal-mining industry, the application would be carefully handled in line with Byrnes's wishes.[5]

The tougher economic policy toward eastern European countries expressed by Byrnes reflected the growing polarization in East-West relations. Clark M. Clifford, special counsel to Truman, submitted a report to the president at the end of September 1946 which articulated new political and economic policy lines to combat what Washington saw as the aggressive and imperialistic policies of the Kremlin. The

Soviet Union, said Clifford, should understand that the United States is a strong military power and will support democracies threatened by the Soviets. Expressing a view advocated by Lane, Clifford stated: "Only a well-informed public will support the stern policies which Soviet activities make imperative and which the United States Government must adopt. The American people should be fully informed about the difficulties in getting along with the Soviet Union, and the record of Soviet evasion, misrepresentation, aggression and militarism should be made public."[6] However, Clifford's views on economic aid to Poland and other eastern European countries were tougher than those of Byrnes. Aid to these countries, Clifford bluntly declared, "will go to strengthen the entire world program of the Kremlin."[7]

Lane could not have been more pleased by the new policy lines being developed in Washington. When he returned to Washington for consultations in October 1946 and saw that his views and those of his staff in Warsaw were close to those of Byrnes, Lane was elated. In a letter to Gerald Keith, chargé d'affaires in Warsaw, Lane wrote: "The general attitude has stiffened a great deal since June. . . . The Russians and their satellites have been, according to reports, insulting in their attitude towards us, which of course is in line with the treatment we have been receiving in Warsaw." He added: "The most encouraging thing here is to know what a very strong line we are taking. . . . As you and I agree, this should pay dividends even as far as Warsaw."[8]

Like Byrnes and other State Department officials, Lane opposed American economic aid to Poland until the Poles were prepared to settle some of the long-standing issues in Polish-American relations. In November 1946 he summed up for Byrnes some of the more important ones such as the refusal of the Polish government to allow American embassy officials access to people who claimed American citizenship, the lack of a satisfactory agreement to compensate Americans for property nationalized by the Polish government, the hostility of the Polish press toward the United States, the continuation of an artificial rate of exchange fixed by Poland at 100 zloty to $1.00, the procrastination by Poland in signing a bilateral aviation agreement, and the refusal of the Warsaw government to acknowledge American observations respecting the holding of free elections as provided in the Yalta declaration on Poland. Unless these issues were addressed, Lane predicted "that Poland and not the United States will be the primary sufferer if our relations are permitted to continue to worsen."[9]

In an effort to break the log-jam in Polish-American economic relations, Poland's minister of industry, Hilary Minc, personally came to Washington and took over the negotiations on the Polish side from

Rajchman, who, despite his wide contacts and ingratiating manner, had failed to get results. Displaying an impressive knowledge of statistics and a keen sensitivity to America's concern that western Europe secure a sufficient supply of coal, Minc told his American counterparts that in 1947 Poland intended to produce approximately 60 million tons of coal. Western Europe, he said, could receive 10 million tons or about 23 percent of its total coal imports for 1947. But the Pole quickly added that increases in Polish coal production in the next three years—from 60 million tons in 1947 to 80 million in 1949—depended upon a $60 million loan for mining equipment and an additional amount from the Export-Import Bank to improve Poland's railway transportation system.[10] The implication was clear: without additional credits, Poland would not be able to deliver its coal to western Europe in amounts that it required.

Minc sought to separate economic from political issues in United States–Polish relations. Like other Polish negotiators, he tried to impress American officials with Polish intentions to establish a more independent economic position between Poland and the Soviet Union. In a discussion on December 18, 1946, with Acheson, Minc met his match. The urbane Acheson was just as determined to link additional American aid with the forthcoming Polish elections as Minc was to avoid it. The Pole argued that elections were ephemeral phenomena, inevitably arousing emotions that soon subsided. Contrary to reports from many diverse sources, Minc claimed, the Polish government did not intend to interfere with the PSL, provided it conducted its activities in a peaceful way. "The Government wished to remove not the ballot but machine guns from the opposition," he declared in an obvious reference to the underground.

Acheson told Minc that political factors were very much involved in American assessments of Poland and could not be divorced from the question of economic aid. In Acheson's account of his discussion with Minc, the undersecretary made it clear to the Polish minister of industry that future American economic aid to Poland was very much tied to the elections: "This country has been very deeply disturbed by three cynical exhibitions of the use of western democratic electoral machinery to produce the most autocratic and repressive results. These experiences had been the two elections in Bulgaria and the recent Rumanian election. If another such example occurred in Poland it would make it next to impossible for this Government to go forward with any extensive economic help for Poland." In a specific reference to the Polish American community, Acheson added: "This was true not only because of the general feeling in the United States

but also because of the large number of Poles and the not unimportant
factor that many of these were located in Michigan, the Senior Senator from which state was the new chairman of the Foreign Relations
Committee of the Senate."[11]

Minc did not realize it at the time but he had received support for
his request for economic aid from a thoroughly unexpected source,
the American ambassador to Poland. Lane had become converted to
the claims of Polish socialists that they genuinely wanted friendly
relations with the United States and that economic aid from Washington was essential to counteract the boasts of the Polish communists
that the Soviet Union was Poland's only true friend. Since it had been
apparent for some time that the PSL would lose the forthcoming
elections, Lane thought it would be prudent if the United States did
not put all its eggs "in Mikolajczyk['s] basket" and instead tried to
drive a wedge between the PPR and the PPS. To Lane, the PPS was
essentially a nationalistic party opposed to a police state and undue
dependence upon the Kremlin.[12] Lane's sudden change of heart toward the PPS has been described by one writer this way: "For that
suspended moment in December 1946 the ascerbic Cold Warrior
made a great deal of sense. The tragedy lies in the fact that Lane
perceived these new alternatives and options too late."[13]

Despite Lane's astonishing advice, the Poles received no satisfac-
tion from American officials concerning a request to the Export-
Import Bank for a cotton loan or to the World Bank for a loan to
expand the Polish coal industry. But Minc's visit did produce a breakthrough on the troublesome issue of compensation to Americans
whose property had been nationalized by the Polish government. The
agreement, providing for the establishment of a claims commission,
paved the way for the release of Polish assets in the United States,
including $27.5 million in gold of the Bank of Poland.[14] Minc's
mission also helped to work out a solution to the unrealistic exchange
rate which had been arbitrarily pegged by Warsaw.[15]

As the wily Minc must have realized, his efforts in Washington to
get more credit had been overshadowed not only by American attention to the promised elections and the way the government bloc
conducted its campaign against the opposition but also by the impact
of Secretary Byrnes's controversial speech, made in Stuttgart, Germany, on September 6.[16] Byrnes's speech has been interpreted in
different ways by historians. Some have seen it as a turning point in
American postwar policy—one which was essentially anti-Soviet in
intent. Others have seen the speech in far less menacing terms. Denise
O. Conover, offers the most persuasive interpretation of the speech

and its place in the context of Byrnes's continuing efforts to reach an accommodation with the Soviet Union: "Rather than just a challenge to the Soviets, it represented an attempt to force issues out into the open, with the hope of clarifying the differences, as well as the similarities, between the Russian and Western positions. It also aimed to provide a more intelligent basis for continued negotiations. Byrnes was not so pessimistic as to believe that the truncation of Germany was inevitable and cooperation with the Russians impossible.[17]

The major thrust of the secretary's remarks concerned Germany. In trying to pressure the Soviets and the French, he emphasized the need for the economic unification of Germany. He also indicated that the United States favored a provisional government for Germany and pledged an American presence there for as long as the occupation lasted.[18] In effect, Byrnes accomplished one of his major objectives: to counteract the Soviets who for some time had sought to create the impression that they were the champions of German unity and economic recovery.

Byrnes's strong bid for the support of the German people included an attempt "to smoke Molotov out" on an alleged Soviet plan "to give Polish territories to Germany."[19] The secretary, completely ignoring the Polish position concerning the lands acquired from Germany, challenged the permanency of the Oder-Neisse boundary, thus forcing the Soviets to support the Polish position on the issue. The political cost to the United States of reopening this sensitive matter was enormous, plunging Polish-American relations to their lowest point since the end of the Second World War.

Predictably the Polish government reacted bitterly. President Bierut told the Polish diet that politicians who thought they could arbitrarily make changes in the national life of a people were "mistaken." He declared: "We have returned to the land where, centuries ago our historical, cultural, and state life took shape, to the land impregnated with the blood, sweat and tears of our fathers and mothers, to the land every inch of which is covered with the sacred ashes of our forefathers. Who can deny us the right to this land?"[20] Gomulka put it more bluntly: "Poland refuses to be any longer a football of other nations. The Polish people refuse to be a people of nomads, of eternal emigrants in search of bread in foreign countries. We wish to live, to work and develop on our own soil, we wish to govern and administer our country according to our needs, we wish to organize our recovered heritage in the west and north with the shortest delay."[21]

Olszewski summoned Lane to the foreign office and brusquely

demanded: "Telegraph to Mr. Byrnes and ask him whether his speech means that the United States has changed its policy toward Poland." Lane refused to oblige but agreed to take up the matter later when he himself had received an official copy of the speech.[22] The intense bitterness of the Poles came out in *Glos Ludu,* the PPR newspaper, which featured a cartoon showing Byrnes standing in front of an American flag that had swastikas and black heads instead of stars and stripes. *Zycie Warszawy,* another procommunist newspaper, succinctly summed up Polish perceptions of American policy when it asked: "What . . . a German United States?"[23]

Polish bitterness toward the United States resulted in a demonstration outside the American embassy in Warsaw. Although Mikolajczyk claimed that the demonstration was staged,[24] there is no doubt that the Poles were outraged by Byrnes's challenge and were certainly capable of participating in that kind of anti-American demonstration. After all, even some priests denounced the United States from the pulpit. A former member of the Polish armed forces, who fought with the British and returned to Poland after the war, exclaimed: "I could not believe it! The United States opposing the Poles, who suffered so much at the hands of the Germans?"[25]

Byrnes's speech seriously undermined the position of the PSL, which had been tied so closely with the United States in the mind of the public. The PPR and the PPS lost no time in portraying Mikolajczyk's party as an enemy of the people. A week after the Stuttgart speech both groups published an open letter to the PSL asking for answers to several questions: "Are you prepared to protect our boundaries in opposition to Byrnes and Churchill? Are you prepared, in the name of our sovereignty, to protest against meddling of Anglo-Saxon reactionary circles in our affairs? Are you prepared to prosecute reactionary bands and bandits? Do you accept our proposal for an electoral bloc?"[26]

Mikolajczyk, who was in Copenhagen attending a meeting at the time Byrnes gave his speech, disagreed with the American position, declaring that the lands acquired from Germany were "for Poland a matter of life and death." His statements, published in the *Gazeta Ludowa* and *Zycie Warszawy,* warned that if the great powers did not want to cause a shock to the Polish body politic, they will recognize the permanency of the Oder-Neisse line.[27] Czeslaw Wycech, a prominent member of the PSL, commented: "History has taught us that to rebuild Germany is not to prepare for peace."[28]

As expected, the Soviets came out in favor of the Poles. Molotov replied to Byrnes saying: "The very idea of involving millions of people in such experiments is unbelievable, quite apart from the cruelty of it, both towards the Poles and the Germans themselves."[29] Even Lane, who soft-pedaled the negative impact of the speech at the time and refused publicly to challenge the State Department's position on the boundary question, privately believed Byrnes had made a mistake and said later in his book that it was "one of the sorest questions plaguing our relations with Poland," which had "made a universally bad impression in Poland."[30]

In retrospect, it is incredible that Byrnes had not anticipated the storm of criticism from Poland. After all, Byrnes himself had proposed at the Potsdam Conference the package deal of which the Polish-German boundary was a major component, though nominally requiring confirmation in a final peace treaty. In view of the elections which were scheduled for January, Byrnes's remarks could easily have been interpreted by the communists in Warsaw and Moscow as meaning that the United States had written off Poland to the Soviets.

After the controversial referendum, there were intensive discussions between the PPS and the PSL concerning the terms on which the Peasant party would enter a government bloc. Wycech and Kiernik, both of whom were well known and ambitious leaders of the PSL, played a key role in these preelection discussions. Some elements within the PPS, anxious to reach an accommodation with the PSL, were prepared to offer up to 40 percent of the seats in a coalition government to the Peasant party.[31] But after the return of the PPS and PPR leaders from talks with Stalin in Moscow, the socialists offered the PSL 25 percent of the representation while it would receive 20 percent of the seats. The rest of the seats would go to the communists and the smaller parties under their control. Mikolajczyk rejected the offer and made some interesting counterproposals. The Peasant party leader was prepared to agree to a bloc list of candidates in eastern and western Poland but in the major sections of Poland, he insisted that free elections be held. In any case, Mikolajczyk wanted the three major independent parties—PSL, PPS, and SP—to receive a majority of the seats.[32] As one authority on the subject has explained, the major advantages for the PSL were that "it would enable [the] PPR to be admitted to the Sejm in larger numbers than if truly free elections were held, the principle of free elections would be adhered to in at least part of the country, and the stipulation that the majority of the seats would be given to three parties would provide a minimum guarantee that the agreement would be respected." It is uncertain whether Mikolajczyk's proposals were ever seriously considered either by the PPS or the PPR.[33]

By early October 1946 the PSL announced it would run its candidates independently from the government bloc. The supreme council of the party, in an effort to dissociate itself completely from Byrnes, declared that "who is with the Germans is against us," and criticized the secretary of state's speech as "a blow at the foundation and the possibility of the development of the country of Poland." It endorsed full cooperation with the Soviet Union, called for an end to the attacks by the regime on the PSL, and warned that unless free elections were held, the strain in the country would deepen "and could plunge our country into indescribable chaos."[34]

In a personal appeal to Stalin a few days later, Mikolajczyk tried to assure the Soviet chief that the PSL was well aware of the importance of Polish-Soviet friendship and described the activities of the PSL to foster that spirit. "This has some considerable results," Mikolajczyk said, "inasmuch as the Polish people have more confidence in the Polish Peasant party as compared to the other parties." The PSL leader emphasized that the intimidation and terror of the PPR against the PSL prejudiced a normalization of the political situation in Poland and created obvious difficulties in strengthening Polish-Russian relations.[35]

After the fraudulent referendum, few Poles had any illusions about the fairness of the forthcoming election. As the election neared, Mikolajczyk talked about the need for international supervision, an idea rejected by Washington and London because it was extremely unlikely Warsaw or Moscow would agree to it.[36] Moreover, even if some kind of international supervision were possible, the western governments probably doubted that the elections would be entirely free, leaving the United States and Britain open to charges of participating in a fraud.

Failing to arouse American and British interest in international supervision, Mikolajczyk considered at one point a boycott, along with instructions to his followers to refuse to pay taxes and to supply food to the government. That inevitably would have brought severe communist countermeasures against the PSL and, as Mikolajczyk may have hoped, western intervention.[37] The boycott idea was rejected because, as Korbonski said, "The Poles might regard a boycott as a capitulation, and the rest of the world might interpret it as a refusal to let elections decide the struggle for our country's liberation. Moreover, the elections will definitely be held and will certainly be fraudulent. But if we boycott them we will not even be able to assert that frauds had been committed, for the absence of our partisans will make it impossible to confirm this."[38]

Mikolajczyk increasingly displayed all the signs of a frustrated leader, fighting for the survival not only of his party but also of his country. Overriding the advice of Washington, he endeavored to secure great power intervention a month before the election by appealing directly to all of the Yalta powers—the United States, Great Britain, and the Soviet Union—who had guaranteed that Poland would have free and unfettered elections. In an impressive twenty-one page memorandum with twenty-six enclosures, Mikolajczyk catalogued in considerable detail the political conditions in Poland which militated against any free expression by the Polish people. His appeal brought Anglo-American protests to the Warsaw and Moscow governments, which promptly rejected them.[39]

Mikolajcyk seems to have entertained some hope that once the elections took place and demonstrable fraud became obvious to diplomatic representatives and correspondents of the United States and Britain, the West might then be prepared to intervene rather than witness the civil war which he predicted.[40] In the final analysis, Mikolajczyk clung tenaciously to the belief that despite the intimidation of his party by the regime, the PSL would score well enough at the polls to impress the communists to force them to allow his party a viable place in the political life of Poland.[41]

As Mikolajczyk desperately searched for ways to prevent political disaster for himself and his party, the United States did not abandon the notion that somehow the PSL would still play a role in the political life of Poland. In the absence of any real policy, the State Department optimistically believed that the elections "would in some measure at least reflect the real situation in the country,"[42] a weak reed, indeed, for Mikolajczyk and his party to cling to.

Meanwhile, after two meetings in Moscow in August and November of 1946, representatives of the PPR and PPS firmed up a united front agreement providing for closer cooperation between the two parties during the electoral campaign and combating the PSL. As a sop to the long-standing criticism of the PPS, which had far greater popularity in the country than the PPR, that it did not have a fair share of positions in the government, Cyrankiewicz became minister without portfolio and Stanislaw Lesczycki became vice-president for foreign affairs.[43] While in Moscow, the communist and the socialist leadership allegedly received personal instructions from Stalin concerning how he wanted the elections conducted. Stalin is said to have told his Polish protégés to keep up the barrage of propaganda that tied the PSL to the underground and the reactionaries. "If you repeat these charges often enough," Mikolajczyk quotes Stalin as saying, "some of the people in the United States and Great Britain will believe you, and they will refuse to join in the protests their government will make."[44] Lane grumped, "And yet . . . [the Russians] have the nerve to tell us that our notes on the elections are a violation of Polish sovereignty."[45] Thus the so-called democratic bloc, consisting of the PPR, PPS, SL, and SD, faced an isolated and demoralized PSL.

One western observer accurately described the Polish elections of January 19, 1947, as a "monstrous fraud."[46] The bloc, headed by the PPR, used almost every conceivable method to compromise, harass, and intimidate the PSL. The attitude of the PPR was summed up by Roman Zambrowski, a member of the party's politburo, on the eve of the election: "Democracy can not mean freedom for the enemies of freedom. While powerful centers of political banditry are still active, while these centers conduct open penetration of legal organizations like the state apparatus, there can be no privilege of democratic freedoms for some persons."[47]

Before the elections, the regime created technical difficulties for the PSL in presenting its lists of candidates, accompanied by the names of their sponsors, to the commissioner general of the elections, Kazimierz Bzowski. The problem was complicated by the arrest of over seven thousand PSL members, including every member of the district and local party organizations. The consequence was that enormous additional burdens fell upon the leaders of the PSL. Mikolajczyk wrote: "I can say out of personal experience that none of us at national headquarters in Warsaw slept more than two or three hours a night for days thereafter. Party members dispatched through the country to see our candidates presented signatures and to inform their sponsors of their district numbers were often arrested before they could complete their missions." The party managed to prepare its slate of candidates and, expecting to use their immunity from arrest, sent forty members of parliament with the lists to fifty-two district commissions. But the ploy was not entirely successful; the immunity of several members was violated and they were arrested.[48]

Arrests and intimidation of members and supporters of the PSL were commonplace. Christopher Buckley, correspondent for the *Daily Telegraph,* reported that after a speech by Mikolajczyk in Lublin, crowds demonstrated for him, yelling, "Long Live Mikolajczyk." Shortly afterward the PSL supporters were arrested and carried away in army trucks. Even people who had sought sanctuary in churches were dragged out.[49] During the last week of December 1946 Lane revealed that 75 out of 854 PSL candidates for election to the Polish diet had been arrested and the names of 40 others had been stricken off the electoral list.[50]

To be sure the army and security police were widely used in a campaign to intimidate the electorate to vote for the bloc. The Polish army established defense-propaganda groups to get into the most remote villages to propagandize for the regime and against the PSL. Orders to these army groups stated:

The PSL must be attacked along these lines: members do not pay taxes or offer public rehabilitation services; they support the underground gangs; they soon will be liquidated by the Government. The question period must be very short. Organizers must prevent discussion or any effort to turn the questions into a line sympathetic to the PSL. If a questioner becomes too brave and asks undersirable questions he must be immediately attacked as an instigator, provocator and hostile towards the Government and the State.[51]

According to Lane the security police forced people to sign endorsements of the government bloc or else risk losing their jobs or places of residence. When arrest or intimidation failed, people were tortured and even murdered. Mikolajczyk estimated that 130 PSL members were liquidated prior to the elections.[52]

The PSL had tremendous difficulties in getting its message to the people because freedom of the press did not exist. The circulation of the party's newspaper, *Gazeta Ludowa,* was arbitrarily limited to 75,000 copies, even though 300,000 copies could have been sold if the regime had allowed it. Copies of the newspaper were in such great demand that people were willing to pay more than three times the normal cost. It was not unusual for cafe and bar owners to buy two or three copies of the *Gazeta Ludowa* and charge their customers five zloty for half an hour's reading time. Censorship, which had been severe before the election, became even more drastic during the election campaign. Fernand Gigon, a French journalist, personally observed how the censor's blue pencil emptied the proofs.[53] Lane commented grimly, "It was indeed saddening to reflect that, although Mikolajczyk's party might number millions, no more than a comparative handful could be told what was going on."[54]

The situation was no better in other forms of communication. The government controlled the radio and allowed Mikolajczyk only two ten-minute periods on the air. Yet, when he did speak, the regime ordered loudspeakers throughout the country to be turned off. In at least one case, thanks to the enterprise of a pro-PSL stalwart in Radomsk, the people heard the Peasant party leader's entire speech. To be sure, Mikolajcyzk's speeches were severely censored—his references to the reign of "rifle, bludgeon and jail" and the bloc's "venomous greed for power" were expunged from his text. Despite the censorship of his speeches, to which he had to submit as a condition to receive radio time, Mikolajczyk's speeches were well received by the listening audience. Sidney Gruson, then a correspondent for the *New York Times,* observed that "M. Mikolajczyk got over a powerful appeal."[55] By raiding and destroying the party's presses, the opposition prevented the PSL from publishing a large amount of campaign literature to appeal to the voters. Little wonder that on election day posters of the PSL were conspicuously absent while those of the opposition were everywhere.[56]

The communists used various methods to confuse and delude the electorate. The day before the polls opened, they sent thousands of telegrams to PSL officials announcing the death of Mikolajczyk in a plane accident.[57] Another ruse, intended to draw away some voters from the PSL and to demonstrate to the West that the regime allowed independent Catholics to express themselves politically, was to permit a new party—the Catholic progressives—to run in a few electoral districts. This so-called independent party was headed by a reactionary who did not enjoy the support of the Catholic church, which endorsed the PSL instead.[58]

The PPR believed that one of the most effective ways to scare the electorate was to stage a few spectacular trials of individuals who were allegedly involved in antistate activities and to link them with the PSL. The trial of Colonel Jan Rzepecki, commander of WIN, began on January 4, 1947, just a few weeks before the elections.[59] And a little over a week before the elections, Count Ksawery Grocholski, a friend of Victor Cavendish-Bentinck, the British ambassador to Poland, was tried on charges of underground activities and conveying secrets to the British. There seems little doubt that the Grocholski trial, which western correspondents were encouraged to attend, was a deliberate effort to divert attention from the communist campaign of intimidation and fraud to win at the polls. Moreover, as one western newsman observed, "The staging of the trial at this time has been effective in confining to Warsaw several foreign correspondents who have arrived to report on the conduct of the elections." Grocholski and two other men were found guilty and sentenced to death.[60]

Before the elections, the communists expected to benefit from the provisions of the new electoral law, passed in September 1946, which had disenfranchised approximately one million people on the grounds that they had collaborated with the enemy during the occupation or were connected with fascist organizations. The law provided the legal basis for the PPR to eliminate not only potential support for the PSL but also the party's candidates in the elections.[61]

As election day neared, the PSL discovered there was virtually no end to the devices the opposition used to prevent the elections from being honest. In Warsaw, the PSL was supposed to have observers at the 166 boards of election. Korbonski, a leading PSL official, had personally handed the appropriate documents to members of the party who were to serve as observers. But all PSL members in Warsaw had been denied entry to the polling centers because they did not have "certificates of morality," an obvious trick to reduce the number of PSL observers on election day. In order to acquire the certificates, the observers had to get letters from the security police. Predictably only twenty-two PSL members were permitted to the polling centers in Warsaw and of these, only six were allowed to remain to the end of election day.[62]

Despite the fact that the regime had arrested PSL candidates, deprived a substantial part of the electorate of the right to vote, monopolized the communications media, intimidated voters by public trials, arrests, and murders, the PPR-dominated bloc was still not entirely certain whether it could win the elections. Obviously fearful that if most Poles voted secretly, they would vote for Mikolajczyk's party, the regime embarked upon a campaign of "open voting" as a demonstration of loyalty. Marguerite Higgins reported that on a 250-mile drive through the country, she personally witnessed the practice at every polling station she visited. But in the cities and in many country districts, large numbers of people insisted upon voting secretly. When confronted by a stubborn voter, the ubiquitous security police did not force people to show their ballots. In Warsaw, Gruson reported that almost everyone he saw voted secretly.[63] However, as Higgins witnessed, it was not always easy to exercise the right to cast a secret ballot:

> There were no screens around the voting booths in any of the precincts. Persons who wished to vote secretly had to turn their backs to the election board and slip their ballots into the envelopes. Some desiring a secret vote folded their ballots in advance (each voter brought his own ballot from home). This still did not afford much secrecy, since those who did not vote openly in this district were automatically considered to be against the

government, a political view which most Poles, in these days of the security police, like to keep to themselves.[64]

One Pole wryly summed up the balloting process: "You put Mikolajczyk in the box but lo and behold, when the votes are counted, out comes Gomulka."[65] The PSL was allowed only thirty-six witnesses, according to Mikolajczyk, at the 5,200 polling places to observe the counting of ballots. Significantly, all the local electoral chairmen were communists.[66] There were several obvious cases of fraud—everything from throwing away ballots marked for the PSL to substituting ballot boxes which were stuffed with slips for the government bloc.[67]

Under these circumstances it was not surprising that the government, releasing the results of the election within forty-eight hours of the closing of the polls, claimed an overwhelming victory for the democratic bloc, winning 444 seats to the PSL's 28 seats in the Sejm. The PPR publicly claimed that the bloc took 80 percent of the votes while the PSL won only 10 percent.[68] There was one man who wanted to know the true results of the election—Stalin. He told the PPR, "I want to see how influential you actually are." According to Mikolajczyk, the PPR informed Stalin that the PSL had actually garnered 79 percent of the mandates.[69]

With the Polish elections of January 1947 the provisional government ended and the communists and their allies moved rapidly to institutionalize their power: a new all bloc cabinet took over the reins of power and an interim constitution, called the "Little Constitution," was adopted by the diet. The major result of the election was the elimination of the PSL—Mikolajczyk, Kiernik, Wycech—from the new cabinet. Although there were changes in thirteen ministries, the major difference between the new cabinet and its predecessor was the absence of the PSL. In effect, the new cabinet became essentially what it had been before the provisional government was constituted—a coalition of the PPR and other left-wing groups which had received political life from the Soviets when the Lublin committee was constituted on July 21, 1944.

In the new cabinet the PPS took seven ministries, one more than in the previous government. The major change was the replacement of Osobka-Morawski as premier by Cyrankiewicz. The PPR had five ministries in the government, losing two seats from the previous cabinet but still holding the major ones in its hands—western territories, industry, public security, and education. Besides, the five positions held by the PPR included a part of the area of the seven former ministerial posts because the ministry of industry was expanded by transferring to its jurisdiction that of foreign trade and supply, previously under the ministries of navigation and foreign trade and of supply and commerce. As before, the PPR controlled ministries not headed by communists through undersecretarial positions.[70]

The other parties in the bloc, all of which were artificial creations of the communists and unable to claim a mass following, picked up the remaining lesser portfolios in the cabinet: 6 went to the SL, 2 to the SD, and 2 to the SP. Within two months, however, one of the positions acquired by the SP—information and propaganda—was abolished and most of its functions were assumed by Berman, the communist undersecretary of state of the council of ministers and still Poland's éminence grise. One American government report noted:

> By the presence in the Cabinet of these three parties (Peasant, Democratic and Labor), the Communist-Socialist ruling group maintains that the peasant masses, the middle-class intellectuals, and the Christian social movement, respectively, participate in the Government on equal terms with the representatives of the industrial proletariat. The fact that the Government is firmly controlled by the Communists and Socialists, however, is evident from the list of the 64 ministerial and undersecretarial posts, 42 of which are held by members of those two parties and only 22 by all other groups combined.[71]

Attempts by the PSL to condemn the elections in the new diet in February brought only jeers from the opposition. Mikolajczyk, leading his small group of twenty-eight representatives, condemned the newly elected bloc: "This group . . . has no right to introduce legislation that will affect the fundamental rights of the citizens." Noting that the mention of God had been taken out of the oath of office that Bierut would take as president of Poland, Mikolajczyk queried, "May I then ask to whom the new President will be swearing?"[72] Perhaps the most impassioned condemnation of the elections was delivered by Zygmunt Zulawski, an elderly socialist of aristocratic bearing. In his speech to the diet, he condemned the way the elections had been conducted and drew analogies between the repression of the communists and the prewar regime of the Sanacja:

> Pilsudski said that the Poles were a nation of morons, and that in their own interest he was justified in educating them by means of the whip. To-day's ruling elite, the best men of our nation, will also say confidentially that, were they to resign from power, terrible things would happen to Poland—white terror and the

blackest reaction. But who has the right to suspect this nation, composed in overwhelming majority of laboring men, of peasants, intellectuals, and workers, of being reactionary merely because it wants to apply its own judgment to questions of social justice, equality, freedom, representation in the Diet, and government?[73]

Only the PSL representatives applauded Zulawski when he finished his memorable address. Commenting on the fact that the old socialist leader suffered from heart disease, Korbonski noted in his diary, "This had been the voice of a man at the grave's edge, and this fact doubled the impact of the address which, from a rhetorical standpoint, was the best heard thus far in the Diet."[74]

Displaying a keen sensitivity to tradition and the forms of legality, the new government decided to draft a new charter that would accomplish two purposes—to codify the economic and social changes made in the country since 1944 without reducing the power of the bloc, and to make certain that the new constitution would bear at least a superficial resemblance to the democratic constitution of 1921 which the communists claimed they were trying to defend. The "Little Constitution," adopted on February 19, 1947, ostensibly an interim charter, established a government apparatus which replaced the constitution of 1921 and made the executive branch supreme over the diet. The "Little Constitution" provided for a *Rada Panstwa* (Council of State), composed of a cabal of six men headed by president Bierut, which effectively ruled the country while the diet was limited to two brief sessions annually.[75] The *Rada Panstwa* represented a continuation of the Presidium of the National Council of the Homeland which had existed from July 1944 to February 1947 and had served as the permanent executive of the provisional government.

The Polish elections precipitated a crisis in the PSL, resulting in the expulsion of the former minister of education, Wycech, and several of his fellow dissenters who favored reaching an accommodation with the communists. Wycech was an opportunist who had joined Mikolajczyk in 1945 in the belief that the PSL would remain a major factor in Polish political life. When the fortunes of the Polish Peasant party declined and finally evaporated in the elections of 1947, Wycech joined Jozef Niecko, another ambitious politician with a penchant for underhandedness, and other left-wing dissenters in the PSL in an effort to replace Mikolajczyk as head of the party and to lead the PSL to a political agreement with the regime. The harried Mikolajczyk was up to the challenge, however. He asserted his authority and succeeded in booting out Wycech, Niecko, and their followers from the PSL in March 1947. Mikolajczyk received wide support for his action from local PSL organizations which opposed compromise with the bloc. The ousted faction, calling themselves the *PSL-Lewica,* held its first conference as a separate party in Warsaw on April 18 and adopted a program of cooperation with the government. The new group also published its own newspaper, *Chlopi i Panstwo (Peasant and State).*[76]

After the elections, the PSL had only a handful of deputies in the diet. Reduced in size and demoralized, the PSL felt it must continue to play some role, albeit a limited one, in the new legislature. The PSL saw its future role as the conscience of the nation: "The role of the PSL deputies' club in the present Sejm may, however, be fruitful through the quiet and dispassionate application of criticism to the activities of the Polish Government, which are continually applauded by the majority."[77] The PSL had no other acceptable option open to it than this limited parliamentary role. Denied any real influence in the political affairs of Poland, the PSL limped along in the months after the election as a minor obstacle to the drive of the PPR to consolidate its power.

The demoralization in the ranks of the PSL was largely due to the profound disillusionment most Poles felt, owing to the lack of any real assistance from the West. "I must state frankly," Korbonski wrote, "that one of the causes of this disintegration is loss of faith in the miraculous recipe for the liberation of Poland that Mikolajczyk brought from London." He added bitterly, "We have been left to our own devices, and now it looks either that Mikolajczyk was cheated by the West or that he has deceived us."[78]

As has been seen, there had never been a "recipe" providing for American intervention to prevent a communist takeover in Poland. At no time did the United States mislead Mikolajczyk and the PSL to expect intervention on their behalf. Even Lane, who made no secret of his sympathy for the PSL and its political fight against the PPR, was careful to explain to his Polish contacts the limitations of American power in the political situation in Poland. Mikolajczyk was well aware of the fact that he could not expect much more than moral and diplomatic support from the United States and Britain when he decided to accept a seat in the provisional government. For a long time he believed that the PSL could go it alone, even though he was less than candid with his followers about the possibilities of western assistance in the future. But the closer the election came, and with it the increased attacks by the bloc against the PSL, Mikolajczyk had second thoughts about the ability of the PSL to survive and tried to get the United States and Britain to intervene in the political situation.

The United States and Great Britain regarded the Polish elections as unsatisfactory and declared that the Yalta commitment concerning free and unfettered elections had not been executed. But neither country challenged the position of the Warsaw government that Yalta was no longer a relevant political question so far as Poland was concerned.[79] The American reaction to the elections was more of an explanation of what had happened than a condemnation of the Polish government.[80] Only one major political figure in the United States, Senator Arthur Vandenberg, completely repudiated the elections and called for a Big Three meeting to consider the question of the Polish government honoring the Yalta pledge concerning free elections.[81]

The British were especially eager to put the Polish elections behind them. The British foreign office said it would gauge its future policy toward Poland "by the performance of the new Polish government." The British recognized in a de facto way the fraudulent elections when it concluded a trade agreement with Poland on April 27, 1947.[82] Mikolajczyk, angered by what he considered the hasty recognition of the results of the elections, told a British correspondent: "But I did feel that you needn't have gone out of your way to give it your blessing, so to speak."[83]

A few days after the elections, Ambassador Lane asked to be transferred to another diplomatic post or be allowed to retire. He explained: "For all practical purposes, my mission to Poland is ended, and I believe that I could do more in educating American public opinion through the writing of articles as a private citizen, or as an envoy in some other country than I can remaining here, where my continued presence would—in the unquestioned absence of publication of our views in Poland—be considered as tacit acquiescence in the recent fraud."[84] The State Department asked Lane to return to the United States where he resigned from the diplomatic service. Lane told Truman he could do more for the cause of relations between the American and Polish people if he became a private citizen "and thus be enabled to speak and write openly, without being hampered by diplomatic convention, regarding the present tragedy of Poland." Lane wrote that Truman "approved my course."[85] Obviously, Truman could not have been very pleased when Lane spent his time attacking Roosevelt and the Yalta agreement and later endorsed Thomas E. Dewey in the 1948 presidential campaign.

V Denouement

The Polish elections were an important element in the growing split between East and West and left the United States with few if any options to prevent the complete satellization of the country. The Polish government, still very much in need of American economic aid, tried to put the best possible face on Polish domestic developments and to emphasize the importance to both countries of Poland's ability to establish a more independent economic position vis-à-vis the Soviet Union. But except for a few individuals in the administration, the United States was no longer seriously interested in extending credit to Poland and even eliminated the Poles as recipients of food assistance under the Foreign Relief Program, despite the fact that Poland had been one of the countries most devastated by the war. Relations between the two countries also continued to plummet because of Washington's insistence on keeping open the question of the permanency of the Oder-Neisse boundary between Poland and Germany.

The deterioration in Polish-American relations was matched by the grim situation in Polish domestic politics. The defeat of the PSL by the communist-dominated bloc eliminated Peasant party representation from the government and it was only a matter of time before Mikolajczyk and other leaders of his party—all of whom feared for their lives—were forced to flee the country. With the PSL removed as a political threat, the PPR began a campaign which called for the absorption of the PPS into a united Polish worker's movement, the final political stage leading to one-party dictatorship.

To offset the negative impact of the fradulent elections, the Polish government appointed Joseph Winiewicz as ambassador to the United States. Winiewicz's apppointment was also intended to remove a long-standing bone of contention in United States–Polish relations—namely, the presence of the unpopular Oscar Lange who served as Poland's first postwar ambassador to Washington. Lange, a Polish-born former professor of economics at the University of Chicago, had been perhaps the most eminent representative of a small, though articulate, group of Polish Americans who criticized the policies and leadership of the Polish government-in-exile and urged close United States–Soviet cooperation during World War II. Stalin had invited Lange, along with the Rev. Stanislaw Orlemanski, a Catholic priest who had organized the pro-Soviet Kosciuszko League, to visit the

Soviet Union in the spring of 1944. Both men accepted the invitation
and returned enthusiastic supporters of a Soviet solution to the Polish
question which had divided the Big Three during the war. The Lange-
Orlemanski visit provoked widespread criticism among Polish Americans because it implied that the United States had changed its policy
of support to the London Poles. After the war, Lange renounced his
American citizenship and accepted the post of Polish ambassador to
Washington. Polish Americans were outraged by the appointment of
a man they considered a traitor.[1] Lange, who also served as Poland's
representative to the United Nations, was not an effective ambassador,
and even the Polish government admitted that it had probably made
a mistake in appointing him.[2]

In contrast to the aloof Lange, Winiewicz tried to cultivate closer
relations with the State Department. Bright and candid, Winiewicz
embarked on an ambitious but hopeless task of attempting to correct
what he perceived as a distorted impression Americans had about his
country. Winiewicz was an erudite man who came from Poznan
where he had edited a newspaper before the war. He later worked in
the ministry of education of the Polish government-in-exile before he
became associated with the Polish provisional government. A realist
who believed that the Poles had to cooperate closely with the Soviets,
Winiewicz also shared the views of many socialists who felt that it was
also important for Poland to maintain close contacts with the West.
Ambassador Lane, impressed by the new Polish appointee, told a
State Department official shortly before he himself resigned as ambassador to Warsaw:

> Winiewicz is a very likeable person, with understanding of the
> other man's point of view, and I feel sure that he will make
> friends easily in the United States and should do a lot to make
> for himself a good position with our Government, the American
> press and his diplomatic colleagues. Whether or not he will be
> forced to follow the Communist line only time can tell, but I
> believe him to be independent enough in his political thinking
> so that he will cooperate wholeheartedly with the Department.[3]

Despite the new ambassador's obvious assets, there was little he
could do to change the course of Polish-American relations. His first
meeting with Truman set the tone for the remainder of his mission
in Washington. The President bluntly told him that the recent Polish
elections were violations of the Yalta and Potsdam agreements. Truman acknowledged that the United States wanted to be on friendly

terms with Poland but the Polish government, he said, would have to make that possible. Then, according to Stanley Woodward, chief of protocol who was present at the meeting, "The President thereupon arose and terminated the visit, something which I have never seen him do before."[4]

The new American ambassador's experience in Warsaw was not much better. Stanton Griffis, born into a Boston Congregationalist family, was a self-made financial tycoon who had no diplomatic experience before Truman summoned him from Palm Beach, Florida, and asked him to represent the United States in Poland.[5] Bespectacled and balding, Griffis was hopelessly naive about Poland and American policy toward it. Before his confirmation by the Senate, Griffis astonished even the most optimistic observers in the Department of State by asserting that Poland would not become a communist nation.[6] To be sure, Griffis's views were appreciated by the Warsaw government which could not help but contrast the new ambassador with Lane who was so disliked by Polish officialdom. Shortly after Griffis arrived in Warsaw, *Zycie Warszawy* observed: "Mr. Stanton Griffis has won us with his benevolence, his evident good-will and sincere desire to repair everything which Mr. Bliss Lane spoiled so long, so perseveringly and so passionately."[7] Griffis, who had a sense of humor, had the strange notion that the application of humor could accomplish significant diplomatic results, despite the failures of his own attempts to be lighthearted with Polish officials. He wrote that if Slavs "could learn to laugh they could more nearly understand us and we might live together in peace and understanding."[8]

Griffis's optimism concerning the possibilities of improvement in United States–Polish relations was quickly tempered by the education he received into the realities of the situation by the American embassy staff in Warsaw and by Polish officialdom itself. After only a short time in Warsaw, Griffis said: "Altogether the atmosphere is surcharged with nervousness and fear and walking through the streets of Warsaw at night one almost has the feeling that the planes should be overhead any minute now."[9] A short time later, Griffis told a friend: "I doubt that in the history of diplomacy any ambassador can point to a more perfect score with the Government to which he has been accredited. So far as I can see, the curve of degeneration in Polish-American relationships has been unbroken since the day of my arrival until the present date."[10]

An important barometer of the deterioration in United States–Polish relations was the enormous attention and unrestrained attack by the Polish press on the United States at the very time Warsaw was asking Washington for more economic help. Even Ambassador Winiewicz was embarrassed by the extremism of Polish editors who, he admitted, "are of inferior mentality and experience, are anxious to curry flavor with the Government and oftentimes, assume a policy more anti-American than even the Government itself desires."[11] Griffis was so upset that he took the Polish press to task for it. He told Janusz Zoltowski of the Polish embassy in Washington that his colleagues in Poland should try to make friends with the United States "instead of continuing ... [a] constant campaign of invective and vituperation." Like Winiewicz, Zoltowski agreed: "I agree with everything you say. The fact is they really want to be friendly but they don't know how to do it."[12]

The tone of the press attacks was exemplified by a large front-page cartoon that appeared in *Szpilki,* a Polish weekly, on June 3, 1947. It depicted the Statue of Liberty in a Ku Klux Klan robe. Liberty held an American flag adorned by swastikas instead of stars and stripes in its right hand and a lash, a bag of dollars, and a tablet in its left hand that read: "Laws Against Workers." Uncle Sam stood in the foreground and was tearing up a sign labelled "UNO" (United Nations Organization). The caption under the cartoon said: "Yankee Risk Taker—Truman Government Against the Achievements of Democracy and Behind the Back of UNO Carries Military Help to Military-Fascist Greece."[13] The cartoon was rather typical of what appeared in the daily and weekly tabloids and magazines. On October 20, 1947, Griffis wrote to a friend and condemned "this kind of tripe." He added: "The one I have before me from this morning's tabloid shows President Truman first dressed as Alexander the Great, later as Julius Caesar, Ivan the Terrible, Frederick the Great, Napoleon, and finally as a haberdasher selling neckties on the street for 5 cents each. The cartoon is headed 'President Truman's dream and reality.' "[14]

By 1947, especially after the bogus elections, the American press had become increasingly critical of the Warsaw government, but it was not preoccupied with Poland as it had been during the war years.[15] Unquestionably, the most unrestrained attacks against the Polish communists came from the Polish American press, which had never made any secret of its hostility toward the communist world.[16] Polish Americans anticipated the shift in attitudes toward the Soviet Union and its satellites that embraced so many important segments of American public opinion—the church, unions, business—by 1947.

While Griffis complained about Polish attacks on the United States, Winiewicz had some justified complaints of his own. The attacks on him in the United States were as severe as those leveled on his predecessor, Lange, who had been described by one Polish American congressman as a "quisling" ambassador. One Detroit newspaper described Winiewicz as "a dangerous emissary" and likened him to Citizen Genet who "grossly affronted" American hospitality. "In the light of incontrovertible facts, under the conditions of a determined and unscrupulous political offensive by Communist despotism against American democracy," the paper stated, "the only effective tactics Mr. Winiewicz's masters can adopt is to call him home." In an article entitled "I Do Not Shake Hands with Agents of Hangmen" in *Nowy Swiat,* a conservative Polish American newspaper long known for its extreme hostility toward Polish and Russian communists, the author criticized a Polish American bishop for welcoming Winiewicz on a visit to Detroit and attacked the ambassador and his predecessor for attempting to break the united front of America's Polonia against the communists.[17]

In one of the Polish American Congress's press organs, the communist Poles were attacked as thieves, cheats, and terrorists. In an article entitled "How Can You Do Business with Bierut," the Polish American Congress asked rhetorically: "Would you care to make a profit dealing with people whom you accuse of immorality, of being Soviet fences, of breaking promises and obligations?"[18] Another Polish American newspaper described the political leaders of Poland in this fashion: "It must be acknowledged that probably no European country has had such rulers in at least the last thousand years. Even the licentious morality of the condottieri of the Renaissance was without doubt on a higher plane."[19]

Since relations between the two countries had deteriorated so badly after the elections, there was little that either Winiewicz or Griffis could do to improve the situation. The time for imaginative bold diplomacy on both sides had long since passed. Griffis and his staff therefore preoccupied themselves with the long and tortuous business of processing the hundreds of applications of Poles who claimed American citizenship, had relatives in the United States, or wanted to emigrate.[20] Griffis betrayed a waspishness concerning American efforts to repatriate children born in the United States but who returned to Poland with their parents. Only "through this geographical accident," he wrote, were these people Americans but "few, if any of them can speak over half dozen words of English." He wrote that "none of them have any understanding of the nation which gave them birth but 'here they come.' "[21] He left little doubt about his elitism, offering to finance personally an orphanage for fifty children so long as he was permitted to screen the children and, in his words, "select only the sons and daughters of the intelligentsia such as of artists, writers, or others having a background susceptible to development by both physical and hereditary gift."[22]

One of the most bizarre, yet humorous, incidents that happened to Griffis in Warsaw was, as he described it, "my battle with the squatters." Seven Polish families had moved into the property of the embassy and refused to leave. Appeals to the Polish government brought amused grins but no willingness to remove the settlers. Griffis placed four radios in rooms adjoining the squatters and literally blasted them with all kinds of music in six or seven languages twenty-four hours a day. After five weeks of that, all but one of the unfortunate people left the compound. But there was an ironic footnote to the episode. The Bulgarian ambassador calmly asserted that the chancery, occupied by the Americans, belonged to Bulgaria, not to the United States.[23] Oddly enough, the Americans were regarded—at least by the Bulgarians—as squatters too!

Throughout 1947 the Poles repeatedly pressed for favorable action on their request for a loan from the World Bank in order to expand their coal production. Even though prominent individuals in and out of the State Department urged that some financial aid be extended to Warsaw, the growing rift between East and West deterred Washington from acting decisively on an issue which would have benefited America's allies in western Europe. Griffis broke with some of former ambassador Lane's lieutenants in the Warsaw embassy and joined the secretary of state for economic affairs, William Clayton, in supporting the Polish request for credits from the World Bank. Like Clayton, Griffis saw an increase in Polish production as an important element in the economic rehabilitation of Europe. But he also saw something else—"a very substantial tie between East and West will have been developed."[24]

The World Bank sent a team to Poland to investigate the Polish request and concluded that a loan of $47 million would support a large increase in Polish coal production. The vice-president of the World Bank, Robert L. Garner, advised that even if the Poles defaulted on the loan it was worth the risk because of the importance of coal to western Europe. There were significant political benefits to be gained too. Garner said that if the World Bank turned down the loan "it will greatly strengthen Russian propaganda claims that Poland and other similarly situated countries have nowhere to turn except to Russia."[25] But hard-line State Department officials such as Charles Bohlen and Llewellyn Thompson opposed the loan, and it was never granted.[26] Nor was the long-standing Polish request for a

$20 million cotton loan favorably acted upon. That forced Warsaw to get its cotton from the Soviet Union. Little wonder the Warsaw government dragged its feet in finalizing the agreement to compensate Americans whose property had been nationalized.[27]

Poland's need for economic aid initially brought a favorable response from Warsaw to Secretary of State George Marshall's speech at Harvard University in which he outlined the essence of the European Recovery Program. The Polish position was quite consistent with the independent line Poland had followed on economic and social matters in the United Nations.[28] Premier Cyrankiewicz declared: "Poland will spare no efforts to strengthen her friendly relations and cooperation with the United States, which in turn may contribute toward a lasting peace and toward economic rehabilitation."[29] The Poles had been prepared to send a delegation to the Paris meeting to discuss details on the Marshall Plan when, because of Soviet pressure, they abruptly changed their position. The official Polish explanation for the reversal was contained in a note on July 9, 1947, in which Poland criticized the intention of the United States to give Germany a dominant role in the reconstruction of Europe.[30] As one Warsaw newspaper put it: "The American policy wishes to have a strong Germany—stronger than all her neighbors. It wants Germany to become the greatest industrial power of Europe."[31] The ascerbic Korbonski, explaining the reason for the change in the Polish position, wrote in his diary: "We were to receive several hundred million dollars for nothing, and they reject it! We soon learned the reasons behind the decision. Cyrankiewicz had received a telephone call from Moscow, which he answered at attention and repeating continually, 'Yes, sir,' whereupon he sent his note of 9th July."[32]

No issue better dramatized just how far relations between the two countries had deteriorated than Washington's reluctance to extend further relief aid to the Poles after the conclusion of the activities of the United Nations Relief and Rehabilitation Administration (UNRRA) in Poland.[33] The Poles argued that they required additional shipments of grain to avert a crisis before the fall harvest.[34] The figures submitted by Polish officials to representatives of UNRRA and the American embassy concerning the anticipated yield of grain in Poland often contained discrepancies, but UNRRA's own estimates convinced Charles Drury, who headed the UNRRA mission in Poland, that Poland's need for additional relief for the remainder of 1947 was very real. Drury believed that if the Polish government was unable to secure supplies of grain from outside sources it would compel the regime to force deliveries on a large scale from the peas-

ants which could provoke a "minor civil war."[35] According to a
report of a special technical committee which studied Poland's post-
UNRRA relief needs, Poland would require in 1947 assistance
amounting to $294 million, of which $173 million should be food.
"These facts mean," the spokesman concluded, "that unless Poland
has assistance in meeting her relief needs, she will be unable to provide
the special foods needed to maintain the health and growth requirements of her children and mothers."[36] As it turned out, UNRRA's
estimates of Polish needs proved to be more accurate than that of the
American embassy in Warsaw, and Poland ended up getting $11
million from the Emergency Food Program early in 1947. Food arrived in April and May of 1947 and averted a threat of hunger.[37]

American embassy officials in Warsaw did not share UNRRA's
views that additional relief be sent to Poland. Gerald Keith, who ran
the American embassy before Griffis arrived in Warsaw, opposed
more relief to Poland by the American government, though he favored the activities of private relief groups. In April 1947 Keith wrote
that since data from the Polish government "have almost always
proved to be underestimated," there was no compelling need for
additional grain shipments to Poland. Besides, even if Poland really
needed more grain, he argued that it could not possibly be bought,
shipped, milled, and distributed before the end of the summer. And
by then the Polish crop would become available.[38] Keith told Marshall: "I believe a line should be drawn between granting relief to
alleviate distress which can be endured and that which might be
granted to prevent serious malnutrition or starvation." He left no
doubt in what category he placed Poland. In the opinion of senior
officers of the American embassy, granting aid to alleviate hardship
deserved sympathy. But it was clear Keith and his American colleagues tied such aid to political objectives:

> That aid to Poland would temporarily improve the standard of
> living and lighten the suffering of many people is undeniable as
> would be the case in almost any recipient country. If however,
> the assumption is correct that funds with which to provide
> assistance are not without limit it would then seem essential to
> determine when aid should be restricted in order to protect
> American interests. To request American people to aid where it
> is not imperative may prejudice support for relief elsewhere such
> as in Greece and Turkey where it may be required for our
> protection.

Leaving no doubt about where he stood on the matter, Keith stated bluntly: "The granting of aid to Poland would in effect result in increasing the power of the Soviets which bitterly oppose us and our way of life."[39]

Keith's comments were echoed in Congress, where there was strong opposition to giving relief to Poland and other countries dominated by communists. In the debate on House Resolution 153, which provided relief to the people of countries devastated by war, Congressman John E. Rankin of Mississippi said he did not intend "to vote a single dime to feed communism throughout the world, if I can help it." Congressman William M. Colmer, also of Mississippi, offered a substitute amendment which provided that no funds be authorized for relief to "those countries whose governments are dominated by the Union of Soviet Socialist Republics." Colmer felt that the nation had to be "coldly realistic," oppose communism "on all fronts," and "fight it with its own weapons." Congressman Joseph R. Bryson of South Carolina, convinced that Americans faced a worldwide threat from communism, felt that the United States should do nothing to support it anywhere.[40]

Secretary of State Marshall, who succeeded Byrnes in the office, believed the United States should furnish relief "to prevent suffering or serious malnutrition" in Poland. If Polish needs could be ascertained, Marshall favored assistance to Poland, provided Warsaw accepted the tough requirements, including full publicity inside Poland concerning the source and purpose of the aid, in House Joint Resolution 153 pending before Congress.[41] Marshall sent Colonel R. L. Harrison, special assistant to the secretary of agriculture and an authority on food matters, to Poland in July of 1947 to determine what Polish relief needs were. After only four days in Poland, obviously too short a time to evaluate the situation properly, Harrison concluded that the Poles could meet their minimum needs without aid from the United States.[42] The superficial investigation surprised even Griffis who asked Harrison how he reached his conclusions in so short a time. Griffis said, "He [Harrison] answered . . . it was very simple. He simply went to the four parts of Poland and looked at the behinds of the citizenry, male and female." The ambassador added, "Confidentially, they are uniformly large."[43] The Department of State quickly accepted Harrison's recommendations and abandoned plans for further relief to Poland. If Washington had indeed offered aid to Warsaw, one questions whether the Polish government would have ever accepted Congress's tough qualifications which required that Americans control the distribution of relief and insisted that aid be given to all people in need, rather than limiting it to those who made the greatest contribution to the reconstruction of the nation, the method practiced by Polish authorities.[44]

The Polish government was astonished by the American action. *Gazeta Ludowa* complained "our effort and our work are the reasons why aid on a broad scale is being refused us. We feel this is inconsistent with economic logic." *Rzeczpospolita* argued that at least 400,000 tons of rye would be needed in 1947 to avert a food shortage, while *Zycie Warszawy* talked about the severe shortage of cattle. The communist daily, *Glos Ludu*, scored the "definite contradictions in [the] Harrison report."[45] *Rzeczpospolita* summed up Polish feelings on the question when it said that the Polish people "had a right to expect help by reason of their contribution to the cause of victory."[46] Ambassador Winiewicz conveyed the same attitude when he somewhat apologetically remarked to State Department officials that, as Churchill had said, an ally should not be ashamed to ask another for necessary assistance.[47]

The Poles tried to convince American policymakers to reverse their decision. Winiewicz emphasized Polish need for grain during the first six or seven months of 1948, a claim endorsed by Trygve Lie, secretary-general of the United Nations.[48] Since even Harrison did not deny the need for food supplements for children and the destitute, Winiewicz worried whether Poland would be able to purchase food in the United States.[49] The Red Cross estimated that there were approximately 2 million people—300,000 were children—to whom the Polish government had not given adequate relief, a claim the American embassy in Warsaw did not dispute. According to the representative of the War Relief Services of the National Catholic Welfare Conference, less than 10 percent of Poland's 6 million children were healthy, 90 percent were underweight, and every fifth child had active tuberculosis.[50] Edward Iwaszkiewicz, Poland's expert on relief matters, drily offered a fairly accurate summary of the Polish relief picture: "In 1947, Poland commenced grain purchases in US out of meager foreign exchange reserves and will have to continue purchases during coming months in order to cover minimum requirements of grain during fall sowing campaign. This fact is [the] best evidence [of] how essential post-UNRRA help was to Poland." He made a telling point when he said that any appraisal of Polish food requirements should be cognizant of the fact that the Polish nation had been undernourished during six years of Nazi occupation.[51]

No postwar issue divided Poland and the United States more than the question of the Oder-Neisse boundary between Germany and Poland. Despite the severe repercussions in Poland following Byrnes's Stuttgart speech, Washington chose to continue a policy that challenged the permanency of the line without any real possibility of changing it. Secretary of State Marshall reopened the controversial question at the council of foreign ministers which met in Moscow in April of 1947. There Marshall declared that Poland should receive territorial compensation from Germany for land ceded to the Soviet Union. "But in deciding what compensation she is entitled to we must consider what territory Poland needs and can effectively settle," Marshall said. "We must avoid making a settlement which would only create difficulties for Poland and for Europe in future years." Marshall worried about the economic impact on Germany of Poland's controlling an area that he claimed had contributed 20 percent of Germany's prewar food supply. That, he said, would force Germany to be industrialized to an even greater degree than the West would like to see. Marshall saw an analogy to the political situation after World War I. He thought that if Poland continued to control lands long under German ownership, it would create an irredenta "which might discredit the democratic forces of Germany and give militant nationalist groups the chance to gain a hold on another generation of German youth." Therefore Marshall recommended that Poland receive southern East Prussia and Upper Silesia but that a boundary commission be established to recommend a permanent German-Polish frontier before a final conference on a peace treaty with Germany.[52] Marshall reiterated the American position again later in the year at the council of foreign ministers in London.[53]

American policy toward Poland and the communist world had crystallized between the fall of 1946 and the spring of 1947. By then the United States had written off Poland in favor of Germany. As Walter Bedell Smith cogently put it, Washington officials considered that the major question was one of Germany versus Poland: "From our . . . point of view . . . it seems more important to keep Germany headed West than to prevent a general turn to the East on the part of Poland."[54] By supporting Germany over Poland, however, Marshall and his lieutenants provided an issue to Polish and Russian communists to continue to attack the United States and to contribute to a feeling of hopelessness on the part of the great majority of pro-West Poles who felt there was no alternative but to give in to communist and Soviet influence. The curious thing about the American position was that there was no genuine means to change the boundary without the agreement of the Soviets who supported the Poles. Even

if there had been a way to return some of the disputed territory to
Germany, it would without doubt have ended up in Soviet hands,
giving Moscow control of a greater portion of Germany than before.

Upon his return to the United States from Warsaw, former ambassador Lane eloquently argued against the American position on the
matter, but he failed to convince Marshall, who bluntly told him that
he would resent Lane's public criticism on the subject. Lane promised
to refrain from doing so.[55] But the next day, May 10, 1947, he wrote
a bitter letter to the secretary, criticizing the Department of State for
arriving at an important policy without consulting with the American
embassy in Warsaw or, for that matter, with the office of Eastern
European affairs of the State Department, which supported Lane's
position. He complained that men like General Lucius Clay in Berlin
and Robert Murphy, the political adviser in Germany, had too great
a role in shaping American polcy. To Lane and senior officials in the
American embassy in Warsaw, the United States should not alienate
the Poles over a boundary issue because when war with the Soviets
broke out—and Lane was certain it would come—it would be important for the United States to have the Poles on its side.[56]

Polish reactions to Marshall's policy statements were predictable.
The official Polish response to the secretary's statement of April 9,
1947, was chillingly correct: the Polish government considered the
question of its western frontier "as being decided and finally settled."
To attempt to change Poland's western frontiers, it declared, would
impair a "just and peaceful solution." The Polish press, however,
more accurately represented the feelings of most Poles, including
those unsympathetic with the communist-controlled government.
Tydzien, a Warsaw weekly, depicted Marshall in a cartoon as a "Geld
Marshall," successor to a German "Feldmarschal." The caption over
the cartoon reflected a common theme in the Polish press about
American policy: "Germany's providential men. The latest statement
by Marshall, the U.S. representative, at the Moscow Conference has
disclosed the true sense of German anxiety: it consists in the common
interest of imperilled international capital."[57] Gomulka made an
emotional speech in which he affirmed that "the land is ours and it
will always remain the boundary of the Polish nation." He touched
the hearts of most Poles when he said that to those who hold different
views, "We reply in the words of our poet, Maria Konopnicka, *Nie
rzucim ziemi skad nasz rod*" ("We shall not desert the land of our
forefathers").[58] In a rare display of agreement with the Warsaw government, even the London Poles criticized American policy.[59] Ambassador Griffis was not exaggerating very much when he wrote: "It

is literally not fanciful to say that the determination to occupy and hold these lands is such that even the pitiful Polish Army might take to the field if the United States, the Great Powers, or any human agency attempted to return them to German control."[60]

There was another emotional issue that deepened Polish resentment toward its wartime ally. Attempts by the Warsaw government to secure the extradition of former officers of the SS and the Wehrmacht, especially those connected with the suppression of the Warsaw Uprising of 1944 and the subsequent destruction of the Polish capital, were denied by American authorities on the grounds that these men were needed in the West for an indefinite period. Among those the Poles wanted repatriated were SS Gruppenfuhrer Heinz Reinefarth, who played a major role in the pacification of Warsaw, General Nikolaus von Vormann, commander of the 9th Army, General Smilo von Luttwitz, who succeeded von Vormann, and SS Brigadefuhrer and Major General of the Waffen SS, Ernst Rode.[61]

The deterioration in United States–Polish relations was matched by the eclipse of the PSL and its leader, Mikolajczyk, as a viable force in Polish political life. By the summer of 1947, some of the leaders of the PSL urged that the party dissolve itself in order to avoid inevitable arrest and prosecution. Presumably the ideas and traditions of the PSL would be kept alive abroad where the top leaders would emigrate. Another wing favored replacing Mikolajczyk and electing a new executive council to collaborate closely with the communist bloc. Still others endorsed the status quo, believing that the PSL could function independently at least through those members who were deputies to the Sejm and were protected by parliamentary immunity.[62]

Meanwhile, the regime escalated pressure on the PSL, convicting two top PSL leaders—Kazimierz Baginski and Stanislaw Mierzwa—on charges of treason, subversion, and espionage. Baginski, a survivor of the Moscow trial of sixteen Polish leaders in 1945, had been rearrested and sentenced to prison in April 1947. He was later pardoned by Bierut. Mierzwa, another victim of the Moscow trial, had received an amnesty in 1946, only to be arrested again by Polish authorities in the summer of 1947. He was tried with seven other Poles in the so-called Krakow Trials in September and convicted on charges of having given information to the American and British ambassadors in Warsaw.[63]

Under these circumstances, it was understandable that there was widespread speculation in and out of Poland concerning the fate of Mikolajczyk himself. In his own account, he related that attacks against him in the Sejm got increasingly more sinister. "What had been inclined to be half-said, or hinted at," he wrote, "was now coming into the open. This kind of attack could only mean that my days were now plainly numbered."[64] By the fall of 1947, the State Department believed that Mikolajczyk would probably be executed just as Nikola Petkov, the peasant party leader of Bulgaria, had been. The State Department recognized that the United States had a moral responsibility to help Mikolajczyk because it was largely owing to American and British pressure that the Polish leader had accepted the Yalta formula and had agreed to join the provisional government in 1945.[65]

Korbonski, who had reliable intelligence sources in the country, apprised Mikolajczyk of the intention of the regime to arrest members of the executive committee of the PSL and suggested a plan of escape for the top leaders of the party. Before the leadership left Poland, Korbonski recommended that the PSL be dissolved in order not to give the communists an opportunity to take over a de facto party and exploit it to their advantage.[66] "Mikolajczyk," Korbonski said, "wanted to be a hero and told me he would stay and sacrifice his life in Poland."[67] Korbonski believed that if Mikolajczyk remained in Poland, "Possibly we may derive considerable political advantage from it, for it will open the eyes of the West to what is happening in Poland. The news that a former premier and vice-premier had been imprisoned and even executed by a firing squad, would arouse the world's conscience."[68]

But Mikolajczyk later changed his mind and decided to escape too. His decision was influenced by information he had received that he, along with other PSL leaders, would be arrested at the next session of the Sejm, scheduled to open on October 27, 1947. The death sentence was a foregone conclusion. Mikolajczyk now believed that his death would serve no useful purpose.[69] Rather, as he told a British audience a month after his escape, it might provoke his supporters to seek revenge, which would provide the communists with "the chance to drown the people's opposition in blood."[70]

Mikolajczyk came to his decision on or before October 17, 1947, the day he asked George D. Andrews, first secretary of the United States embassy, for American assistance to get him out of the country.[71] Andrews reported Mikolajczyk's request to Griffis who did not hesitate to extend help. "He was our man, our duty was clear," Griffis said, "and we were not long in aiding him." He added: "We had arranged and fostered his return to Poland, he was the hope of the great democratic nations, and it seemed to all of us that, diplomatic hanky-panky notwithstanding, we had to save this man from death."[72]

Officials of the American and British embassies worked quickly and suggested several possible methods and routes of escape for the Polish leader. Andrews returned to see Mikolajczyk and offered three alternatives: first, smuggling him out in an empty coffin in an American convoy which was to return the bodies of American airmen who had been shot down over Poland during the war; second, carrying him in the trunk of Griffis's Chrysler to the Czechoslovakian frontier; and third, helping him to get to Gdynia where he would board a British ship. Mikolajczyk chose the last alternative. On October 20, 1947, carrying only a toothbrush and a revolver and wearing a crumpled American raincoat and slouch hat that Griffis had given to him, Mikolajczyk got into the back of a truck which took him to Gdynia. Despite the long and dangerous trip—the truck passed nine control points and had several blowouts—Mikolajczyk made it to the Polish seaport where he boarded the *Baltavia,* which sailed early the next morning for England.[73]

Before his flight, Mikolajczyk had pleaded with Griffis to allow Maria Hulewicz, who the American ambassador erroneously claimed was the wife of the Polish leader, to accompany him, but Griffis refused, saying later, "I could not run the risk of permitting a double hazard."[74] But if Hulewicz made it to Czechoslovakia, the United States military attaché in Prague was prepared to assist her from there. Unfortunately, Hulewicz, who tried to escape with W. Bryja, treasurer of the PSL, and M. Dabrowski, were caught at the Czechoslovakian frontier.[75] Baginski and his wife, taking another route, reached the American zone. Shortly after Mikolajczyk's departure from the Baltic coast, Korbonski and his wife also managed to escape from Gdynia for Sweden on a Swedish ship. Korbonski was most critical of Mikolajczyk for not revealing to his followers his plans to escape and for urging Korbonski to delay his own departure in order to insure the success of his escape. "All this indicated cold and ruthless calculation and complete absence of any human feeling," Korbonski later wrote bitterly.[76]

The departure of Mikolajczyk and other opposition leaders no doubt brought a sigh of relief from the Warsaw regime which now was spared the problem of liquidating them. As Piotr Wandycz has said, "It is likely that the Communists viewed Mikolajczyk's flight as good riddance."[77] The regime, which rapidly assumed control of the PSL through such willing tools as Wycech, Banach, and Niecko, took special delight in making a point of Mikolajczyk's "shameful" flight and his loss of followers in Poland.[78] *Glos Ludu* called for the liquidation of the remainder of Mikolajczyk's followers "once and forever from the political life of the country."[79] In the Sejm Mikolajczyk was described as "Poland's best export."[80]

The officials of the PSL who had failed to escape and were apprehended at the Czechoslovakian frontier revealed the involvement of the American embassy in Warsaw in Mikolajczyk's flight. Griffis flatly denied helping Mikolajczyk, who once he got to London labeled the Warsaw government's allegations "a pack of lies."[81] Mikolajczyk even wrote a fictional account of his escape in his book, *The Rape of Poland,* published in the United States in 1948, and carefully avoided any reference to American or British involvement in his escape. But Ambassador Griffis set the record straight by giving an essentially accurate account of the episode in his book, *Lying in State,* published four years later.[82]

The Warsaw government had sufficient evidence implicating not only Andrews but also Monroe W. Blake, the second secretary of the American embassy, in the operation. Andrews had been transferred to another diplomatic post, but Blake, who was still in Warsaw, was declared persona non grata in a note handed to Griffis by the Polish foreign minister. The Poles agreed to withdraw the note after Griffis promised to transfer Blake, whose tour of duty in Warsaw was nearly over anyway.[83]

With the leadership of the PSL safely in the hands of reliable protégés of the regime, the PPR escalated pressures on the PPS for a merger, a proposal that had been given major public expression in an address by Gomulka on May Day, 1947. Despite communist pressures, however, the Socialist Party Congress, meeting in Wroclaw on December 14, 1947, was not very receptive to the idea. The PPS argued that it could play an important role as an independent party, especially as a link between leftist socialists in western Europe and the communists. But Stalin had other ideas and pressured Cyrankiewicz, head of the PPS, to reverse himself and press for union with the PPR. After purges within the two parties had been completed, the merger finally occurred in December of 1948 with the creation of a new party, now called the *Polska Zjednoczona Partia Robotnicza* (PZPR) (Polish United Worker's party).[84]

The departure of Mikolajczyk from Poland meant that, with the exception of Czechoslovakia, the last major opposition leader in eastern Europe had been forced out of the political arena. His escape provided an epilogue to the elections of 1947 which had belied the hopes and expectations of the United States that Poland could somehow be prevented from becoming entirely a Soviet satellite. Griffis summed up the limited role of American diplomacy in Poland at the end of 1947 when he wrote home, "Under all the circumstances, it is difficult to see any justification for the maintenance of an Embassy or Consular Service here except for (a) the use of the Embassy merely as a symbol of indestructible American friendship for the Polish people and as a listening post; (b) the maintenance of a Consular Service for the protection of bona fide American citizens and interests."[85]

VI Relief and Repatriation

One of the most visible and rewarding areas of American contact with Poland in the immediate postwar period was through the relief assistance that had been sent to the Polish people. In view of the tense political relations between Warsaw and Washington, it was inevitable that even relief would become politicized by both sides. Nevertheless, millions of Poles benefited from American relief provided through the United Nations Relief and Rehabilitation Administration (UNRRA) and several major private agencies, including the Red Cross, War Relief Services of the National Catholic Welfare Conference, the American Relief for Poland, and the American Joint Distribution Committee.

Closely tied to relief was the related question of repatriation which affected thousands of Poles in displaced persons camps and soldiers who had fought with the western allies during the war. In many ways the repatriation issue was even more political than relief because a large number of Polish civilian and military refugees abroad were staunchly anticommunist and refused to return to Poland. Although the repatriation question was eventually resolved, there were many people who, despite their preference to live in the West, reluctantly ended up back in Poland.

Plans to extend relief to the Poles began during the summer of 1944. UNRRA negotiated with the Polish government-in-exile, whose representatives played an important role in the early sessions of the organization. But the creation of the Polish committee of national liberation in July 1944, and its recognition later as the government of Poland by the Soviet Union, immediately raised a political issue concerning UNRRA aid to the people of Poland. In response to an invitation from Osobka-Morawski to Herbert H. Lehman, director general of UNRRA, to send technical experts to Poland, Lehman announced early in October of that year that a delegation under the leadership of John P. Gregg would be sent to Poland. The delegation, consisting of experts in the fields of supply, public health, displaced persons, and welfare, was to form the nucleus of an operating mission when UNRRA began to send supplies and provide services to Poland.[1]

Gregg was an excellent choice for the position. He had served for a year in Poland with the American Relief Administration after

World War I, and came to UNRRA from the War Production Board with an experienced background in supply and production. In announcing the appointment of Gregg's delegation, UNRRA, anxious to maintain a scrupulous neutrality in the political struggle between the London Poles and the Lublinites, issued a carefully worded press release stating, "The proposed relief operations for the people of liberated Poland, the director general stated, are being undertaken in accordance with the desires of the Polish Committee of National Liberation in Lublin and the Polish Government in London."[2] Unfortunately, the Lublin Poles did not grant the necessary entry visas to the UNRRA group, provoking Gregg to resign in despair.[3]

In March of 1945 Lehman appointed Mikhail A. Menshikov, deputy director general of the headquarters bureau of areas of UNRRA, to succeed Gregg. Menshikov's appointment was a disappointment not only to Ambassador Lane but also to many Poles.[4] Lehman may have believed that the appointment of a Russian would cut through bureaucratic red tape and facilitate the UNRRA aid program to Poland. But unfortunately Menshikov's appointment simply underscored to the Poles the dominant role of Moscow in their country and, for that matter, in eastern Europe.

Menshikov was to negotiate a formal agreement with the Polish provisional government, establish a permanent mission, survey conditions within the country, and ascertain the relief needs of the Poles. Only after the United States and Great Britain extended diplomatic recognition to the reconstituted Warsaw government did the UNRRA mission receive its visas to enter Poland. Menshikov proved too accommodating in his dealings with the Warsaw government, giving the Poles complete control over the distribution of supplies, agreeing to unrealistic limitations on the size of the UNRRA staff, and assuring Polish authorities that no regional offices for the organization would be needed. This naturally limited the ability of UNRRA officials to monitor the distribution of supplies adequately at a time when Congress was considering further appropriations for the organization.[5]

The first shipment of UNRRA supplies to Poland arrived in April 1945 at Constanza, Rumania, from where goods had to be shipped by rail. Pilferage was a problem until Polish guards began in August to accompany the rail shipments. It was not until September that the first ship, the S.S. *Nishmaha,* arrived with UNRRA supplies at Gdynia. Even Ambassador Lane was there for the historic event, underscoring the American role in the aid program to Poland. Rail facilities had been so badly destroyed by the war that it took approximately one month for the goods to make their way to Warsaw, only 250 miles away.[6] With the opening of Gdynia and Danzig the much more time-consuming overland route was no longer used.

Menshikov was succeeded by Charles M. Drury, a Canadian, who became head of the permanent UNRRA mission to Poland in September 1945. Without waiting for visa clearance, he flew to Warsaw with his staff the following month so that Lehman could honestly assure the United States Congress, then considering further appropriations for UNRRA, that UNRRA's Polish mission was in full operation.[7] Educated at the Royal Military College, Drury was a pragmatist who avoided politics and dedicated himself to overseeing the aid program to Poland. He got along well with Polish officials, especially Minc. He persuaded the Poles to remove the limitations on the size of the UNRRA staff agreed to earlier by Menshikov and to open six regional offices—Katowice, Krakow, Lodz, Poznan, Gdynia, and Warsaw—in January 1946. A seventh office was established in Stettin that September.[8]

State Department officials were not very fond of Drury. Lane suggested that Drury's wife had "communistic tendencies and that Drury himself, being personally ambitious and weak, has permitted himself to follow her lead." Ray Atherton, the American ambassador to Canada, dubbed Drury an "ardent," if naive, propagandist for the communist-dominated Warsaw government.[9]

UNRRA aid to Poland became an emotional issue, exploited by Warsaw and Washington to serve their own political interests. Early in 1946 UNRRA was forced to cut back on grain shipments because of shortages. Gomulka claimed that the reductions were politically motivated, a charge Polish historians have tied to alleged American efforts to influence the Polish elections.[10]

The reductions in grain deliveries were exploited by Gomulka and other communist leaders, who insisted that hungry people were in no position to vote intelligently and that the promised elections would therefore have to be postponed. Even Drury, who was described as getting along "like a house on fire" with Polish officials, admitted that the entire grain question was used by the communists "to discredit, insofar as possible, Mr. Mikolajczyk and the Peasant Party." Both the PPR and the PPS encouraged the belief among urban workers that the peasants were hoarding stocks of grain and suggested that bands of workers be organized and, war communism style, raid villages and confiscate the grain. Drury deplored the strategy, arguing that estimates of indigenous stocks of grain by the ministry of supply were "entirely out of line with reality" and were confusing to UNRRA officials. When he complained to officials that his mission needed the "real figures" concerning the local wheat situation in order to formulate recommendations, Drury succeeded in getting the Polish government to admit that there was no foundation to the allegations of hoarding. As a matter of fact, peasant stocks of seed for planting in the spring were extremely low, but that played politically into the hands of the communists because Mikolajczyk's ministry of agriculture was responsible for providing the seed. Drury told Lehman "that the current political situation has not made the provision of food to the people of Poland any easier."[11]

Neither the Poles nor the Soviets were willing to accept UNRRA's explanation that food deliveries were tied to world grain shortages and that cutbacks affected all recipient countries, not only Poland. The Soviet ambassador to Poland, Viktor Lebedev, bluntly told Lane: "Let's not be diplomatic. You know as well as I that the person who pays is the person who controls. It is absurd that the poor United States has not enough grain for Polish needs." He added that if the United States sent more grain to Poland, he and Gomulka would call the American ambassador, "Tovarich Lane."[12]

UNRRA officials in New York were angered by Polish charges. Senior Deputy Director General R.G.A. Jackson told his staff that it was unfortunate for the Poles "to bite the hand that is feeding them." The new director general, Fiorello LaGuardia, a staunch advocate of relief to the Poles, said, "Here I am fighting to get more help for Poland. This kind of talk may be good politics at home, but it is very bad for getting food. . . . I am too good a friend of Poland to stand for any kicking around like this." The Polish government soon realized it had gone too far, and so later changed its position by publicizing UNRRA's explanation of the food situation and took the unprecedented step of allowing the mission in Poland to review before publication subsequent Polish statements concerning UNRRA aid.[13]

As East-West tensions increased in 1946, the American public did not look favorably upon UNRRA, preferring a unilateral relief program to replace it. Congressional sentiment for continuing UNRRA had eroded so much that one government official had to promise Congress he would not return after 1946 for additional funding, even though he was well aware that the need for relief in Europe in 1947 would continue.[14]

Administration officials were unsympathetic with UNRRA too. Stimson claimed Lehman "never got hold of the reality of the job." Lane, who had once strongly endorsed UNRRA aid, later attacked it because it benefited the communists, a theme repeated by his successor in Warsaw. Acheson saw UNRRA supplies going "to the wrong places and were used for wrong purposes." Former president Herbert Hoover, who had visited Poland in March of 1946 and was appalled by the grim situation that faced the Polish people, had recommended aid to the Poles. But by the end of the year he also favored an end to UNRRA operations.[15]

Truman, whose attitude toward UNRRA had cooled shortly after he came to the presidency, had no intention of providing more funds —the Untied States paid almost 75 percent of the cost—to UNRRA after December 1946. After that date Washington would do what the State Department had urged for a long time—namely, act unilaterally, rather than through an international organization in its relief activities in Europe.[16]

The major burden of the criticism in the United States against UNRRA concerned aid to countries which were largely under communist control. Since Poland was the largest single beneficiary of UNRRA aid the operation of the aid program there predictably came in for special scrutiny. During the months of UNRRA's operation in Poland there were constant references to the existence of pilferage, black-marketing, and discrimination.[17]

These problems, though exaggerated by some critics, were inevitable in a program under which distribution was entirely in the hands of the Polish government. Although the Polish government had pledged to UNRRA that it would not discriminate according to race, religion, or political opinion in doling out the aid, the ration card system, established by Warsaw, favored some groups over others. For example, holders of a class one ration card, which called for the highest allowances, included bureaucrats, government employees, and employees of private industries which sold 75 percent of their output to the government. Lower rated ration cards went to older people, pensioners, and employees of private industries which sold smaller percentages of their goods to the state. More than half of the population—people who lived on farms and were considered self-sufficient and those who ran their own businesses or worked in private industries which did not sell to the state—did not benefit from the UNRRA aid. Yet the situation in the Polish countryside was often worse than in the cities. People within the Kielce bridgehead, for example, lived in mud huts and desperately needed relief. LaGuardia, who visited one of the hundreds of villages in the area, was so shaken by what he had seen that he told his son who accompanied him,

"Never forget what you're seeing here. If you ever think you're badly off, remember how these children lived."

Polish authorities claimed that food and other scarce commodities should be shared on the basis of the amount and nature of the work performed. Also, they claimed that the rationing system should be used as a wage subsidy, apportioned according to the wages the individual earned. As Drury explained, "The necessity for this system is that 20 percent of non-agriculture manpower working in the nationalized section of the economy receive low controlled wages while the 80 percent working under free enterprise are paid on higher but widely differing wage scales. The large agriculture community, supplying their own food and selling their surplus products in the free market at high prices, are outside the rationing system because of their privileged position and free market profit." Drury's explanation, however, did not contradict the position of critics who argued that the Polish government used the UNRRA supplies to subsidize itself.[18]

Moreover, the system conspicuously ignored some groups most in need of relief, among them the sick, aged, children, and repatriates. After pressuring Polish authorities, the UNRRA mission in Warsaw managed to convince the regime to give a daily milk allotment to all children under twelve years of age in Warsaw and to provide supplementary rations for pregnant women and nursing mothers.[19]

Even Drury did not deny that some abuses existed. One criticism he did not deny was that bureaucrats received free food allotments out of UNRRA supplies, but he claimed that when abuses were brought to the attention of the Polish authorities they were usually corrected. According to the official historian of UNRRA, only four hundred out of five thousand complaints concerning the misuse of UNRRA aid were considered well founded and referred to the Polish government for action. Drury flatly denied the oft-repeated criticism that communism or cryptocommunism was a criterion in determining an individual's eligibility for receiving UNRRA goods, a view contradicted by Ambassador Lane.[20]

Much was made in the American press over the appearance of UNRRA goods on the free market. *Life* magazine strongly criticized the fact that UNRRA goods were peddled on Warsaw's streets and hotels. "At Warsaw's Hotel Polonia," the article said, "if you are willing to pay the price, you can drink vodka cocktails made with UNRRA grapefruit juice intended for Poland's undernourished children." The fact was that ration card holders could and did resell any item they wanted. Fruit juices, a novelty to Poles at that time, were eagerly sold for bread. A quart of juice brought ten pounds of bread, four pounds more than even a package of American cigarettes.[21]

An episode involving LaGuardia and Lane perhaps best illustrated just how politicized UNRRA had become. LaGuardia, a colorful but tactless politician, told the press shortly before the Polish elections in 1947, "There has been meddling on the part of diplomatic representatives in Poland. I have always stated that it would be far better if ambassadors would look after the interests of their own country rather than interfere in the politics of the country to which they are accredited." After the Polish elections, in response to a question from a correspondent from the *New York Herald Tribune* who asked him if he thought the Poles had a fair and free election, LaGuardia snapped, "Better than anything ever held in South Carolina, North Carolina, Virginia, Georgia, Alabama and Tennessee; there is no comparison. Better in every way." To be sure, Lane took issue with LaGuardia's indirect criticism of him. "What I regret very much is that a person of your experience, particularly because of your having headed a great humanitarian project which was designed *not* to have any political connotation whatever, should take it upon yourself to express a political opinion quite contrary, to use an understatement, to the facts."[22]

Lane reminded LaGuardia that when he had visited Poland in August of 1946 he had promised to write a letter to the Polish premier concerning treatment of American citizens in Poland, yet he never did so. Instead, when the question of the status of Poles who claimed American citizenship was later brought up by a correspondent, LaGuardia bluntly replied, "Everybody in Poland who has ever been to the United States claims American citizenship." Lane politely wrote him, expressing "regret" that as "a champion of human rights [you] did not fulfill your promise to me." When quizzed later by an Associated Press representative who referred to Lane's contention that LaGuardia had welshed on his promise, the Little Flower yelled: "He's a goddamn liar!"[23]

Poland received over $480 million worth of aid from UNRRA during the period 1945–1947, making it the largest single beneficiary of this international program. Foodstuffs accounted for more than 40 percent of the relief, though UNRRA also sent large amounts of clothing, textiles, medical and sanitation equipment, and agricultural and industrial goods.[24] For example, UNRRA provided more than 50 percent of all the trucks in Poland, $11 million worth of seed, $5 million worth of nitrate and phosphate, 151,000 horses, 17,000 cattle, 2,685 box cars, 871 gondolas, and 105 locomotives.[25]

One of the more unusual episodes that occurred in connection with the UNRRA program involved a white stallion. The horse, later to be known as the "White Stallion of Gdansk," had broken loose at the dock. He found a duckboard lying over a drainpipe and played seesaw on it. The workers sent the horse thirty miles away from Gdansk, only to find him back on the seesaw a short time later. After a few more attempts to locate the horse elsewhere, the stallion always found his way back to his favorite seesaw. He was allowed to spend his days as the UNRRA mascot at Gdansk.[26]

One of the unique contributions by UNRRA to Poland was the provision of modern apparatus for the Madame Curie Institute for cancer research. This included x-ray machines, equipment for laboratories and operating rooms, and grams of radium.[27]

Polish officials were unanimous in their expressions of gratitude for UNRRA aid. Berman candidly admitted that UNRRA assistance had been a major factor in the economic revival of the country. Rusinek, unveiling a plaque at a ceremony commemorating UNRRA's aid, was poetic: "Here was a friend and here were good men. There was a crime and here was assistance; there was devastation and here construction." The Soviet ambassador, Lebedev, dolefully said that when UNRRA ended, "it will be a sad moment indeed for the Poles, as U.N.R.R.A. has been doing great work in helping this country, especially at the most desperate period immediately after liberation." Mikolajczyk was even more complimentary: "Without UNRRA and the unflagging determination of the Polish people to rebuild even a country dominated by a despotic alien rule, Poland would have perished."[28] Minister Minc told the UNRRA council,

> It can be said that UNRRA was the first international organization which brought real and substantial assistance to humanity suffering as a result of the war. Obviously, it is possible to criticize the activities of UNRRA; but without these activities, famine would have prevailed in many European countries, if not throughout the world. As far as my country is concerned, the fact that we have revived our industry, which has today reached 71 percent of pre-war production; the fact that we have partially reconstructed our ports, so that their activity is now 58 percent what is was of pre-war; the fact that it has been possible to sow two-and-a-half millions of hectares of uncultivated land; all this we owe to the industry and courage of the Polish population, but also to the generous help given by the friendly nations and by UNRRA.[29]

There seems to be little doubt, too, that most Poles were well aware of the American role in the UNRRA program. Since most items carried a "made in U.S.A." or "shipped from U.S.A." label on them, it is not very surprising that the aid was popularly referred to as "UNRRA-Amerikanski." As one American observer in Warsaw said at the time, the Polish people "talk of the new Poland and the 'wonderful America' which is sending UNRRA ships."[30]

In retrospect, it is difficult to see how American involvement in UNRRA could have been continued beyond 1946–1947. Public opinion in the United States no longer supported a program that even apologists for it have not denied buttressed communist regimes in eastern Europe.[31] Little wonder, then, that in a day of rising Cold War passions the United States decided to end its support of this international relief agency and to follow a unilateral program of aid. It would be presumptuous to assume that the United States could or should have remained oblivious to the political currents that buffeted UNRRA since it was established in 1944.[32]

Apart from UNRRA, a large number of private relief organizations operated in Poland after the war. Unlike UNRRA, these organizations provided supplies and services directly to the beneficiaries of the aid or through reliable Polish groups such as the Polish Red Cross, Caritas (Catholic Charities), and the YMCA. To be sure, the total amount of relief by these organizations did not bulk as large as that provided by UNRRA. But the relief activities of these groups did meet needs unfulfilled by UNRRA and continued after the end of UNRRA operations in Poland. The largest American relief organizations which operated in Poland after the war included the American Relief for Poland, American Red Cross, War Relief Services of the National Catholic Welfare Conference, and the American Joint Distribution Committee. In 1945–1946 these organizations had sent approximately $20 million worth of aid to Poland, consisting primarily of foodstuffs, clothing, medicines, and hospital supplies.[33]

The American Relief for Poland had been established in the spring of 1938 as the *Rada Polonii Amerikanskiej* (the Polish American Council). The *Rada,* which brought together several Polish American fraternal organizations, was a relief organization that unified the humanitarian effort in the United States on behalf of the Polish war victims. The organization underwent two changes in name—first to Polish War Relief when it became a member agency of the National War Fund and, after the war, to the American Relief for Poland. The organization embraced virtually all Polish American groups in the United States, including the three major fraternals—the Polish National Alliance, Polish Roman Catholic Union, and the Polish Women's Alliance.[34]

During the war years, the *Rada* was unable to conduct direct relief in Poland, but it did make arrangements with the Red Cross for the distribution of medicines and drugs in Poland. Thousands of food packages, too, were sent to needy people in Poland and to Polish soldiers in prisoner-of-war camps. The organization also provided clothing and medicines for Polish refugees in Africa, India, the Near East, and Mexico, made contributions for the care of members of the Polish armed forces by the Polish Red Cross and Polish YMCA, and gave funds for the purchase of a mobile hospital and the maintenance of the Paderewski Hospital in Edinburgh, Scotland.

After the war, the American Relief for Poland operated through five regional offices centered in Warsaw, Poznan, Krakow, Gdynia, and Lublin. It maintained its own warehouses in Poland and a fleet of sixty trucks to distribute the aid. Actual distribution was carried out by Polish organizations—Caritas, Cekos, and the Polish Red Cross.[35]

Like UNRRA, the American Relief for Poland did not entirely escape political attacks at home and abroad. One long-time critic, KNAPP, disapproved of the idea that the organization even sent representatives to Poland because it implied that Polonia accepted the Yalta political settlement regarding Poland, something these conservative Polish Americans adamantly refused to do. KNAPP was a persistent critic of the way the organization was run, arguing that "all of Polonia should have a voice in matters concerning the activities of the Rada Polonia."

Rather than support an organization that gave legitimacy to a communist-dominated regime, KNAPP urged Polonia to embark on other projects, such as pressuring the American government to determine whether the thousands of aid packages Polish Americans had sent to Poland actually got to their addressees.[36] The State Department was flooded with complaints from Polish Americans that few if any of the packages reached their relatives in Poland. No doubt part of the explanation was the fact that not many Poles could afford the tariff which the Polish government levied on the packages from the United States. Senator Leverett Saltonstall of Massachusetts agreed with Polish American criticism that the United States had not done enough to help American citizens maintain mail and parcel post contact with their relatives.[37]

The first shipload of aid to Poland after the war from the American Relief for Poland was delayed until the end of 1945 because of bureaucratic red tape, much of which was Warsaw's fault. But this did not prevent Michael Szyszko, vice-minister of agriculture, from suggesting that the aid had been delayed deliberately because of "persons under the influence of the Polish London government" within the organization. Since the *Rada* received some of its funds from the United States government, one American apologist for the Warsaw regime urged that Congress investigate the long delay in supplies raised by the *Rada* reaching Poland.[38]

Under the leadership of Henry Osinski,the American Relief for Poland cooperated with other relief agencies in the country and in the opinion of both the American embassy in Warsaw and the Poles themselves made a significant contribution toward meeting the needs of the Polish people. In addition to its operations in Poland the American Relief for Poland also carried out an extensive program of aid to Polish displaced persons in Germany, France, Switzerland, and elsewhere.

By the end of August 1946 almost $4 million worth of aid had been received by Poland. In 1947 the American Relief for Poland prepared a budget calling for $12.5 million, half of which was to be cash and the balance in gifts-in-kind. The organization's funding came from several sources—the National War Fund, War Relief Services of the National Catholic Welfare Conference, and voluntary contributions of affiliated groups and individuals.[39] The organization was fortunate in drawing the support of many prominent Americans without blood ties to Poland such as Hugh Gibson, former minister to Warsaw who served as honorary chairman of the organization, Arthur Bliss Lane, Clare Boothe Luce, James A. Farley, Cardinal Francis J. Spellman, and Cardinal Samuel A. Stritch.[40]

Like UNRRA and the American Relief for Poland, the American Red Cross experienced delays in getting clearance from Polish authorities to enter Poland. It was not until September 1945 that two Red Cross officials accompanied Ambassador Lane on a flight to Warsaw, even though they still had not received entry visas.[41] The Red Cross worked closely with the American Relief for Poland, even allocating supplies to it for distribution. By September 1946 the dollar value of Red Cross aid which had arrived in Poland from the United States exceeded $6.5 million. The aid consisted primarily of clothing, shoes, medical supplies, and bedding.[42]

The War Relief Services of the National Catholic Welfare Conference under the direction of George Szudy in Poland made all of its distributions through Caritas, the Polish Catholic welfare organization which operated through twenty-five district offices in Poland. By

September 1946 nineteen shipments valued at $2,577,684 had arrived in Poland. An additional $1.5 million had been spent to purchase relief supplies for Polish refugees in the period from August 1943 to September 1946. By February 1947 War Relief Services reported to its headquarters in New York that the organization's aid had reached 5.4 million needy people. Of special significance was the organization's priority to aid Poland's children, 2 million of whom were homeless.[43] War Relief Services could take pride in the fact that it had responded to the plight of children and the aged, groups who were discriminated against by Polish authorities when they allocated UNRRA supplies. Szudy's organization reported, "our relief shipments are reaching 490 orphanages serving 24,500 children; 945 preschool feeding programs that reach 46,800 children; 220 old age homes that serve 15,400 aged; approximately 230 kitchens that serve warm meals to 2,243,893 persons; 600 clinics and 300 hospitals that are making excellent use of the medicines you are sending to Poland."[44]

The American Joint Distribution Committee, first headed by David Guzik and later by Wilhelm Beim, was an American Jewish agency which assisted not only Jews but also Christians. In the seven-month period extending from June to December of 1946, the committee had contributed approximately $6 million in cash or kind.[45] Other American agencies or groups with a strong American component included the Anglo-American Quaker Relief Mission, which was committed especially to providing food supplements to children; the Cooperative for American Remittances to Europe, which facilitated the dispatch of relief parcels to Poland; the Unitarian Service Committee, which specialized in giving medical advice and care; the General Conference of Seventh Day Adventists, which collected funds in the United States to purchase food for distribution in Poland;[46] and the YMCA, which not only fed and clothed thousands of people but also cared for fifteen thousand boys. An additional six thousand children were looked after in YMCA day camps.[47]

Ambassador Lane was correct when he stated that beyond the material assistance which these private agencies gave to the needy people of Poland they helped to rebuild "the bridge of understanding and affection between the American and Polish peoples, which had been closed to traffic during the Nazi occupation."[48]

World War II had resulted in major migrations of the Polish people which took the form of mass expulsions and voluntary movement of refugees. After the Nazi invasion of Poland in 1939 thousands of soldiers and civilians fled to Hungary and Rumania, and from there many went to France where General Wladyslaw Sikorski had temporarily established a Polish government-in-exile prior to its departure for England. Most Poles, however, were victims of German and Soviet policies that expelled or forcibly transferred them from their homes. In 1939 and 1940 1.5 million Poles were expelled from western Poland, which was incorporated into the Third Reich. About the same time, approximately 1.5–2 million Poles and Jews who lived on the Soviet side of the Molotov-Ribbentrop Line were deported to the Asiatic provinces of the Soviet Union.[49] A small portion of them, a little over 100,000 soldiers and civilians, managed to leave the Soviet Union in 1942 for Iran under General Wladyslaw Anders.[50] Then there were 3.5 million Poles deported to Germany as slave laborers.[51] By the time the war ended in Europe the bulk of Polish refugees were in western Europe and the Soviet Union, though thousands of Poles were also scattered in Africa, India, the Middle East, and Mexico. Little wonder, then, that the problem of repatriating the Poles in the West constituted a major issue in Poland's relations with the United States.

Most Polish refugees in the West decided to return home after the war. Between November 1945 and June 1947, 569,727 Poles, most of whom came from the American and British occupation zones of Germany, had been repatriated.[52] Polish sources claim that more than 2 million people returned home from the West between 1944 and 1949. Most of the refugees—85 percent—returned in the period 1945 –1946.[53] Approximately 40 percent of the Polish intelligentsia who were in Great Britain decided to return home.[54] Many of these intellectuals, though unsympathetic with communism, wanted to return and help rebuild their country. In view of the high losses suffered by the Polish professional class during World War II, it is easy to understand why the Polish government encouraged these people to return. Still, as late as February 1947 UNRRA cared for 335,117 Polish refugees, most of whom were in the Allied occupation zones of western Germany. A large proportion of them refused to return home.[55] Many had originally come from eastern Poland and had bitter memories of the treatment they had received at the hands of the Russians. As one observer pointed out, these Poles "would commit suicide rather than return to Poland."[56]

The United States and Great Britain were agreeable to the repatriation of Poles who wanted to return to Poland. And as the flood of displaced persons (DP's) clogged the communications system and strained the food resources of the West, Washington and London became increasingly anxious to oblige the Warsaw government. Warsaw mistakenly charged that the Americans and British refused to allow Polish citizens to return home. And when queried by the West about the need for early and fair elections in Poland, the Polish government was quick to tie the repatriation issue to it. The sooner the repatriation of Polish refugees took place, Warsaw said, the sooner the elections would be held.[59]

In fact, American authorities were so eager to oblige the Warsaw government that by August of 1945 the United States wanted to repatriate ten thousand DP's a day but Polish authorities could only handle half that number. No doubt part of the problem was the refusal of the Soviets to provide enough gasoline for the trucks transporting the Poles out of Germany to Poland. Once the repatriation of Russians from the West had been completed—and they had priority over other groups—American authorities suggested foot marching as many Poles as possible out of the western zones in Germany before the end of 1945.[58]

American eagerness in expediting the repatriation of Poles eastward gave rise to charges that contrary to its official policy the United States forced refugees to return to Poland. By the end of 1945 reports circulated that Polish citizens had been involuntarily repatriated from the American zone in Germany. One report claimed that an entire Polish regiment had been involuntarily sent back from France.[59]

Understandably, Polish Americans took an active interest in the fate of their kinsmen. KNAPP, an affiliate of the Polish American Congress, was one of the first Polish American organizations to become actively involved in the problem, devoting many issues of its *Biuletyn Organizacyjny* to the question and enlisting the aid of Senator Arthur Vandenberg. Vandenberg proposed to the State Department that a special representative who enjoyed the confidence of Polonia be sent to the American occupation zone in Germany and to Poland itself to deal with repatriation matters. The State Department did not like the idea, noting that the issue came under the purview of the American ambassador to Poland.[60] Besides, Byrnes told Vandenberg that if incidents of involuntary repatriation did occur, "I can assure you that they have been exceptions rather than the rule in the administration of clearly defined military directives in pursuance of United States policies."[61]

Vandenberg, satisfied that there was no convincing evidence to prove conclusively that involuntary repatriation of Poles was practiced, rejected suggestions from KNAPP that a congressional investigation of the matter be launched. In a letter to KNAPP's president,

Walter Cytacki, Vandenberg said, "I am very sure that our insistent inquiry (both here and in Germany) will result in extreme care by the State Department and by the army that there will be no involuntary repatriation hereafter. . . . But we must continue to be vigilant."[62]

Cytacki dropped the matter for the moment and then appealed to Vandenberg to do something to see that postal and parcel post communications between Polish Americans and their families and friends in DP camps in the American zone in Germany were established. Vandenberg apprised Byrnes of Polonia's concerns, and by the end of November of 1945 postal and parcel post contact between the United States and Polish citizens in the American zones in Germany and Austria was inaugurated.[63]

The question of involuntary repatriation was also a major issue of concern to the Polish American Congress, headed by Charles Rozmarek, an able if sometimes demagogic leader who also was president of one of Polonia'a major fraternals, the Polish National Alliance. One of Rozmarek's strengths was that he was bilingual, unlike many Polish American leaders who did not feel comfortable speaking English.[64] Moreover, he had broad contacts within the large Polish American community.

Throughout the latter part of 1945 the Polish American Congress unleashed a constant barrage of criticism against involuntary repatriation of Polish refugees. To force these people to return to a communist-dominated Poland, Rozmarek said in August, "would be a cruel injustice and a flagrant violation of our American tradition of justice and humanity." Rozmarek claimed that "hundreds of thousands of Poles" were arbitrarily classified as Soviet citizens and returned to the Soviets, a charge some students of the subject today confirm.[65] But after Rozmarek visited the DP camps in Europe, his organization altered its attacks and emphasized the conditions in these camps which convinced Polish refugees reluctantly to accept repatriation.

Rozmarek, accompanied by Ignacy Nurkiewicz, vice-president of the Polish American Congress, and Charles Burke, who later headed the office of the Polish American Congress in Washington, D.C., went to Germany and visited DP camps in the American and British zones of occupation in the late summer and early fall of 1946.[66] Rozmarek later recounted that "we went there with open minds, expecting a certain amount of distress, but wholly unprepared for the indescribable conditions we encountered." The Polish American leaders blamed UNRRA for making Polish DP's endure conditions "in which life itself becomes unbearable" and for becoming "an instrument of coercion and a political weapon employed by Soviet Russia to force repatriation on Displaced Persons to serve its own selfish purposes." The indictment by the Polish American leaders called attention to the not too subtle methods of officials to discourage the Poles to remain in the DP camps. Rozmarek declared "UNRRA has embarked on a course to make life so miserable for Displaced Persons that they will accept repatriation as the lesser of two evils."[67] Nurkiewicz said much the same thing: "We came away with the conviction UNRRA policies were deliberately designed to force the inmates of the camps to go back to Poland, even though many of them would do so at peril of their lives."[68]

Food was used as a political weapon—cutting down rations and offering little or no variety was apparently a common practice.[69] At the time the Polish Americans were in Germany, UNRRA embarked upon another strategy—promising to give Polish DP's in Germany who returned to Poland before the end of 1946 two months extra food rations. This was part of LaGuardia's campaign to get as many Polish DP's home as soon as possible.

Even the United States military establishment in Germany, headed by General Joseph T. McNarney, supported the pressure tactics on the Poles. McNarney stated: "I urge all Polish displaced persons in the U.S. Zone of Germany to take advantage of this new plan for a 60-day food ration, available to all who return to Poland during the period from October 1 to December 31, 1946. The U.S. Army and the American people firmly believe that your future lies in Poland, helping to rebuild your devastated country." McNarney went on to admonish the Poles that they faced worse economic conditions if they remained in Germany than if they returned to Poland,[70] a view contradicted by the large number of Poles who returned or tried to return to the West after having been repatriated. As one observer at the time noted, once the Polish DP's learned of the poor food situation in Poland, "repatriation ... dropped over night."[71] McNarney, not shrinking from scaring these unfortunate people who had already been victimized by so many for so long, told the Polish DP's: "It is impossible for the United States to continue operating assembly centers and camps indefinitely. Emigration to another land holds little hope for fulfillment at present, although the United States has attempted to initiate international action. Conditions for resettlement in any country will not be easy. Substantial improvement in your economic conditions in another country over economic conditions in

Poland is very doubtful. Poland needs you. Again, I urge you to return to your homeland while several months of moderate weather remains."[72]

Once the Poles decided to accept the inducement of additional rations, the head of the UNRRA mission in Warsaw told the Polish DP's that UNRRA employees "are now packing this food at Dziedice and Szczecin, and will personally deliver it to the repatriates as they arrive."[73] The LaGuardia-sponsored food offer did not produce the desired results because he did not understand that the Poles who refused to return home either feared political reprisals or did not want to live under a system of government installed by the Kremlin. No wonder so many Polish refugees regarded UNRRA's offer as an insulting attempt to trade on their misery.[74]

Apparently UNRRA officials believed that the less attractive housing conditions were the more likely the Poles would go home. Rozmarek complained that as soon as the DP's made a more decent life for themselves by planting a garden and starting a school for their children, they were shifted to another camp "where bare walls and ruined barracks are the only things left by the previous occupants."[75] Under these circumstances, deep-seated resentments by Polish refugees toward UNRRA officials were inevitable.

Polish camp leaders were convinced that a well-organized cultural life was the last thing UNRRA officials wanted to see developed because it encouraged the DP's to remain in Germany. Rozmarek reported on one camp that had schools, a theater, choir, library, pharmacy, and a mimeographed newspaper. He related, "Before moving the inmates to another camp, UNRRA confiscated text books, school supplies, sporting and recreational equipment, music sheets and sewing machines, presented to the camp by a relief organization. The departing Poles were permitted to take only clothing and bedding with them." Rozmarek's claim was supported by a directive from UNRRA's Stuttgart office which read: "Effective October 1st, 1946, all educational, recreational and other cultural activities are to be discontinued in all camps caring for one hundred or more Polish Displaced Persons."[76]

In the feverish campaign to induce the Poles to leave the DP camps, UNRRA officials directed that Polish refugees should not be employed. One office memorandum declared: "Do not employ Poles—repatriate them, as they must go home . . . no such thing as a unrepatriable Pole. . . . Hire outsiders, even Germans, to replace essential Poles, but fire Poles and get them home."[77]

What especially concerned the delegation of the Polish American

Congress was the large number of Polish youths who fled from Poland after the war but were not accorded DP status. Apparently many of these men had belonged to the Polish underground during the war. Rozmarek charged that "when caught out of bounds by American or British military police, they are handed over to Soviet authorities and they disappear never to be heard of again."[78]

UNRRA denied the claims of the Polish American leaders, but the denials were not entirely convincing. When LaGuardia took issue with the attacks, the *Narod Polski* noted that "the cocky LaGuardia denied" what the Polish American leaders had said. But, it added, "We believe the delegation of the Polish American Congress which was there and LaGuardia was not and saw that which LaGuardia did not see."[79] Rozmarek's charges were borne out by William Henry Chamberlin who also had visited the DP camps in Germany. Chamberlin wrote:

> Although there has not been forced repatriation, except in a few borderline cases, very strong pressure is being put on the Poles to return to their Soviet-dominated country. People in the camps are denied any semblance of the Four Freedoms. They are permitted to read only the propaganda of the Soviet puppet government. Independent Polish newspapers are not allowed to circulate in the camps.
>
> There is continual shifting from one camp to another. Schools and recreation grounds are arbitrarily closed. Those Poles who are performing guard duty, under American command, are given very inferior conditions, as regards pay and rations, compared with those of American soldiers.[80]

Although Rozmarek and Chamberlin stopped short of charging that Polish DP's were forcibly repatriated to Poland, it is clear that only a fine distinction exists between physically forcing individuals to do something against their will and creating intolerable conditions that induce them to choose an alternative they would not normally select in less intimidating circumstances.

One issue which became a source of considerable controversy was the use by American military authorities in Germany of liaison officers whose loyalty was to the Polish government-in-exile in London, not to Warsaw. The Polish government, supported by the Kremlin, wanted the London Poles expelled and liaison officers appointed by Warsaw to replace them. UNRRA believed that the officers representing the London Poles hindered the repatriation of Polish DP's. But American military authorities were quite satisfied using the London

Poles as liaison officers. "These men," LaGuardia said, "have stated that they are not going to return home. It would have been better for the Polish Government to have had their own liaison officers in the Displaced Persons' Camps, who could have dispelled their doubts, concerning a decision to return home."[81]

Frank Januszewski of KNAPP condemned the suggestion that the London Poles be replaced by "murderers and spies" who would bring "methods of political criminal terrorism by that government." He did not understand why the United States was treating Warsaw as a permanent de jure government. "In other words," he told Vandenberg, "by treating the *provisional* Government in Warsaw as a *regular* Government, we are violating the Yalta agreement ourselves."[82] On his part, Rozmarek suggested but he did not follow up a proposal that an American adviser be appointed to act as a liaison between Polish DP's and military authorities in Germany and Austria to represent the interests of the Poles.[83]

Despite the fact that UNRRA Resolution 92 recommended "that only those persons who have been properly nominated by presently recognized governments shall be accredited to the occupying authorities and military authorities, and permitted to serve as liaison officers," American military officials in Germany and Austria did not completely implement it with respect to the London Poles who continued to exert considerable influence in the DP camps. Assistant Secretary of State Clayton, who headed the American delegation to UNRRA's Fifth Council session in August 1946, complained that the current role of the London Poles "is certain to be a cause of continuing embarrassment to the United States Government and exerts a retarding influence on repatriation of Polish displaced persons." Clayton admitted that the Warsaw government had been lax and even uncooperative in providing liaison officers in sufficient numbers, which he implied may have required continued use of the London Poles. But, he said, the "United States will be blamed in large measure for [the] ineffectiveness of Warsaw Polish liaison officers and nonrepatriation of large numbers of Poles as long as our military authorities maintain [their] present unfriendly attitude toward Warsaw Poles in contrast to [their] friendly attitude toward London Poles."

Clayton wanted Washington to send a strongly worded directive to American military authorities in Germany and Austria depriving officials of the former London Polish government of any influence whatsoever with respect to Polish DP's.[84] By the middle of August 1946 the War Department instructed its officers in Germany and Austria to eliminate any influence of the London Poles and to invite the Warsaw government to provide liaison and welfare officers to promote the repatriation of Polish refugees from the West. The United States political adviser for Germany, Robert Murphy, told Secretary of State Byrnes that the State Department's intention to remove the influence of the London Poles would also affect the supervision of guard and labor companies and that it would take more time to reorganize them. Murphy had high praise for the loyalty and efficiency of the Polish officers from London who, he said, would still be of great value to screen, select, and influence nonrepatriable DP's to resettle in other countries. "In that operation, when it arises," Murphy noted, "we can expect little or no assistance from [the] Warsaw Poles."[85]

The most controversial group of Polish refugees in the West that the Warsaw regime wanted repatriated was the Polish army which had fought with the British after the Germans overran Poland in 1939. The Polish army, which had also fought in France before its collapse in June of 1940, was reorganized in Scotland. Polish naval and air units were reorganized too, and, as is well known, Polish fighter units fought with distinction during the Battle of Britain. After Hitler invaded the Soviet Union, the Soviet and Polish government-in-exile came to an understanding, allowing the creation on Soviet soil of a Polish Army, composed of men and officers in Soviet internment camps, under the command of General Wladyslaw Anders. Stalin never really wanted armed Poles in the Soviet Union and so allowed Anders to evacuate approximately 115,000 troops and civilians to Iran in 1942.[86] These troops, combined with the Carpathian Brigade which had fought at Tobruk, were organized into the Polish II Corps, which played a major role in the Italian campaign from the capture of Cassino to the fall of Bologna. Meanwhile, British-based Polish troops participated in the liberation of France, Belgium, and Holland. After VE Day, the Polish II Corps under Anders's command remained in Italy as part of the British army of occupation.

The official position of the United States and Great Britain concerning the repatriation of members of the Polish armed forces was no different from their position toward civilians. Both governments officially opposed forced repatriation and stood by the Potsdam understanding of the Big Three that veterans who decided to return to Poland "shall be accorded personal and property rights on the same basis as all Polish citizens."[87] For all the claims by the Warsaw government that it wanted Polish veterans repatriated, there was a curious lack of cooperation with the British to effect a speedy and efficient return of those men who wanted to return. Mikolajczyk and

Lane claimed—correctly as it turned out—that the Polish government was apprehensive about having a large number of soldiers from
abroad in Poland at the time of the elections. It was reported that
those who had already returned home were kept out of Warsaw.[88]

General I. Modelski, head of the Polish military mission sent to
Britain to negotiate the repatriation of Polish soldiers under British
control, himself admitted that Warsaw deliberately intended to slow
down the process of repatriation. Warsaw insisted that all men who
elected to return to Poland be subjected to a screening process. The
British, on the other hand, favored sending as a group all men who
wished to return as soon as possible without the time-consuming
process of screening.[89] Obviously the Warsaw government hoped to
screen out older veterans who might be less sympathetic with the
regime than younger, more adaptable men. Then, too, Warsaw probably feared a large military influx which might constitute a political
threat to a government not yet completely controlled by the communists. It was not an idle fear; after all, Mikolajczyk himself favored a
return of Polish veterans as units so that they could act as a democratic corps in the Polish army to offset the men who had been
indoctrinated by the Soviets.[90]

The Polish government was especially concerned about the continued presence under arms of the Polish II Corps in Italy. These battle-
experienced veterans, most of whom came from eastern Poland,
which the Kremlin absorbed into the Soviet Union, hated the Russians, and few of them chose repatriation to Poland. Warsaw claimed
that Anders's corps carried out subversive activities against the Polish
government. Polish communists were convinced that Anders's units
aided the antiregime underground and claimed that the Polish civil
war would end once Anders and his troops were disbanded. On
February 6, 1946, foreign minister Molotov made a speech in which
he alluded to the maintenance of "anti-Soviet armies" in central
Europe, which threatened world peace.[91] At one point, the Soviets
tried to cripple Anders's forces by demanding that the British turn
over 30,000 of his men on the grounds they were really Soviet citizens.
The British refused. The Soviets even included Anders's men among
those who fought with the Nazis against the allies and demanded their
return on that basis. Secretary Byrnes, not very well informed about
the contribution of Anders's men to the Allied victory in Italy, weakly
challenged the Soviet assertion and reiterated the Anglo-American
position against involuntary repatriation.[92]

Early in 1946 the Soviet delegate to the United Nations, Andrei
Vyshinsky, voiced Yugoslavian charges that Polish troops in Italy had

moved toward the Yugoslavian frontier and had recruited anti-Tito groups in Italy into their units. Vyshinsky characterized the actions as "a possible future threat to peace, calm, and order on the Yugoslav-Italian frontier." British foreign secretary Bevin denied the charges.[93] In retrospect, it appears that the Yugoslav-Soviet claims were part of a carefully orchestrated attack at a time when Yugoslavian troops moved into the Venezia Giulia area.

Of the 249,000 members of the Polish armed forces abroad in 1945, 105,000 chose to return to Poland. General Anders opposed repatriation.[94] "All our rights as a nation are being wiped out," he declared. Homebound soldiers, he said, would "go not to Poland but to Russia, not to a free life, but to captivity." Despite the fact that Anders had promised not to interfere with those who decided to return to Poland, men in his command who chose repatriation were made to feel as though they were traitors.

Major General Klemens Rudnicki, commander of the Polish 1st Armored Division in occupied Germany, threatened: "We shall return to Poland—but only with arms in hand."[95] Anders and most of his staff were anxious to preserve the nucleus of a Polish military force which would return, Pilsudski-style, to Poland in a war between the West and the Soviet Union that most Poles in western Europe believed was inevitable.

The Polish II Corps had become a political embarrassment to Britain, so the units were recalled to Britain in the summer and early fall of 1946 and disbanded. Although the British government preferred that the veterans return home, it pledged itself to help those who remained in the West to resettle. To help the Poles build a future, the British established a Polish Resettlement Corps in which they received training in agricultural and industrial activities which helped them return to civilian life.[96] At first, the Polish government condemned the resettlement corps as "a military organization under military discipline." Using a law of 1920 which authorized the government to take away Polish citizenship from soldiers who joined a foreign organization, the Warsaw regime applied it to General Anders and seventy-five of his staff officers. Enrollment in the Polish Resettlement Corps began in January 1947, and 103,000 Poles joined it.[97]

Although several European governments expressed a willingness to admit former Polish veterans into their countries, the United States was slow to respond to the needs of this group of refugees, which was consistent with the apathy and, in some cases, the hostility of American public opinion on the issue. Even Polish Americans were slow to call for congressional efforts to provide a home for these former Allied troops.[98] It was not until late in 1946 that the Polish American Congress mounted a campaign that Polish veterans be permitted either to enlist in the United States army of occupation and be granted American citizenship or to join Polish civilian refugees in settling in Alaska.[99] Later, when Congress considered passage of the Stratton Bill which provided for the entrance of 400,000 DP's into the United States over a four-year period, Rozmarek appeared before the House immigration subcommittee and pleaded that an amendment be added to provide for former Polish soldiers who, he said, were entitled to enter the United States "if only as a reward for the invaluable service they rendered America as our gallant fighting allies." It was not until 1950 that H.R. 4567, amending the Displaced Persons Act of 1948, allowed 18,000 former Polish veterans to enter the United States.[100]

To be sure, the Polish American Congress was equally interested in the fate of the thousands of Polish civilians who refused to go back to Poland and wanted to find a home somewhere in the West. After the return of his delegation from Europe in 1946, Rozmarek made several recommendations aimed at opening the doors of the United States to Polish refugees. He called for revision of immigration laws that would allow unused quotas during the war to be filled by DP's. While still in Europe, Rozmarek had recommended to secretary Byrnes that 150,000 Polish DP's be admitted to the United States. "For its participation in Yalta, which deprived displaced persons of a free homeland," he declared, "the United States must accept its full responsibility in this challenging crisis on moral as well as on humanitarian grounds." Leaving no doubt about his views concerning the Big Three settlement on Poland, he added a stinging rebuke: "If there had been no Yalta in 1945 there would be no Displaced Persons problem in 1947."[101]

It was not until April 1947 that the American Committee for the Relief of Polish Immigrants was incorporated. Popularly known as the Polish Immigration Committee, the organization made its headquarters in New York City and received assistance from the Polish American Congress and the American Relief for Poland. Before the passage of the Displaced Persons Act of June 25, 1948, the organization's activity was confined to assisting a number of DP's who had relatives in the United States to fill Poland's unused wartime immigration quotas, helping Poles born in America or naturalized Americans who were in Poland or other parts of Europe and had been unable to return to the United States during the war, and influencing the passage of private bills by Congress to allow several hundred Polish war victims to remain in the United States.[102]

VII Polish Americans and the Polish Question

During World War II most Polish Americans supported the Polish government-in-exile and regarded the Soviet Union as an atheistic despotism which intended to force the communist system upon the Polish people. From May 1944 most Polish Americans were organized in the Polish American Congress, which represented approximately 6 million Americans of Polish ancestry. Through the Polish American Congress, they tried but failed to influence American policy toward the Soviet Union over the questions of Poland's postwar boundary in the east and the complexion of the future government of Poland. President Roosevelt had misled not only the Polish American Congress but also Polish officials in London that he intended to do far more for Poland than he was willing or able to accomplish.

When Polish Americans became aware of the results of the Yalta Conference, which confirmed the cession of a large chunk of Polish land east of the Curzon Line and provided for the framework of a coalition government dominated by communists, the Polish American Congress was the first major bloc of anti-Soviet Americans to condemn the Yalta agreements and recommend that the administration take steps to deal with the Polish situation. For all its attacks against the Yalta and Potsdam agreements, the Polish American Congress did nevertheless support Polish land acquistions to the Oder-Neisse line and criticized secretaries Byrnes and Marshall for suggesting revisions in favor of the Germans.

But the zealous fervor of the Polish American Congress in 1945 and 1946 in condemning the Soviets and criticizing American policies toward the Polish and Soviet governments did not find a responsive audience either in Washington or in the American public at large. The proposals of the Polish American Congress in dealing with Warsaw and Moscow were seen as too extreme and even dangerous until the American public came around later in the 1940s to share many of the views advanced by Polish Americans. That is why the Truman administration maintained an aloof attitude toward Rozmarek and other leaders of the Polish American Congress and its affiliates.

Predictably during these years, the Polish American Congress drew

closer to officials associated with the Polish government-in-exile, criticized American loans to Warsaw, had misgivings about the distribution of UNRRA aid in Poland, welcomed Mikolajczyk when he fled
from Poland to the United States, and launched a major attack on the
communists through the Committee to Stop World Communism.

No issue had unified the Polish American community as much as
the Yalta decisions concerning Poland. Polish Americans perceived
American policy on the Polish question as a cynical disregard of the
ideals contained in the Atlantic Charter and a deliberate effort to
appease the Soviet Union, which they regarded as the inveterate
enemy of the entire free world. Since almost every Polish American
family had a relative in Poland, a country that had lost lands to the
Soviets and from which a large proportion of Polish Americans had
emigrated to the United States, it is not surprising that they were very
bitter about the wartime settlements concerning Poland.

The Yalta decision on Poland had provoked immediate and sharp
criticism from the Polish American Congress. Rozmarek called Yalta
a "moral abdication of the Atlantic Charter" and implied that Roosevelt and Churchill were as guilty as Stalin in delivering a blow to
Poland. *Dziennik Zwiazkowy (Alliance Daily)*, the widely read publication of the Polish National Alliance, bitterly criticized Roosevelt
and Churchill for abandoning western ideals and sacrificing Poland
at Yalta. In one issue of the newspaper a cartoon showed Stalin's
police whipping Poles who trudged off to labor camps in the Soviet
Union. The Poles passed a sign ostensibly bearing the words of the
Big Three at Yalta: "We will create a strong, free and prosperous
Poland."[1] The Polish American Congress *Bulletin* bitterly declared:
"We want to be on record in claiming that America has lost her way,
that we have again missed, miscalculated, squandered, frustrated, and
deeply hurt the heart and soul of America."[2]

When Truman assumed the presidency, Polish Americans hoped
that he would take a tougher stand against the Soviet Union on behalf
of Poland. But it became increasingly apparent that once the government in Warsaw was reconstituted according to the Yalta formula,
Washington paid less attention to the Polish problem. One of the
persistent themes which characterized the Polish American press was
that the Truman administration no longer really cared about Poland
and that Polonia should act in defense of the interests of the Polish
nation. "So long has the Polish question taxed the diplomatic brains
and the conscience of the world, that from sheer exhaustion, perhaps,
this lamentable settlement has been accepted with something akin to
relief," the Polish American Congress said. "The world is too weary

to protest. And for Poland, justice sleeps."[3] Late in October of 1945 officers of the Polish American Congress issued a statement saying, "As Poland's independence is being strangled by a Soviet military noose, there is not a single word of protest from our government. This silence only intensifies the mental, physical and spiritual anguish of the people of Poland."[4]

Following a series of articles which described the difficult and often brutal conditions the Polish people had to endure, *Narod Polski,* published by the Polish Roman Catholic Union, asked: "Why Doesn't the United States Interest Itself More in Poland?" No longer was this influential Polish American newspaper optimistic as it once had been that the United States would help free Poland from communism. *Narod Polski* joined *Zgoda* in boldly suggesting that somehow Polonia could save Poland.[5] To that end, the Polish American Congress launched a "Million Dollar Drive" to propagandize the Polish cause. Since the Polish nation could not act as its own spokesman, the Polish American Congress declared: "we must speak for them and plead their cause before the bar of public opinion." Interestingly enough, the campaign was at least partially intended to combat discrimination against Polish Americans in the United States. With headquarters in Gary, Indiana, the campaign hoped to raise $1 million, most of which would be used to purchase advertisements in newspapers. General Bor's visit to the United States and his extensive speaking tour was a part of the "Million Dollar Drive."[6] When Rozmarek's delegation left the United States to inspect DP camps in Europe, *Zgoda* described the trip as "the first act in defense of the Polish Nation." It added: "Thanks for this help of Polonia—the struggle for freedom, independence and sovereignty—the Polish people shall win."[7] Finally, in order to be able to exert greater political pressure, delegates of the Polish American Congress authorized funding for the purchase of a building in Washington, D.C., for the national headquarters of the organization and voted to have its national convention in the nation's capital in May 1948.[8]

The Truman administration was unwilling to take measures which would insure that the promised elections in Poland would indeed be free and unfettered. Rozmarek urged Truman to insist upon guarantees that would enable allied supervision of the Polish elections.[9] No such guarantees had been provided for at Yalta and Truman did not press the matter at Potsdam.[10] As has been seen, whatever opportunity may still have been left to alter the conditions that would make Poland more independent was lost at the Potsdam Conference when the United States failed to link its agreement to the Oder-Neisse line with concessions from the communist side concerning the political future of Poland.

To Polish Americans the Big Three meeting at Potsdam simply confirmed the partition of Poland that condemned millions of unwilling people into the Soviet sphere of influence. The pledge of the Polish provisional government of national unity to hold free and unfettered elections as soon as possible did not impress Polish Americans. Speaking on behalf of the Polish American Congress, Rozmarek saw little hope for free elections unless they were supervised by the allies and the Russians withdrew their troops from the country. Even the Big Three agreement permitting the Warsaw government to administer former German territories up to the Oder-Neisse line was regarded by the Polish American Congress as an extension of Soviet frontiers westward "unless Poland is rehabilitated to a free democratic life of her own." In its August-September 1945 *Bulletin,* the Polish group bitterly declared: "It was not Russia but *America* that broke Poland."[11]

Speaking on behalf of the Polish American Congress, Rozmarek told Truman on October 20, 1945, that the United States was not bound by Roosevelt's agreements at Tehran and Yalta because they were made without the knowledge or approval of the United States Congress and the American people. He criticized Truman, too, for recognizing the Warsaw government before the promised free and unfettered elections had actually been held, instead of "merely promised." Rozmarek returned to an oft-repeated Polish American theme —"If Russia would only withdraw its armies and stop interfering in Poland's internal affairs, Poland's troubles would come to a swift end."[12] The position of the Polish American Congress was endorsed by Congressman Thomas S. Gordon of Illinois, a Polish American who chaired a congressional investigating committee that had recently returned from Poland. Gordon told a Pulaski memorial rally that "all the Poles want is to get rid of the Soviet Army and the government backed by Soviet bayonets." He added, "They want America and the whole world to redeem the pledges which were given to them and become a free, democratic and independent nation."[13]

Convinced that the promised elections would have no value without adequate guarantees, Rozmarek asked the administration to withdraw recognition from the Warsaw regime and reestablish relations with the former Polish government, still in exile in London, until free elections under Allied supervision were possible.[14] By the end of 1946 the Polish American Congress refined its position by proposing that the United States withdraw recognition from the Warsaw regime and extend recognition to the president of the Polish republic in London as the only legal representative of the Polish nation until free elections were held under the supervision of the United Nations. Picking up on a theme implied earlier in the Polish American press, Rozmarek's organization also recommended that meanwhile the Polish American Congress should serve as a trustee of the rights of the Polish nation.[15] Rozmarek appears to have had little real hope that the free elections would ever be held in Poland and apparently believed that if Truman withdrew recognition from Warsaw and extended it to the London Poles at least the "moral blunders" of Yalta and Potsdam would be redressed.[16]

Rozmarek's views were echoed by other leaders within the Polish American community. The Rev. A.A. Skoniecki, a prominent and articulate leader of the Coordinating Committee of American-Polish Associations in the East, pointed out that the Polish people "out of fear and hunger will vote the way they are told." A leader in New England's Polonia at the time later observed, "No reasonable Polish American expected free elections in a country occupied by Soviet troops and police. Most Polish Americans strongly endorsed Rozmarek's call to withdraw United States recognition from the Warsaw regime as the legal government of Poland."[17] But the Truman administration had no intention of withdrawing recognition from the Warsaw government and disingenuously told the Polish Americans that the current regime in Poland had been established "by the Poles themselves and was not imposed upon the Polish people by the United States, Great Britain and the Soviet Union."[18]

Rozmarek's stance came increasingly closer to that of KNAPP's leadership who stubbornly refused to accept the legality of the Yalta agreement, continued to recognize the London Poles as the legal political representatives of Poland and condemned Mikolajczyk for his willingness to participate in the Warsaw government. KNAPP deplored what it described as American weakness in the face of Soviet aggression and wondered disapprovingly if the "home of the brave" was to become "the home of cowering appeasers."[19]

KNAPP's interest in the fate of General Leopold Okulicki highlighted the organization's conviction that the United States had an obligation to protect individuals formerly associated with the Polish government-in-exile, a government Washington had once recognized as the legal representative of the Polish people. Okulicki was the former commander of the *Armia Krajowa* (Home Army) and one of the underground leaders who had been arrested and tried by Soviet authorities in the summer of 1945. Januszewski appealed to General

Dwight D. Eisenhower to intervene on behalf of Okulicki "to do whatever is within your power as the former Supreme Commander of the United Nations Forces in order that one of our most loyal generals and comrades at arms be assured humane treatment dictated by common decency." The State Department said the United States could not do anything for Okulicki because of the Kremlin's policy of not entertaining requests about people who were citizens of another country. Januszewski was not satisfied; he told the State Department:

> The United States Government, however, has not only the right but also a duty to intervene in the above matter. The United States Government deprived General Okulicki and his comrades of protection under their legal Government by withdrawing recognition from the Constitutional Government of the Republic of Poland in London. In withdrawing recognition the United States assumed an obligation of safeguarding General Okulicki and his comrades from persecution for their activities undertaken under orders from the legal Polish Government at a time when the said Polish Government was recognized by the United States and allied with the United States.

The State Department did not want to pursue the matter, provoking an irate Januszewski to tell it "that the present Administration is evading in a manner deserving the sharpest criticism, action in behalf of its Polish ally, when it is definitely committed to such action."[20]

KNAPP was equally outraged by the refusal of the State Department to grant a visa to General Kazimierz Sosnkowski, former commander-in-chief of the Polish army, to enter the United States to speak to Polish American audiences. Sosnkowski, a brilliant intellectual, was a follower of the Pilsudski political school and shared the old Polish dictator's hatred of the Soviets. Since KNAPP's membership was ultranationalistic and Russophobic—some of its leaders were former "colonels" in Pilsudski's government—it is not surprising that the organization espoused the cause of Sosnkowski so zealously. KNAPP angrily told the secretary of state, "If this man and his army were good enough to fight with us thru all the war, why can't he be good enough to come to our country now?"[21] The New York division of the Polish American Congress labeled the refusal to grant the general a visa an "outrage," especially in view of the fact that the State Department allowed communist leaders to enter the country "to destroy democracy."[22]

Polish Americans reacted bitterly to the Polish elections of January 1947. Rozmarek sent a telegram to Secretary of State Marshall and urged the United States to repudiate the elections and to withhold recognition from "the counterfeit government" in Warsaw. He called for the ouster of Poland from the United Nations and demanded an immediate investigation by the United Nations of the situation in Poland. Echoing a theme that the Polish American Congress had repeated since the end of the war, Rozmarek described the election as "a warning of destiny that annexation of all Europe, Asia and eventually of America will take place by similar methods as in Poland, unless stern and effective measures are adopted by the United States, the only country capable of stopping Russia's ruthless drive for world domination."[23] The *Narod Polski* bemoaned the elections as the "blackest" day in the history of the Polish people, while the editor of *Zgoda* wrote, "The Polish nation went through another painful and bitter tragedy." The day after the elections, the *Dziennik Zwiazkowy* headlined its issue: "There Were No Free Elections in Poland. Miko-lajczyk Demands Annulment."[24]

Polish Americans saw the political situation in Poland as part of a scenario of Soviet expansionism that would sooner or later engulf the entire world. Increasingly the rhetoric of the Polish American Congress and its affiliates become more shrill and extreme, a consequence of the bitterness, frustration, and hopelessness so many Americans of Polish ancestry felt at this time. The Polish American Congress believed that it had a duty not only to inform the American public about the situation in Poland but also to instruct Americans in the dangers of continuing to placate a menace that it considered even worse than Nazi Germany.

After Rozmarek's trip to Europe, his rhetoric became more alarmist, offering solutions to Soviet expansionism that the administration had no intention of adopting. Shortly after his return to the United States in the latter part of 1946, Rozmarek confided that he was pessimistic about the chances that peace would last very long. "Nurtured by Moscow, the cancerous growth of communism is spreading," he said. "It is painfully evident that Russia is playing an evil role in the postwar world. Already two-thirds of Europe, with a population exceeding that of the United States, is encoiled by the Red Octopus." He claimed that what astonished democratic elements in Europe was not Soviet aggression but the failure of American leaders "to summon enough courage to call off the Soviet bluff about American imperialism by turning the tables to point an accusing finger at the only instigator of a new war—Soviet Russia."[25] Rozmarek claimed that European statesmen told him that the United States did not have to lose a single soldier because it had a monopoly on the atomic bomb, "the only thing that can convince Russia that criminal aggression does not pay." Rozmarek approved of a policy of atomic diplomacy against the Kremlin and rejected schemes to control America's monopoly of the weapon.[26] Later he said, "The threat of the atomic bomb can be used successfully to force Russia to remove her armies, puppet governments and fifth columnists from territories not held by her after the first world war." He added, "The atomic bomb is the only thing that can check war."[27]

Concern in Polish American circles about communist expansionism also focused on the alleged threat at home. Rozmarek told a Polish American audience during a celebration of Polish Constitution Day on May 5, 1946, that "we wholeheartedly endorse the move to purge all communists, and those of the same mind as communists, . . . from our government payrolls! Washington has too long been under their destructive influence."[28] The *Narod Polski* urged Secretary of State Marshall shortly after his appointment to fire communist advisers in the State Department and to appoint some Polish Americans who had a realistic understanding of the world situation. In February 1947 the Polish American Congress voted to set up its own "Committee on Un-American Activities" to ferret out and publicize all foreign agents who sought to destroy America and strongly supported the work of the House Un-American Activities Committee.[29]

When Truman announced aid to Greece and Turkey early in 1947 Polish Americans for the first time since the end of World War II rallied to the administration and heartily endorsed Washington's tougher foreign policy toward the Kremlin. Rozmarek told fifty thousand Americans of Polish descent during a celebration of the 156th anniversary of the Polish Constitution in May 1947 that the Polish American Congress was in full agreement with the Truman Doctrine and boldly suggested that it be applied to Poland, which he reminded his listeners was "the first victim of combined Nazi and Communist aggression."[30]

Rozmarek's proposal was echoed by some of the Polish American Congress's most articulate affiliates—the Polish Roman Catholic Union and KNAPP.[31] Henryk Kogut, the head of KNAPP, told Truman that the president's announcement of aid to Greece and Turkey opened a new chapter in history that canceled the mistakes of Yalta. Kogut warned, however, that Soviet aggression would not be stopped until the United States understood that its security lay on the Niemen.[32] For all the administration's talk about stopping Soviet expansionism, Rozmarek was disappointed that Washington did not repudiate the Yalta agreement. If Washington disavowed the Yalta agreement, Rozmarek felt that it would destroy the legal basis for Soviet claims to eastern Poland and provide the foundation to restore freedom to the countries of eastern Europe.[33]

American policy concerning the German-Polish boundary ironically found most Polish Americans in agreement with the Warsaw government which they had anathematized since its recognition by the United States. Secretary Byrnes's speech at Stuttgart in September of 1946, just two months before the congressional elections, had a major impact on the Polish American community. Rozmarek labeled Byrnes's suggestion to revise the Oder-Neisse boundary "a horrible miscarriage of justice." He asked sardonically, "Why weren't the Poles informed in the first place that territory assigned to them at Potsdam was only for the purpose of giving it back to the Germans and making the Polish settlers face the pitiful tragedy of eviction?"[34] Like most Polish American leaders, Rozmarek believed that Polish acquisitions from Germany did not compensate the Polish nation for losses to the Soviets in the east. In fact, a spokesman for one major Polish American organization, the Coordinating Committee of American-Polish Associations in the East, considered Poland's postwar boundary with Germany in reality a Soviet frontier "because all of Poland belongs in fact to Russia."[35] KNAPP attacked Byrnes for building up Germany and sacrificing Europe.[36]

The Polish American press, reflecting the deep emotional commitment of Polish Americans to the existing Polish-German frontier, scored Washington for suggesting even the slightest revision in the boundary. On September 10, 1946, *Dziennik Zwiazkowy* published a cartoon showing a large ugly woman who represented Germany being courted by Byrnes and Molotov, both of whom were offering Polish land to her. The following day the same newspaper featured a cartoon with the headline, "Another Blow to the Polish People." It depicted a man—who represented the Polish people—lying on the ground between one boulder on his legs and another one about to fall on his body. The rock on his legs represented lands in the east taken by the Soviets while the other, representing Byrnes's proposal made at Stuttgart, carried the caption: "New Partition of Poland for the Benefit of Germany."[37] In 1947, when Secretary of State Marshall picked up on Byrnes's suggestion concerning a revision of the Polish-German frontier, Polish Americans again made it unmistakably clear that they considered Washington's policy on the issue "regretable and painful."[38]

Despite Mikolajczyk's urging that the United States extend credits to the Polish government, the Polish American Congress opposed it, believing that employing American economic wealth without exacting a quid pro quo from Warsaw was unwise. In May 1946 Rozmarek told a Polish American audience in Chicago that his organization disapproved of promised loans to Poland without securing a commitment from Warsaw concerning the holding of free elections. Since the credits had been approved without restrictions, Rozmarek asserted that the United States was bound to send an investigating team to Poland to insure that the money was used for the benefit of the Polish people and "not for the purposes of financing the enemies of Polish freedom."[39]

As has been seen, the Polish American Congress had severely criticized UNRRA procedures and operations in connection with the care and welfare of Polish refugees in DP camps in Germany and Austria. Though it favored continued aid to the Polish people, the Polish American Congress urged that American officials supervise the distribution of UNRRA aid, thereby preventing the Warsaw regime from using political criteria in granting relief.[40] However, most Polish Americans appear to have favored the continuation of relief to Poland and probably agreed with Congressman George Sadowski of Michigan when he criticized the Truman administration for ending American support of the UNRRA program: "It is said 'but they (Communist Satellites) have a government that we do not like.' And I say in reply, so what? The people of that nation also may not like their government, but governments come and governments go, but nations and people live forever."[41]

Still, not all Polish Americans were anticommunists. A minority of Americans of Polish ancestry supported the Warsaw government and defended Soviet policies in eastern Europe. During the war years the Kosciuszko League, organized by the Rev. Stanislaw Orlemanski in November 1943, and the American Polish Labor Council, organized a few months later, were pro-Soviet and endorsed Stalin's policies in Poland. Leo Krzycki, who headed the American Polish Labor Council and the American Slav Congress, was the major spokesman in the United States for the postwar Warsaw government. In fact, when the Lublin committee was organized by Stalin, Krzycki described himself as its leading representative in the United States.[41] He echoed the Warsaw government's charges that General Anders's army encouraged terroristic bands in Poland, criticized the reception General Bor had received in the United States in the spring of 1946, and urged Washington to follow a friendly policy toward Warsaw by giving "economic help in the form of a loan to Poland." Krzycki's appeals and letters to the State Department were widely publicized by the Polish press in Warsaw.[43]

Krzycki, described by Rozmarek as a "completely misguided individual,"[44] toured Poland and the Soviet Union in 1945 and 1946, and later published his experiences in a pamphlet entitled *What I Saw in the Slavic Countries.* He had a lengthy interview with president Bierut, who awarded him one of Poland's most coveted awards, the *Polonia Restituta.* After his meeting with Bierut, Krzycki came away with the conviction that Poland was not a lackey of Moscow. He later met Stalin, whom he compared to Abraham Lincoln.[45]

The dissatisfaction of Polish Americans with the failure of the Truman administration to prevent communist domination over Poland made them vulnerable to Republican party strategy which exploited the issue in the congressional elections of 1946. Januszewski, a long-time Republican, encouraged Senator Vandenberg and other Republican leaders to wage a campaign directed at the voter with eastern European ties. He told the senator, "We must win elections by taking away the votes of those Democrats who comprehend the suicidal trend of the present administration's international policy." Januszewski added emotionally, "The Republican party [can] save itself in the next election by saving America. There is one positive way to save America from catastrophe: Save Europe and Asia from slavery!"[46]

Vandenberg, regarded by Polonia as "a proven friend of Poland and the Polish people,"[47] acknowledged the fact that Americans of Polish ancestry were well organized, but he had doubts about their political wisdom and sophistication. Instead of repudiating the Yalta agreement, Vandenberg believed that it was far more prudent to insist that the Warsaw and Moscow governments fulfill the decisions reached at the Yalta and Potsdam conferences.[48] He shared the views of other Republican leaders who refused to repudiate the Yalta agreement. Vandenberg, bristling at the suggestion that he was not tough enough in postwar dealings with the Soviets, told Januszewski that if he was defeated in the November elections, that would confirm the Soviet allegation that his views did not "reflect the opinion either of my country or my large Polish constituency."[49]

The attitude that the Roosevelt and Truman administrations had betrayed Poland was a pervasive one in Polish American circles. Byrnes's Stuttgart speech, which received wide coverage and commentary in the Polish American press, had a significant impact on reinforcing the belief that Washington had written off Poland to the

Soviets and now favored Germany. One prominent Polish American leader in Massachusetts, commented, "I could not believe my ears when I read what Byrnes had said in Stuttgart. It was another sell-out."[50]

Dramatic evidence of Polish American disaffection with the Democratic party in 1946 came shortly before the elections when Republican candidates were asked for the first time in thirty years to speak to a meeting of a politically important civic organization in the heart of northwest Chicago's Polish section. Even Polish American congressmen were criticized by some of their kinsmen for joining "in the betrayal of free Poland by their silent approval of the Truman leadership." Chicago's War Veterans Committee completely disavowed the Democratic party and urged Polish Americans to vote Republican.[51]

To be sure, the Republicans made every effort to appeal to the ethnic voter, especially those with eastern European roots, by charging that the Democrats were soft on communism and talking constantly about their "betrayal" of Poland. State Department officials even complained about the embarrassing questions that were raised during the campaign concerning American credits to the Polish government.[52]

Ironically, contrary to some claims,[53] the president of the Polish American Congress, Charles Rozmarek, did not endorse any congressional candidates in the elections. Possibly Rozmarek's inexperience in partisan politics and his fear of jeopardizing support within the Polish American community may have influenced his decision to keep the Polish American Congress neutral in the 1946 elections.[54] One experienced Polish American leader astutely observed that even though many leaders within Polonia favored the Republicans over the Democrats in 1946, they realized that the Democratic party was still widely regarded as "the poor man's party" and were reluctant to endorse, at least openly, Republican candidates.[55]

The results of the elections revealed the degree to which traditionally Democratic-voting Polish Americans had turned away from the Democrats. In the Polish American second congressional district of Chicago, a Republican, Richard Vail, defeated the incumbent, William Rowen. In the Polish American seventh congressional district, the Republicans won by 46,000 votes. Polish American support for Democratic candidates in the Illinois at-large congressional seat showed a significant decline since the early 1940s. In Pennsylvania, Republicans took away seats from Democrats in counties with large numbers of Polish voters. In Detroit, Republicans took two Democratic house seats, revealing considerable defection by Polish Americans from the Democratic party.[56] In Detroit, the share of the Democratic party's vote dropped dramatically—19.1 percent—compared to its previous vote in congressional elections or to the Democratic vote in non-Slavic wards.[57] There is little doubt that Polonia's ironclad allegiance to the Democratic party was broken by the Republicans in 1946. It appears equally true that American foreign policy played a major, if not decisive, factor in the number of Polish Americans who shifted their votes to the Republican party.

After Mikolajczyk's escape from Poland, he went to England before coming to the United States at the end of 1947. He was well aware of the divisions within Polonia concerning his association with a government that had been legitimized by the Yalta agreement. The Polish American right wing, represented by KNAPP, was the most aggressive in attacking Mikolajczyk for forsaking the Polish government in London and joining a regime it considered composed of Soviet agents. The attacks against Mikolajczyk were especially severe in such right-wing newspapers as *Nowy Swiat* and *Dziennik Polski.*[58]

Though Rozmarek's position was close to that of KNAPP and the London Poles, he, like Mikolajczyk, also appreciated the need for unity among various groups of Poles in what was now perceived as a long-term struggle against communism. Despite KNAPP's attacks against Mikolajczyk, Rozmarek was keenly aware of the role a statesman of Mikolajczyk's stature could play in Polonia's crusade against communism. As a realist, Rozmarek understood too that Mikolajczyk would have to make peace with Polish Americans who found it difficult to accept his association with the Warsaw regime. In order to do that Mikolajczyk would have to condemn the Yalta agreement. Only then would Polonia accept him with open arms. Early in December 1947 *Dziennik Zwiazkowy* warned that anyone who did not repudiate the Yalta agreement could not expect cooperation from Polish Americans.[59]

Mikolajczyk, accompanied by Korbonski and Baginski, who were also prominent leaders of the PSL leadership in exile, went to Chicago and met with leaders of the Polish American Congress in December 1947. During the discussions there, officials of the Polish American Congress talked almost exclusively in terms of the Yalta agreement and the need for its repudiation. It was equally clear that Mikolajczyk and his colleagues believed that the American Polonia placed too much emphasis on the agreement. They emphasized the fact that the validity of the Crimean decisions concerning Poland was a matter which should be left up to the American government. Mikolajczyk argued that those who agreed to participate in the reconstituted postwar Polish government were not party to the agreement; they simply tried to execute it. Besides, the PSL leaders pointed out, to challenge the Yalta decisions raised serious questions about Poland's boundaries, including Poland's substantial acquisitions in the West. At one point, Baginski, obviously annoyed by the unrealistic views of Polonia's leaders, astutely observed, "Why is there so much talk about Yalta and not about more important matters such as the loss of [Polish] independence?"[60] The implication was clear—if the Yalta agreement had been fulfilled, Poland would be an independent nation.

After two days of discussions on December 15 and 16, 1947, the leadership of the Polish American Congress and the PSL in exile came to an agreement which called for the unification of all forces to try to restore Polish freedom and to combat communism, condemned the Warsaw government as an alien agency "foisted" upon Poland through false elections, labeled the Yalta agreement "an evil," and proclaimed "the duty" of all Poles to defend Poland's western frontiers. By this understanding, Mikolajczyk and his colleagues recognized the work of the Polish American Congress on behalf of the Polish cause, and likewise Rozmarek and other leaders of the congress welcomed the PSL leaders to the United States with the expectation that cooperation between both groups would benefit a free Poland.[61]

Although the Rozmarek-Mikolajczyk agreement met with wide support within the Polish American community,[62] the Polish American right wing did not accept the understanding. KNAPP withdrew from the Polish American Congress, regarding Rozmarek's agreement with Mikolajczyk as a major blunder, equaled only by his endorsement of Roosevelt for the presidency in 1944. Shortly thereafter, the Polish Roman Catholic Union, which resented Rozmarek's dictatorial methods, also left the Polish American Congress. For a long time many members and leaders had bristled over Rozmarek's administration of the Polish American Congress, criticizing his reluctance to accept suggestions and initiatives which originated from the leadership of affiliate organizations.[63]

The united front between the two Polish groups did not last long. Mikolajczyk, who could be disingenuous, fell out not only with his PSL colleagues but also with the leadership of the Polish American Congress, preferring to be the unchallenged spokesman for a free Poland. Mikolajczyk, who had a somewhat condescending attitude toward Polish American leaders like Rozmarek and other Polish leaders in exile, including the London Poles, was interested in linking himself with other exiled peasant party leaders from eastern Europe and was encouraged to do so by the State Department.[64] In fact, the

State Department's single-minded attention to Mikolajczyk annoyed other prominent Polish émigrés who were involved in political activities in the United States. Juliusz Lukasiewicz, former Polish ambassador to the Soviet Union and France before World War II and himself an émigré, complained that the "Voice of America" and the BBC focused only on Mikolajczyk and ignored the activities of other Polish leaders.[65] One historian observed that Mikolajczyk "played a lone hand, organized and dismissed his own committee, and carried on his own policies in second exile."[66]

The views of the Polish American Congress concerning the menace of communism were shared by the former ambassador to Poland, Arthur Bliss Lane, who also hoped that the differences among Poles and Polish Americans could be overcome in order to serve the interests of a free Poland. After his resignation from the diplomatic service, Lane, like Rozmarek, became obsessed with the threat of communism to the free world. He toured the United States and spoke to audiences on the theme. He wrote a popular book, *I Saw Poland Betrayed,* published in 1948, criticizing American policies toward the Kremlin which had resulted in a communist government in Warsaw. "Although the principal responsibility for Poland's fate must be placed on the Nazi and Soviet governments," Lane wrote, "certainly the United States and Great Britain cannot escape a share in the tragic betrayal."[67] American liberals had to bear responsibility too, Lane said in a radio broadcast in April 1947, "in condoning under Soviet domination what they formerly castigated under Nazi domination."[68]

It was natural that Lane, a former ambassador to Poland during one of the most critical periods in its history and a man who strongly believed in the threat of communism to the United States and the rest of the free world, should support the efforts of Rozmarek and other leaders of the Polish American Congress in organizing a committee whose major objective was to stop the advance of world communism. In the winter of 1947 Lane joined Judge Blair F. Gunther to serve as cochairman of the Committee to Stop World Communism. Gunther was a prominent Polish American leader who was censor of the Polish National Alliance and president of the western Pennsylvania division of the Polish American Congress.[69]

The objectives of the Committee to Stop World Communism were to alert the American public to the dangers of communism in Poland and other eastern European countries and to encourage public support of policies that would check it, to unify Americans of eastern European ancestry to fight against the spread of communism in the United States and abroad, to support democratic elements in Poland

and other communist-dominated countries through welfare services, information, and moral support, and to expose communist fifth-column infiltration in the United States, especially in labor groups.[70]

The committee expected to achieve these objectives through a massive information campaign, focusing especially upon educational programs among workers and ethnics because, in the opinion of the committee, "these are key areas of attempted communist penetration and trickery." The committee observed, "Of great value in this will be the help of patriotic organizations like the Polish American Congress, whose members have long recognized the dangers of communist expansion and are already active in these key points of communist operation."[71]

Lane spent considerable time writing to prominent individuals and soliciting their support for the activities of the committee.[72] But Rozmarek's insistence on controlling the committee and limiting the activities of the public relations firm hired to achieve many of the goals of the organization soured Lane so much that he resigned his position early in 1948.[73] Despite Lane's resignation and Rozmarek's failure to broaden the scope and activities of the Committee to Stop World Communism, it is significant that by 1947 the views of Polish Americans about the Soviet Union and its satellites were now shared by most Americans and that the Truman administration had come around to a policy of toughness toward the Kremlin which American Polonia had advocated several years earlier.

VIII Conclusions

United States postwar relations with Poland were conditioned by the arrangements reached at the Yalta Conference. By agreeing to an imprecise understanding which provided no enforcement mechanism to insure that an expanded provisional government in Warsaw would hold "free and unfettered elections," the United States took a major step in dissociating itself from Poland and eastern Europe. Neither Roosevelt at Yalta nor Truman at Potsdam pressed for international supervision of the promised elections, and thus implied American recognition of a Soviet sphere of influence over Poland. At Potsdam, it was possible for Truman to have linked the future Polish elections with American agreement to the Oder-Neisse boundary between Poland and Germany, as the British had suggested. But as American diplomacy at Potsdam revealed, Washington was more concerned about Germany than it was about Poland. When Truman brought up the promised Polish elections at Potsdam, he, like Roosevelt before him, made it appear that the Polish question was more of an issue in American domestic politics than it was a foreign policy matter of grave concern to Washington.

The United States had an exaggerated faith in the impact that economic measures would have in preventing Poland from falling completely into the Soviet orbit. Poland's need for postwar credits, American officials believed, would help to moderate the situation in Warsaw and allow the Polish Peasant party under the leadership of Stanislaw Mikolajczyk to play a role in Polish political life. The United States did not tie credits to Poland to political conditions, though ambassador Arthur Bliss Lane and other hard-line State Department officials favored such a quid pro quo. The refusal of Secretary of State Byrnes to do so was consistent with his policy toward the Kremlin during most of 1946 which was based on a search for compromises that would get the Soviets to agree to the postwar peace treaties and a four power pact.

The most compelling reason to grant credits to the Poles without linking them with the future elections was the fact that Polish coal was needed to help western Europe to recover economically. Much of the economic aid from Washington to Warsaw would ostensibly be used to increase coal production and to transport a great deal of it to the West. Yet American credits were extended to Poland before the controversial Polish referendum of June 1946, despite the atmosphere of intimidation and harassment of the opposition in which the campaign was conducted.

Credits did not have the expected results in improving the American political position in Poland. While credit and other economic negotiations were under way in Washington between American and Polish officials, the PPR-dominated government in Warsaw expanded its political control over the nation, concentrating on eliminating the PSL and its supporters as a force in Polish politics.

The exaggerated expectations of the United States to be able to influence matters in Poland were matched by Mikolajczyk's unrealistic belief that the PSL would have a meaningful place in the political life of postwar Poland. Mikolajczyk, despised by the right-wing emigration for compromising with the communists and taking a seat in the postwar provisional government in Warsaw, became a symbol for most Poles who wanted an independent country. Mikolajczyk returned to Poland without guarantees from either the United States or Great Britain, but he tried to exploit the illusion of western commitments to him in his dealings with the leadership of his own party as well as with the opposition. It is difficult to determine how effective the ruse was because the PPR initially was interested more in concentrating upon the reconstruction of the country than it was in combating the PSL. But as the PPR increased its grip over Poland, it was clear to the Polish communists and their patrons in Moscow that the PSL had little more than the rhetorical and moral support of the United States.

The closer the promised elections came, the more evident it became that neither Washington nor Mikolajczyk had any realistic political strategy other than to hope for the best. As Philip Moseley said, "hope, divorced from power, is not a policy."[1] Washington still clung to the naive notion that the PSL would not be entirely excluded from Polish political life while Mikolajczyk vainly hoped that somehow the United States would become involved in the desperate struggle for survival in which the PSL found itself. In the end, the PPR won the rigged elections and the PSL was reduced to impotence and political irrelevance.

After the Polish elections of 1947 relations between the two countries rapidly deteriorated. Despite the obvious importance of Polish coal to the recovery of western Europe, Washington refused to grant additional credits to Poland to expand its coal industry. Even the needs of the Polish people for relief aid in order to fill the gap left by the end of UNRRA operations in Poland did not find a sympathetic audience in Washington. That is why the continued activities of private relief organizations filled important, if not crucial, gaps in western relief to Poland.

Although Secretary Byrnes's Stuttgart speech is often seen as a turning point in American policy toward the communist world, it was probably even more significant as a turning point in Polish perceptions of the United States. By challenging claims to the Oder-Neisse boundary, Byrnes helped to unify the Polish people behind the communist-controlled government and undermined the position of Mikolajczyk and the PSL, which had been so closely tied to the United States. Moreover, his speech shattered the idealistic expectations of most Poles that the United States could be depended upon to change the political situation in Poland. Secretary Marshall's later challenges to the permanency of the Oder-Neisse boundary confirmed in Polish minds the belief that it was better to join in the tasks of the nation's recovery than to engage in a hopeless struggle to dislodge the communists.

Polish Americans tried but failed to influence American policies toward Poland and the Soviet Union. The policies of the Roosevelt and Truman administrations toward Poland had unified Polonia in the United States to such an extent that these policies became the major issue to which the Polish American Congress addressed itself for years. Despite its size, organizational ability, and propaganda activities, the Polish American Congress was no more able to change the direction of American policy toward Warsaw and Moscow in the immediate postwar years than it had been during the war. Nevertheless, the views of this large articulate body of Americans presaged what the American public in general came to believe about the communist world later in the 1940s and early 1950s.

Bitterness and disillusionment with the foreign policy of the United States predictably made Polish Americans vulnerable to a conspiracy theory concerning the fate of Poland. Polish Americans believed that Washington's deliberate appeasement of the communists enabled the Kremlin to gain control over Poland and charged that communists in the Department of State were responsible for influencing the direction of foreign policy. Polish Americans were so unhappy with the Truman administration that in 1946 large numbers of them defected from the ranks of the Democratic party, helping the Republicans to win control over the United States Congress. But after Truman announced aid to Greece and Turkey, signaling a tougher policy toward the Kremlin, Polish Americans strongly endorsed the Truman Doctrine, finding renewed confidence in the political party which they believed had let them down for so long.

It is difficult to see how the United States could have influenced affairs in Poland after World War II without far greater exertions than it was able or willing to make. Unfortunately, the time for the United States to have established an effective American presence in Poland had passed. As this study has shown, the communization of Poland in the period 1945–1947 was less the result of communist defensive reactions to American challenges than it was the consequence of Washington's having habituated the Kremlin to deal with political issues in eastern Europe without the United States during the war years. Such was the bitter legacy for the United States and Poland.

Notes

CHAPTER I

1. See Richard C. Lukas, *The Strange Allies: The United States and Poland, 1941–1945* (Knoxville: University of Tennessee Press, 1978).
2. Ibid., pp. 153, 161; "Letter from Stalin," *Newsweek*, XXV (May 28, 1945), 56.
3. "The Polish Provisional Government of National Unity," July 17, 1945, in Office of Strategic Services/Department of State Intelligence and Research Reports, Roll 9. Hereinafter cited as OSS/DS Reports.
4. Jan Krzysztof Kwiatkowski, *Komunisci w Polsce: Rodowod, Taktyka, Ludzie* (Brussels: Polski Instytut Wydawniczy, 1946), pp. 95–97; Arthur Bliss Lane, *I Saw Poland Betrayed: An American Ambassador Reports to the American People* (Indianapolis: Bobbs-Merrill, 1948), p. 148; Interview with B.B. Kopecki (pseud.), June 28, 1979, Warsaw, Poland; Wladyslaw Pobog-Malinowski, *Najnowsza Historia Polityczna Polski, 1864–1945. Tom Trzeci: Okres 1939–1945* (London: Gryf, 1960), p. 804. Lane went so far as to say that Bierut's physical appearance, complete with clipped moustache, reminded him of Adolf Hitler. Lane, *I Saw Poland Betrayed,* p. 133.
5. Interview with Kopecki; Stanislaw Mikolajczyk, *The Rape of Poland* (New York: McGraw-Hill, 1948), pp. 231, 233; Lane, *I Saw Poland Betrayed,* pp. 134, 140, 225. The principal unit within the ministry of public security was the security office *(Urzad Bezpieczenstwa),* commonly known as the "Bezpieka." Berman and his wife, a leading Warsaw dentist, lived in the same apartment house as Mikolajczyk. They did not speak to each other. Arthur Bliss Lane, "How Russia Rules Poland," *Life,* XXIII (July 14, 1947), 112.
6. Nicholas Bethell, *Gomulka: His Poland, His Communism* (New York: Holt, Rinehart and Winston, 1969), pp. 2–6, 8–9, 97–98, 123; Mikolajczyk, *The Rape of Poland,* p. 232.
7. Kwiatkowski, *Komunisci w Polsce,* pp. 101–2; Anna Louise Strong, *I Saw the New Poland* (Boston: Little, Brown, 1946), pp. 84–87. One critic wrote that Osobka-Morawski "justifies the comment that the era of village scribes and schoolmasters is upon us." Stefan Korbonski, *Warsaw in Chains* (New York: Macmillan, 1959), p. 27.
8. Kwiatkowski, *Komunisci w Polsce,* pp. 102–4, 99–100. Mikolajczyk claimed that Rola-Zymierski "was a communist behind his nonparty facade." Mikolajczyk, *The Rape of Poland,* p. 211.
9. Kwiatkowski, *Komunisci w Polsce,* p. 105; Ltr., Lane to Durbrow, December 20, 1945, in Arthur Bliss Lane Papers, Yale University Library, box 69, folder 1247. Hereinafter cited as Lane Papers, YU/L; Statement by Mikolajczyk, undated, in Stanislaw Mikolajczyk Papers, in Hoover Institution of War, Revolution and Peace, box 42. Hereinafter cited as Mikolajczyk Papers, HI.
10. Mikolajczyk is extensively discussed in Lukas, *The Strange Allies.*
11. Ibid., p. 132.
12. Rose points out that the United States at Potsdam had no goal to root out the

Soviets "or even to contest Soviet control over Eastern Europe." Lisle Rose, *Dubious Victory: The United States and the End of World War II* (Kent, Ohio: Kent State University Press, 1973), p. 277.

13. Briefing Book Paper, June 29, 1945, in U.S., Department of State, *Foreign Relations of the United States, Diplomatic Papers. The Conference of Berlin (The Potsdam Conference), 1945.* (2 vols.; Washington, D.C.: United States Government Printing Office, 1960), I, 714–15. Hereinafter cited as *FRUS: Potsdam;* memo of press and radio news conferences, August 22, 1945, in James F. Byrnes papers, folder 556, Clemson University Library. Hereinafter cited as Byrnes papers, CU/L.

14. Ltr., Robert I. Gannon, et al. to Truman, July 10, 1945, in Harry S. Truman Papers, Official File, box 1297, Harry S. Truman Library. Hereinafter cited as Truman Papers, HST/L. Herbert Hoover, who had been traveling at the time, was unable to sign the memorial. But he told Christopher Emmet, Jr., "I am all for it, and you may include my name if it is not too late." George J. Lerski (comp.), *Herbert Hoover and Poland: A Documentary History of a Friendship* (Stanford, Calif.: Hoover Institution Press, 1977), pp. 49–50.

15. See Lukas, *The Strange Allies,* pp. 107–27, 142–43. Also see Chapter VII infra.

16. Polish American Congress, *Story of the Polish American Congress in Press Clippings, 1944–1948* (Chicago: Alliance Printers and Publishers, n.d.), pp. 64–65.

17. Minutes by Department of State, Fifth Plenary Meeting, July 21, 1945; report by the subcommittee on Poland, July 21, 1945; statement on the Polish question, July 21, 1945; statement on the Polish question approved by the Heads of Government, July 21, 1945, in *FRUS: Potsdam,* II, 206–7, 216, 1120–24.

18. Mikolajczyk suggested to American officials that the guarantees include freedom for noncommunist political parties, removal of Soviet troops and security forces from the country, and international control over the elections. Memo by Mikolajczyk, undated, but handed to Harriman on or about July 25, 1945, in ibid., pp. 1129–30.

19. Ibid., p. 490; 518, note 23; W.T. Kowalski, *Polityka Zagraniczna RP, 1944–1947* (Warsaw: Ksiazka i Weidza, 1971), p. 56.

20. Minutes by Thompson, First Plenary Meeting, July 17, 1945; Cohen Notes, First Plenary Meeting, July 17, 1945; Minutes by Thompson, First Meeting of the Foreign Ministers, July 18, 1945; Draft Proposal by the Soviet Delegation, July 18, 1945, in *FRUS: Potsdam,* II, 55–56, 61, 71–72, 78–79, 1110.

21. Minutes by Thompson, Second Plenary Meeting, July 18, 1945; Cohen Notes, Second Plenary Meeting, July 18, 1945, ibid., pp. 91–93, 97–98.

22. Ibid., pp. 1110, 91–93, 97–98. The Big Three were in basic agreement on how Polish assets should be disposed and how to deal with Polish soldiers abroad. See protocol of proceedings and final communiqué of the Potsdam Conference, ibid., 1490–91, 1508–9. Also see Chapter VI below.

23. Memo, with enclosures, Modzelewski to Harriman, July 10, 1945, ibid., I, 757–77; Mikolajczyk, *The Rape of Poland,* pp. 138–39; Mikolajczyk statement to Executive Council of PSL, October 6, 1945, in Mikolajczyk Papers, box 38, HI.

24. Quoted in George Glinka-Janczewski, "American Policy toward Poland under the Truman Administration" (unpublished Ph.D. dissertation, Georgetown University, 1965), p. 158, n. 1.

25. The Cadogan letter and Churchill's remarks to the House of Commons are

quoted in Elizabeth Wiskemann, *Germany's Eastern Neighbours: Problems Relating to the Oder-Neisse Line and the Czech Frontier Regions* (London: Oxford University Press, 1956), pp. 80–82.

26. Lukas, *The Strange Allies,* pp. 131–33.

27. Wiskemann, *Germany's Eastern Neighbours,* pp. 82–85; 83, n. 9; 85, n. 1; Lukas, *The Strange Allies,* p. 137.

28. The Big Three statement on Poland made at Yalta is quoted in Lukas, *The Strange Allies,* pp. 140–41.

29. Memo by H.P. Meiksins, April 9, 1945, in Records of European Advisory Commission, box 16, in National Archives. Hereinafter cited as EAC/NA.

30. Eduard Mark, " 'Today Has Been a Historical One:' Harry S. Truman's Diary of the Potsdam Conference," *Diplomatic History,* IV (Summer, 1980), 324–25.

31. Minutes by Department of State, Fifth Plenary Meeting, July 21, 1945, in *FRUS: Potsdam,* II, 208–9, 215.

32. Ibid., pp. 210–14. Churchill made much of the alleged fact that German land claimed by Poland was essential as a source of food for Germany. Less than half of the land acquired by the Poles was arable and did not constitute a major source of food for the Third Reich. And these lands were no more important to Germany from an industrial point of view either. The territory lost to Poland accounted for only 7.6 percent of total German industrial production on the eve of World War II. See W.M. Drzewieniecki, *The German-Polish Frontier* (Chicago: Polish Western Association of America, 1959), pp. 126–27, 129, 132.

33. Minutes by Department of State, Fifth Plenary Meeting, July 21, 1945; memo by the United States Delegation, July 24, 1945, in *FRUS: Potsdam,* II, 211–13, 217–21, 335. Churchill placed the figure at 2.5 million Germans. De Zayas says that there were 4 million Germans in the area while another million tried to return. See Alfred M. de Zayas, *Nemesis at Potsdam: The Anglo-Americans and the Expulsion of the Germans* (London: Routledge and Kegan Paul, 1977), p. 86.

34. Quoted in Glinka-Janczewski, "American Policy toward Poland under the Truman Administration," p. 158, n. 1.

35. Memo of Clayton-Mikolajczyk conversation, July 28, 1945; memo of Depres-Minc conversation, in *FRUS: Potsdam,* II, 455, 478–79; Kowalski, *Polityka Zagraniczna RP,* p. 53. Ludwik Rajchman, an opportunist with extensive American and British contacts, was also there.

36. Memo by Mikolajczyk, July 24, 1945, in U.S., Department of State, *FRUS: Potsdam,* II, 1140–41; Kowalski, *Polityka Zagraniczna RP,* p. 52.

37. Minutes by Thompson, Ninth Plenary Meeting, July 25, 1945, in *FRUS: Potsdam,* II, 384.

38. Memo by Mikolajczyk, July 26, 1945, ibid., pp. 1528–29.

39. Minutes by Bohlen, Truman-Molotov meeting, July 29, 1945; proposal by the United States Delegation, July 29, 1945, ibid., pp. 472–76, 1150.

40. Minutes by Bohlen, Truman-Molotov meeting, July 29, 1945, ibid., p. 472; briefing book paper, June 29, 1945, I, 746.

41. Diary entry by Mikolajczyk, July 29, 1945, in ibid., II, 1539; Kowalski, *Polityka Zagraniczna RP,* p. 58. Mastny says that Polish stubbornness on this issue revealed that Stalin's dominance over his Polish protégés was less than absolute. Vojtech Mastny,

Russia's Road to the Cold War: Diplomacy, Warfare, and the Politics of Communism, 1941–1945 (New York: Columbia University Press, 1979), pp. 299–300.

42. Minutes by Bohlen of Byrnes-Molotov meeting, July 30, 1945; minutes by Department of State at Tenth Meeting of the Foreign Ministers, July 30, 1945; proposal by the United States Delegation (German reparations), July 30, 1945; proposal by the United States Delegation, July 29, 1945; proposal by the United States Delegation (western frontiers of Poland), July 30, 1945, in *FRUS: Potsdam,* II, 480–85, 921, 1150–51. The package presented by Byrnes appears to have been suggested by Joseph Davies. See Davies Diary, July 28, 1945, box 19, in Davies Papers, Library of Congress. Hereinafter cited as Davies Papers, LC.

43. Byrnes-Molotov meeting, July 31, 1945, in *FRUS: Potsdam,* II, 510; James F. Byrnes, *Speaking Frankly* (New York: Harper, 1947), p. 85; James F. Byrnes, *All in One Lifetime* (New York: Harper, 1958), p. 302.

44. Minutes by Department of State, Eleventh Plenary Meeting, July 31, 1945; protocol of proceedings of the Berlin Conference, August 1, 1945; communiqué of the Berlin Conference, August 2, 1945, in *FRUS: Potsdam,* II, 510–20, 1485–86, 1490–92, 1508–9. As finally agreed, the Soviets would receive 15 percent of industrial equipment from the western zones of occupied Germany in exchange for an equivalent value of food, coal, and other products from their zone of occupation; in addition, the West agreed to hand over 10 percent of industrial equipment without payment or exchange from the Soviets.

45. Mikolajczyk, *The Rape of Poland,* p. 140; Kowalski, *Polityka Zagraniczna RP,* p. 57.

46. Byrnes, *All in One Lifetime,* pp. 299–300.

47. Winston S. Churchill, *Triumph and Tragedy* (Boston: Houghton Mifflin, 1953), p. 672.

48. John C. Campbell, *The United States in World Affairs, 1945–1947* (New York: Harper, 1947), p. 178.

49. Kowalski, *Polityka Zagraniczna RP,* p. 59.

50. Davies Diary, July 31, 1945, box 19, in Davies Papers, LC.

51. Byrnes, *Speaking Frankly,* pp. 191–92.

52. Martin F. Herz, *Beginnings of the Cold War* (Bloomington, Ind.: Indiana University Press, 1966), p. 140.

CHAPTER II

1. See Chapter I where the six political parties of postwar Poland are identified.

2. Freda Bruce Lockhart, "Meeting with Mikolajczyk," *Nineteenth Century and After,"* CXLIII (January, 1948), 4; Andrzej Korbonski, *Politics of Socialist Agriculture in Poland: 1945–1960* (New York: Columbia University Press, 1965) pp. 115–16; Mikolajczyk, *The Rape of Poland,* p. 136.

3. Glinka-Janczewski, "American Policy toward Poland under the Truman Administration," p. 214; Wladyslaw Gora, *Polska Rzeczpospolita Ludowa, 1944–1974* (Warsaw: Ksiazka i Wiedza, 1974), p. 216.

4. S. Harrison Thomson, "The New Poland," *Foreign Policy Reports,* XXIII (December 1, 1947), 228; Norbert Kolomyjczyk, *PPR: 1944–1945* (Warsaw: Ksiazka i Wiedza, 1965), pp. 174–76.

5. Stefan Korbonski, *Warsaw in Chains* (New York: Macmillan, 1959), p. 241. Years later, commenting on Soviet stealing from Poland and other countries, Truman talked about the "destructive attitude" of the Soviets which, he said, "is based on the teachings of Jenghis Khan and Tamerlane." Robert H. Ferrell, ed., *Off the Record: The Private Papers of Harry S. Truman* (New York: Harper and Row, 1980), p. 333.

6. M. K. Dziewanowski, *The Communist Party of Poland: An Outline of History* (Cambridge, Mass.: Harvard University Press, 1959), pp. 190–92; Zbigniew K. Brzezinski, *The Soviet Bloc: Unity and Conflict* (Cambridge, Mass.: Harvard University Press, 1960), p. 112.

7. Piotr S. Wandycz, *The United States and Poland* (Cambridge, Mass.: Harvard University Press, 1980), p. 313. For example, in the 1920s and 1930s Jews numbered about 25 percent of the party but that figure increased to 50 percent in the urban areas of Poland. Moreover, most of the top leaders of the Polish communist movement were Jews. Jan B. de Weydenthal, *The Communists of Poland: An Historical Outline* (Stanford: Hoover Institution Press, 1978), pp. 26–27.

8. Richard Hiscocks, *Poland: Bridge for the Abyss?: An Interpretation of Developments in Post-War Poland* (London: Oxford University Press, 1963), pp. 96–97, 121.

9. Dziewanowski, *The Communist Party of Poland,* p. 193.

10. "Pro-Soviet Political Forces in Central European Countries," November 6, 1946, in OSS/DS Reports, Roll 3; Korbonski, *Politics of Socialist Agriculture,* pp. 118–19.

11. Dziewanowski, *The Communist Party of Poland,* p. 189.

12. Interview with Stefan Korbonski, June 20, 1980, Washington, D.C.

13. Ltr., Oak to Lane, February 29, 1947, in Lane Papers, box 26, folder 492, YU/L. Cyrankiewicz's critics accused him of being a closet communist during the period 1945–1948. Korbonski, *Warsaw in Chains,* p. 231; Mikolajczyk, *The Rape of Poland,* p. 232. Stanton Griffis, Lane's successor in Warsaw, painted an uncomplimentary picture of him. He said his "head resembled a billiard ball with eyes." Stanton Griffis, *Lying in State* (Garden City, N.Y.: Doubleday, 1952), p. 163.

14. Dziewanowski, *The Communist Party of Poland,* p. 189.

15. "R," "The Fate of Polish Socialism," *Foreign Affairs,* XXVIII (October, 1949), 127.

16. Hiscocks, *Poland: Bridge for the Abyss,* pp. 99–100; ltr., Zulawski to Drobner, November 14, 1946, in Mikolajczyk Papers, box 45, HI.

17. Dziewanowski, *The Communist Party of Poland,* p. 190; Korbonski, *Politics of Socialist Agriculture,* pp. 111–12, 116, including n. 63; Gora, *Polska Rzeczpospolita Ludowa,* p. 153. Polish historians claim that the capitalists flocked to the PSL while the peasants gravitated to the SL. Gora, ibid., p. 157.

18. Statement by Mikolajczyk, undated, in Mikolajczyk Papers, box 42, HI.

19. "Rozmowa Prezesa Stanislawa Mikolajczyka z Premjerem Winstonem Spencerem Churchillem w dniu 9-go Czerwca 1945 r;" "Ocena Sytuacji Politycnej," notatka Prezesa Mikolajczyka, June 6, 1945, in Mikolajczyk Papers, box 34, HI. Also see his comments in Mikolajczyk, *The Rape of Poland,* p. 134.

20. Korbonski, *Warsaw in Chains*, p. 43.

21. Interview with Korbonski.

22. Interview with Paul Zaleski, June 18, 1980, Washington, D.C.; Korbonski, *Warsaw in Chains*, pp. 19–20, 31; Newsclip, *New York Times*, October 23, 1945, in Davies Papers, box 66, LC; I. Brant, *The New Poland* (New York: Universe, 1946), pp. 47, 91.

23. Mikolajczyk conveyed some of his views to Lane. See msg., Lane to Secretary of State, September 20, 1945, in U.S., Department of State, *Foreign Relations of the United States, Diplomatic Papers: 1945*. Volume V: *Europe* (Washington, D.C.: United States Government Printing Office, 1967), pp. 372–74. Hereinafter cited as *FRUS*, V, 1945.

24. See Korbonski's comments for the impact of the Hungarian elections on the PSL and the release from prison of two of the sixteen Polish leaders who had been tried in Moscow in June, 1945. Korbonski, *Warsaw in Chains*, p. 47.

25. Dziewanowski, *The Communist Party of Poland*, p. 201.

26. Lockhart, "Meeting with Mikolajczyk," p. 3.

27. Korbonski, *Warsaw in Chains*, p. 208.

28. Lockhart, "Meeting with Mikolajczyk," p. 9; interview with Zaleski.

29. Lockhart, "Meeting with Mikolajczyk," p. 9.

30. Korbonski, *Politics of Socialist Agriculture*, p. 117; "Poland: The House on Szucha Avenue," *Time*, XLVIII (December 9, 1946), 32–33.

31. Mikolajczyk, *The Rape of Poland*, pp. 147–48; *Gazeta Ludowa*, November 14, 1945.

32. Mikolajczyk, *The Rape of Poland*, p. 151.

33. Memo, "Do Komitetu PPR i Centralnego Komitetu Wykonawczego PPS, dnia 22 Lutego 1946 r," and "Protokol Posiedzenia Rady Naczelnej Polskiego Stronnictwa Ludowego, 26 i 27 Maja 1946," in Mikolajczyk Papers, box 34 and box 38, respectively, HI; Gora, *Polska Rzeczpospolita Ludowa*, pp. 205–06. Mikolajczyk knew he would not get what he wanted from the PPR, and intended to have the PSL come out for a separate list. He even anticipated that he and his party might be asked to leave the government. In that eventuality, he wanted the United States and Britain to take the position that the action of the Warsaw regime violated one of the major conditions attached to American and British recognition of the Polish government. Msg., Lane to Secretary of State, February 26, 1946, in U.S., Department of State, *Foreign Relations of the United States, 1946*. Volume VI: *Eastern Europe: The Soviet Union* (Washington, D.C.: United States Government Printing Office, 1969), pp. 406–8. Hereinafter cited as *FRUS*, VI, 1946.

34. Korbonski, *Politics of Socialist Agriculture*, p. 122.

35. Mikolajczyk, *The Rape of Poland*, pp. 155–60; "The Peace: Red Seeds of a Polish Civil War," *Newsweek*, XXVII (May 27, 1946), 36; "Poland: Report from Warsaw," *Time*, XLVII (May 13, 1946), 40, 45. The American chargé d'affaires wrote to Ambassador Lane, who was in Paris at the time: "We are rapidly seeing a deterioration of the situation here." He pointed out that the government prohibited PSL activities in two districts in Poland and quoted a Polish leader who believed that this was a trial balloon before the regime did the same thing in other parts of Poland. Ltr., Keith to Lane, April 15, 1946, in Lane Papers, box 24, folder 465, YU/L. The security police

appear to have been responsible for the murders of Wladyslaw Kojder, a member of the executive committee of the Polish Peasant Party, and Boleslaw Scibiorek, who had merged his peasant organization with Mikolajczyk's. Both men died in the latter part of 1945.

36. Statement by Mikolajczyk, undated, in Mikolajczyk Papers, box 42, HI.

37. "Protokol Posiedzenia Rady Naczelnej Polskiego Stronnictwa Ludowego, 26 i 27 Maja 1946."

38. Mikolajczyk, *The Rape of Poland,* pp. 156–157.

39. U.S., Department of State, "Policy and Information Statements," May 1, 1946, pp. 1–2, 11, in Byrnes Papers, CU/L.

40. Gora, *Polska Rzeczpospolita Ludowa,* pp. 151–52, 156, 162–63, 167; Stanislaw Arnold and Marian Zychowski, *Zarys Historii Polski: Od Poczatkow Panstwa do Czasow Najnowszych* (N.C.: Wydawnictwo Polonia, 1962), pp. 183–84; memo, Keith to Secretary of State, April 9, 1947, in DS/NA, RG 59, box 3426. One ploy used by the security police to link the PSL and the underground was to raid PSL offices, steal membership cards and then plant them on prisoners rounded up from the underground. Korbonski, *Warsaw in Chains,* p. 81.

41. *Gazeta Ludowa,* February 20–21, 1946.

42. Interview with Korbonski; "Pro-Soviet Political Forces in Central European Countries."

43. Stefan Korbonski, *The Polish Underground State: A Guide to the Underground, 1939–45.* (Boulder, Colo.: East European Quarterly, 1978), pp. 238–40.

44. Arnold and Zychowski, *Zarys Historii Polski,* p. 180.

45. Korbonski, *Warsaw in Chains,* p. 232.

46. Ibid., p. 53.

47. Ibid., pp. 66, 224.

48. Ltr., Lane to Durbrow, March 11, 1946, in Lane Papers, box 69, folder 1251, YU/L.

49. Korbonski, *The Polish Underground State,* p. 242.

50. Richard F. Starr, *Poland, 1944–1962: The Sovietization of a Captive People* (Baton Rouge: Louisiana State University Press, 1962), p. 243. A new agreement was not signed until April 1950.

51. See Chapter III.

52. Interview with Pelagia Lukaszewska, August 1, 1980, North Miami Beach, Florida.

53. Janusz Gumkowski and Kazimierz Leszczynski, *Poland under Nazi Occupation* (Warsaw: Polonia Publishing House, 1961), pp. 215–16. Brzezinski puts it this way: Poland lost 220 out of every 1,000 of its citizens compared to the Soviet Union which lost 40 out of 1,000. See Brzezinski, *The Soviet Bloc,* p. 9.

54. S. Harrison Thomson, "The New Poland," p. 232.

55. Wandycz, *The United States and Poland,* p. 309.

56. Mikolajczyk, *The Rape of Poland,* p. 131; Brant, *The New Poland,* p. 15.

57. Gumkowski and Leszczynski, *Poland under Nazi Occupation,* p. 217; Wandycz, *The United States and Poland,* p. 310; M. Zlotowska, "I Came Back from Poland," *Harper's Magazine* CXCIII (November, 1946), 428–29.

58. Statement by Mikolajczyk, undated, in Mikolajczyk Papers, box 42, HI.

59. Kowalski, *Polityka Zagraniczna RP*, p. 62; Thad Paul Alton, *Polish Postwar Economy* (Westport, Conn.: Greenwood Press, 1974), p. 25.

60. Wiskemann, *Germany's Eastern Neighbours*, pp. 238–41.

61. O. Halecki, *A History of Poland* (New York: Roy, 1943), pp. 296–97; Hiscocks, *Poland: Bridge for the Abyss*, p. 94.

62. Wiskemann, *Germany's Eastern Neighbours*, p. 97, including n. 4; memo, chairman, Reporting Board to Durbrow, June 17, 1946, in RG 59, box 6381, DS/NA.

63. Wiskemann, *Germany's Eastern Neighbours*, pp. 114–19; 218, n. 2; de Zayas, *Nemesis at Potsdam*, pp. 103–30. The Soviets dismantled and shipped property from these former German lands as war booty. There was a good deal of looting and stealing by the Soviet army soldiers as well. Some Poles from other parts of Poland came to the area and joined the Russians in the looting too. Korbonski, *Warsaw in Chains*, p. 87.

64. Wiskemann, *Germany's Eastern Neighbours*, pp. 211, 216, 218.

65. Thomson, "The New Poland," p. 229; "Nationalization Laws and American Investments in Poland," August 5, 1946, in OSS/DS Reports, Roll 9; Hiscocks, *Poland: Bridge for the Abyss*, p. 122; Czeslaw Milosz, *The Captive Mind* (New York: Vintage, 1955), p. 157.

66. "Nationalization Laws and American Investments in Poland;" U.S. Department of State, "Policy and Information Statements," May 1, 1946, in Byrnes Papers, CU/L. A major American holder of Polish property before World War II was Anaconda Copper.

67. The 80 percent figure most likely included the peasants and workers in privately owned firms. Hiscocks, *Poland: Bridge for the Abyss*, p. 123.

68. "The Polish Provisional Government of National Unity: An Appraisal of the First Half Year," December 3, 1945 in OSS/DS Reports, Roll 9; Polish Press Agency *Bulletin*, October 1, 1945.

69. R.R. Betts, ed., *Central and South East Europe, 1945–48* (Westport, Conn.: Greenwood Press, 1971), p. 145. According to one scholar, "Wincenty Pstrowski, a Silesian coal miner, is credited with having initiated socialist competition. He died at the age of forty-four." Starr, *Poland, 1944–1962*, p. 104, n. 48.

70. Korbonski, *Politics of Socialist Agriculture*, pp. 76, 86, 90. Church property was unaffected by this agrarian reform.

71. Statement by Mikolajczyk, December 1, 1947, in Mikolajczyk Papers, box 42, HI.

72. Hiscocks, *Poland: Bridge for the Abyss*, p. 125.

73. Msg., Keith to Secretary of State, April 10, 1947, in RG 59, box 6381, in NA.

74. Milosz, *The Captive Mind*, p. 156. There was considerable freedom for Polish writers during this time, provided they did not criticize Soviet institutions. "Socialist realism," like the collective farm, was not even mentioned yet. Ibid., pp. 101, 157.

75. Korbonski, *Politics of Socialist Agriculture*, pp. 135, 153.

76. Alton, *Polish Postwar Economy*, pp. 269, 280. Still Polish historians claim that Poland could only depend on help from the Soviet Union, not the West. Kowalski, *Polityka Zagraniczna RP*, pp. 221ff.

77. Lane, *I Saw Poland Betrayed*, pp. 160–62; Polish American Congress, *Bulletin*, August-September, 1945, p. 21; Interview with Korbonski.

78. Stanley J. Zyzniewski, "The Soviet Economic Impact on Poland," *American Slavic and East European Review,* XVIII (April, 1959), 209, n. 9.

79. Betts, *Central and South East Europe,* p. 152.

80. Kowalski, *Polityka Zangraniczna RP,* pp. 62, 369–70, n. 5; memo of conversation by Durbrow, November 9, 1945, in Matthews-Hickerson Files, box 17, DS/NA; Mikolajczyk, *The Rape of Poland,* pp. 141–42.

81. Betts, *Central and South East Europe,* p. 152; memo of conversation by Armour, December 12, 1947, in U.S., Department of State, *Foreign Relations of the United States, 1947.* Volume IV: *Eastern Europe; The Soviet Union* (Washington, D.C.: United States Government Printing Office, 1972), pp. 468–69.

82. Memo of conversation with attachments, December 16, 1946, in RG 59, box 6381 in DS/NA.

83. Msg., Caffery to Secretary of State, July 11, 1947, in U.S., Department of State, *Foreign Relations of the United States, 1947.* Volume III: *The British Commonwealth: Europe* (Washington, D.C.: United States Government Printing Office, 1972), p. 328. Also see msg., Secretary of State to Embassy, United Kingdom, May 16, 1947 and memo of conversation by Dunn, January 6, 1947, ibid., pp. 509, 839. Hereinafter cited as *FRUS,* III, 1947.

84. Poland, Central Board of Planning, *Polish National Economic Plan* (Warsaw: Central Board of Planning, 1946), pp. 7ff.

85. Hiscocks, *Poland: Bridge for the Abyss,* p. 126; Alton, *Polish Postwar Economy,* p. 22.

CHAPTER III

1. Briefing Book Paper, June 29, 1945, in *FRUS: Potsdam,* I, 784–85.

2. Msg., Harriman to Secretary of State, April 4, 1945, in *FRUS,* V, 1945, 817–20.

3. Msg., Harriman to Secretary of State ad interim, June 28, 1945, in *FRUS: Potsdam,* I, 728.

4. Msg., Harriman to Acting Secretary of State, June 26, 1945, ibid., pp. 785–87.

5. Msg., Grew to Lane, July 12, 1945, in *FRUS: Potsdam,* I, 788–79; memo of conversation [unsigned], July 25, 1945 and memo by Mikolajczyk, June 25, 1945, in *FRUS: Potsdam,* II, 403–6, 1525–27. Poland also had a great need for livestock. See Chapter II above.

6. Briefing Book Paper, June 29, 1945, in *FRUS: Potsdam,* I, 714–15.

7. "Who's Important in Government," in Lane Papers, box 70, folder 1256, YU/L. Lane also studied Polish. He did not speak it very well but could read Polish newspapers. Ltr., Lane to Chramiec, October 15, 1945, in box 69, ibid.

8. Vladimir Petrov, *A Study in Diplomacy: The Story of Arthur Bliss Lane* (Chicago: Henry Regnery, 1971), pp. 244–45, 260–62. One scholar has said that Lane's "thinly veiled hatred of the Lublin Poles merely made an already difficult situation worse, and the rhetoric of Lane, often flagrantly anti-Soviet, circumscribed the opportunities of the United States to influence the course of events in post-war Poland." John N. Cable, "Arthur Bliss Lane: Cold Warrior in Warsaw, 1945–47," *Polish American Studies,* XXX (Autumn, 1973), 66.

9. Msg., Lane to Secretary of State, August 6, 1945, in *FRUS,* V, 1945, 361–63. Despite Polish agricultural needs, the State Department did not send an agricultural expert to the American embassy in Warsaw for almost a year, and an economic counselor, promised to Lane in July 1945, did not arrive until June 1946. Lane, *I Saw Poland Betrayed,* p. 146. The congressional team, consisting of Frances P. Bolton, Karl E. Mundt, Thomas S. Gordon, and Joseph P. Ryter, visited Poland in late August.

10. Msg., Lane to Secretary of State, October 13, 1945, in *FRUS,* V, 1945, 388–90. Also see p. 390, n. 27.

11. Msg., Lane to Secretary of State, September 20, 1945; msg., Lane to Secretary of State, September 25, 1945; msg., Lane to Secretary of State, September 26, 1945; msg., Lane to Secretary of State, October 4, 1945; msg., Lane to Secretary of State, October 13, 1945, ibid., pp. 372–74, 376–79, 380–81, 383–86, 388–90.

12. Msg., Lane to Byrnes, November 14, 1945, ibid., pp. 414–17. Also see Lane's account of this meeting in his book. Lane, *I Saw Poland Betrayed,* pp. 229–30.

13. Ltr., Lane to Durbrow, October 22, 1945, in Lane Papers, box 69, folder 1245, YU/L.

14. Msg., Lane to Secretary of State, October 15, 1945, in *FRUS,* V, 1945, 391–92; Petrov, *A Study in Diplomacy,* p. 237. Also see p. 245, n. 26.

15. Msg., Lane to Secretary of State, October 13, 1945, in *FRUS,* V, 1945, 388–90; Lane, *I Saw Poland Betrayed,* p. 227.

16. Msg., Acheson to Lane, September 21, 1945; msg., Byrnes to Lane, November 9, 1945, in *FRUS,* V, 1945, 374–76, 411–12. Several days earlier Byrnes told Lane that he could remind the Polish government that the Yalta and Potsdam agreements obliged it to hold free elections which "would undoubtedly contribute materially to popular support in this country for any program of aid to Poland which might be under consideration." Msg., Byrnes to Lane, November 2, 1945, ibid., pp. 398–99.

17. Memo of conversation by Underwood, October 1, 1945, ibid., 382–83.

18. Ltr., Durbrow to Lane, December 1, 1945 in Lane Papers, box 23, folder 446, YU/L.

19. Memo, Young to Acheson, October 25, 1945; msg., Lane to Byrnes, November 30, 1945, in *FRUS,* V, 1945, 392, 423–25, including n. 6; 410, note 71; Lane, *I Saw Poland Betrayed,* p. 152; ltr., Lane to McNarney, March 12, 1946, in Lane Papers, box 69, folder 1251, YU/L.

20. Memo of conversation by Durbrow, November 8, 1945, in *FRUS,* V, 1945, 400–4; memo of conversation by Durbrow, November 9, 1945, in Matthews-Hickerson Files, box 17, DS/NA.

21. Aide memoire, Polish Embassy to Department of State, December 5, 1945; memo of conversation by Durbrow, December 5, 1945, in *FRUS,* V, 1945, 427–30; ltr., Durbrow to Lane, November 29, 1945, in Lane Papers, box 25, folder 484, YU/L.

22. Msg., Lane to Byrnes, November 13, 1945; msg., Byrnes to Lane, November 24, 1945; msg., Lane to Byrnes, November 29, 1945, in *FRUS,* V, 1945, 412–14, 419–20, 422–23.

23. Denise O'Neal Conover, "James F. Byrnes, Germany and the Cold War, 1946" (unpublished Ph.D. dissertation, Washington State University, 1978), p. 41. For the importance of the four power treaty and the peace treaties with the Balkans to Byrnes, see Byrnes, *Speaking Frankly,* pp. 172ff. and *All in One Lifetime,* pp. 318–19.

24. Geir Lundestad, *The American Non-Policy towards Eastern Europe, 1943–47: Universalism in an Area not of Essential Interest to the United States* (Oslo: Universitetsforlaget, 1978), p. 209.

25. Msg., Lane to Secretary of State, November 9, 1945, in *FRUS,* V, 1945, 409–11.

26. Lundestad, *The American Non-Policy towards Eastern Europe,* p. 209.

27. Msg., Lane to Byrnes, November 16, 1945; msg., Byrnes to Lane, December 1, 1945; msg., Lane to Byrnes, December 4, 1945; msg., Acheson to Lane, December 13, 1945; msg., Lane to Secretary of State, December 19, 1945; msg., Lane to Secretary of State, December 22, 1945, in *FRUS,* V, 1945, 417–18, 425–27, 430–35.

28. Memo, transatlantic telephone conversation between Stettinius and Byrnes, January 31, 1946, in U.S., Department of State, *Foreign Relations of the United States,* 1946. Vol. VI: *Eastern Europe; The Soviet Union* (Washington, D.C.: United States Government Printing Office, 1969), pp. 387–91.

29. For Januszewski's role in KNAPP and the Polish American Congress, see Lukas, *The Strange Allies,* pp. 107–27.

30. Ltr., Januszewski to Vandenberg, January 12, 1946, quoted in Waclaw Jedrzejewicz, *Polonia Amerykanska w Polityce Polskiej: Historia Komitetu Narodowego Amerykanow Polskiego Pochodzenia* (New York: National Committee of Americans of Polish Descent, 1954), pp. 162–63. Ignacy Matuszewski, a major force behind the organization of KNAPP and regular contributor to the right-wing Polish American press, played an important role in drafting the Januszewski letters to Vandenberg. Interview with Waclaw Jedrzejewicz, June 17, 1980.

31. John N. Cable, "The United States and the Polish Question, 1939–1948" (unpublished Ph.D. dissertation, Vanderbilt University, 1972), pp. 415–16.

32. Memo, transatlantic telephone conversation between Stettinius and Byrnes; Peter H. Irons, " 'The Test is Poland:' Polish Americans and the Origins of the Cold War," *Polish American Studies,* XXX (Autumn, 1973), 57.

33. Memo, transatlantic telephone conversation between Stettinius and Byrnes; U.S., Department of State, *Bulletin,* February 10, 1946, p. 209. According to Lane, Byrnes's remarks were not published in the Polish press. Lane, *I Saw Poland Betrayed,* p. 191.

34. Cable, "The United States and the Polish Question," pp. 422–23.

35. *New York Times,* January 26, 1946; msg., Keith to Byrnes, February 3, 1946, in *FRUS,* VI, 1946, 392. Mikolajczyk was asked by the communists to issue a statement denying participation of the security police in political murders. He refused. See msg., Lane to Secretary of State, February 19, 1946, ibid., pp. 395–98.

36. Draft msg., Lane to Secretary of State, February 2, 1946 (not sent), in Lane Papers, box 69, folder 1250, YU/L; Petrov, *A Study in Diplomacy,* pp. 254–55; Lane, *I Saw Poland Betrayed,* pp. 230–31.

37. Msg., Byrnes to Keith, January 26, 1946, in *FRUS,* VI, 1946, 384–85.

38. Msg., Byrnes to Lane, April 22, 1946, ibid., pp. 432–33. Lane said "through the export of Poland's Silesian coal to France and Italy, those countries would be enabled to export products marketable in the United States, and so build up a dollar balance for Poland in New York." Lane, *I Saw Poland Betrayed,* p. 144.

39. Msg., Acheson to Byrnes, January 22, 1946; ltr., Clayton to Martin, February 13, 1946 in *FRUS,* VI, 1946, 382–84, 393–95. The *New York Times* claimed that

Vandenberg was instrumental in having the conditions placed on the loan. *New York Times,* April 25, 1946.

40. Msg., Acheson to Byrnes, January 22, 1946; msg., Byrnes to Lane, March 8, 1946; ltr., McCabe to Lange, April 22, 1946, in *FRUS,* VI, 1946, 382–84, 408–9, 433–35.

41. U.S., Department of State, *Bulletin,* May 5, 1946, pp. 761–62; aide memoire, Polish Embassy to Department of State, April 30, 1946, in *FRUS,* VI, 1946, 440. Also see p. 431, n. 22.

42. Msg., Lane to Secretary of State, February 22, 1946; msg., Lane to Secretary of State, March 14, 1946, ibid., pp. 398, 412–14; 387, n. 28.

43. Ltr., Lane to Matthews, March 1, 1946, in Lane Papers, box 69, folder 1251, YU/L. Also quoted in Lane, *I Saw Poland Betrayed,* p. 195.

44. Msg., Lane to Byrnes, April 21, 1946; msg., Lane to Byrnes, April 25, 1946 in *FRUS,* VI, 1946, 431–32, 436–37.

45. Petrov, *A Study in Diplomacy,* p. 257.

46. Memo of conversation by Durbrow, April 24, 1946; memo of conversation by Elbrick, June 25, 1946, in *FRUS,* VI, 1946, 437, n. 27; 467; memo of conversation by Elbrick, June 25, 1946, in Matthews-Hickerson Files, box 3, DS/NA.

47. Memo, British Embassy to Department of State, May 20, 1946, in *FRUS,* VI, 1946, 454–55.

48. Ltr., Lange to Acting Secretary of State, April 30, 1946; msg., Lane to Byrnes, May 1, 1946, ibid., pp. 438–40, 441–43.

49. Msg., Lane to Secretary of State, March 21, 1946, in DS/NA; *FRUS,* VI, 1946, 412, n. 84; 468, n. 75; Lane, *I Saw Poland Betrayed,* pp. 163–64. Lane said by the time he left his diplomatic post, there were 100 people in Polish prisons who claimed to be Americans. One of them, Stanislaw Tupaj, had been executed. ibid., p. 168.

50. Memo of conversation by Acheson, May 2, 1946; msg., Byrnes to Acheson, May 6, 1946; memo of conversation, May 20, 1946, in *FRUS,* VI, 1946, 443–45, 448–49, 453; Lane, *I Saw Poland Betrayed,* pp. 238–39. In the midst of this delicate situation, the PPR still risked alienating Washington by attacking the influential senator from Michigan, Arthur Vandenberg, who was critical of loans to Warsaw, as "a sworn and deserving follower and defender of Hitler." The Polish minister for foreign affairs, Modzelewski, described the PSL as a "ward of Mr. Vandenberg." "Poland: Report from Warsaw," *Time,* XLVII (May 13, 1946), 40, 45; *FRUS,* VI, 1946, 475–76.

51. Msg., Acheson to Byrnes, May 15, 1946; msg., Lane to Byrnes, June 14, 1946; memo of conversation by Thompson, June 25, 1946; memo, Department of State to British Embassy, July 12, 1946, in *FRUS,* VI, 1946, 450–51, 459–60, 466–67, 474–75. Also see p. 450, n. 54, and p. 490, n. 3.

52. Memo of conversation, May 25, 1946, in DS/NA, box 6381; msg., Byrnes to Acheson, May 17, 1946 in *FRUS,* VI, 1946, 451–52; Lane, *I Saw Poland Betrayed,* p. 239.

53. Msg., Lane to Byrnes, May 4, 1946, in *FRUS,* VI, 1946, 448.

54. Msg., Byrnes to Acheson, May 17, 1946; memo, Elbrick to Matthews, May 21, 1946 in *FRUS,* VI, 1946, 452, 455–56; ltr., Elbrick to Lane, May 13, 1946, in box 24, folder 465, Lane Papers, YU/L; Lane, *I Saw Poland Betrayed,* p. 238–39. See Chapter II supra.

55. Ltr., Lane to Elbrick, June 17, 1946; ltr. Lane to Elbrick, June 19, 1946 in Lane Papers, box 25, folder 470, YU/L. Lane also worried about the artificially high value placed on the zloty which could be used to repay loans to the United States. Lane urged: "If it cannot be properly imposed as a new condition to the Exim [*sic*] credit it should certainly be included in any other extension of credit which [the] Polish Government may seek." Msg., Lane to Byrnes, July 15, 1946, in *FRUS*, VI, 1946, 476–78.

56. See Lukas, *The Strange Allies*, Chapter IV.

57. Msg., Lane to Secretary of State, June 10, 1946; memo, with enclosure, Lane to Secretary of State, June 21, 1946, in DS/NA, box 3426; memo of conversation by Thompson, June 21, 1946, in *FRUS*, VI, 1946, 462–66; 465, n. 69.

58. *Dziennik Zwiazkowy*, May 4, 1946; May 6, 1946. In Milwaukee Polish Americans erected a huge electric sign on the tower of the city hall to welcome Bor. Polish American Congress, *Delegates Newsletter*, May, 1946, p. 2.

59. Msg., Byrnes to Lane, June 11, 1946 in RG 59, box 3426, in DS/NA. Later attempts by Polish American leaders to convince the State Department to issue a visa to General Anders failed. Memo Acheson to Hickerson, March 18, 1947, in Lane Papers, box 26, folder 495, YU/L.

60. See n. 41 supra.

61. Dziewanowski, *The Communist Party of Poland*, p. 195; Lane, *I Saw Poland Betrayed*, p. 244; memo, Keith to Secretary of State, April 9, 1947 in RG 59, box 3426, DS/NA.

62. Korbonski, *Warsaw in Chains*, pp. 116–17; Interview with Korbonski.

63. Ibid.; Jan Borkowski, "Ksztaltowanie Sie Antymikolajczykowskiej Opozycji w Kierownictwie Polskiego Stronnictwa Ludowego, 1946–1947," in Polska Akademia Nauk, Instytut Historii, *Polska Ludowa: Materialy i Studia* (Warszawa: Panstwowe Wydawnictwo Naukowe, 1962), I, 98ff.

64. Korbonski, *Politics of Socialist Agriculture*, p. 124. Karol Popiel, who headed the Labor party, joined the PSL in opposing the elimination of the senate because it would remove a body which could be used against a communist-dominated chamber of deputies. Popiel was eventually squeezed out from the leadership of the party by a proregime supporter, Dr. Feliks Widy-Wirski.

65. Lane, *I Saw Poland Betrayed*, pp. 241–42; *New York Times*, July 1, 1946.

66. H.W. Henderson, *Why Don't the Poles Go Home?* (Glasgow: 1946), pp. 19, 21–22.

67. *New York Times*, July 3, 1946.

68. Arnold and Zychowski, *Zarys Historii Polski*, p. 185.

69. Mikolajczyk, *The Rape of Poland*, p. 164.

70. Ibid., p. 167; Lane, *I Saw Poland Betrayed*, pp. 243–44.

71. Msg., Byrnes to Lane, July 27, 1946, in *FRUS*, VI, 1946, 485–87; U.S., Department of State, *Bulletin*, September 1, 1946, p. 422.

72. *New York Times*, August 29, 1946; "After the Referendum," *Poland of Today*, September, 1946, pp. 1–2, 6.

73. No objective account of Polish-Jewish relations during World War II exists in the English language. One highly touted account of the Holocaust, Lucy S. Dawidowicz's *The War against the Jews, 1933–1945* (New York: Holt, Rinehart and Winston, 1975), is badly flawed by the author's hostility toward the Poles. The weaknesses of her

treatment of the subject are well documented in Richard Adamiak's, "Dawidowicz's War against the Poles," *Perspectives,* May–June, 1980; July–August, 1980; November–December, 1980, pp. 568, 580–81, 600–1.

74. See the books by Wladyslaw Bartoszewski and Zofia Lewin: *Ten Jest z Ojczyny Mojej* (Krakow: Znak, 1966); *Righteous among Nations* (London: Earl's Court Publications, 1969); and *The Samaritans* (New York: Twayne, 1970). Also see Kazimierz Iranek-Osmecki, *He Who Saves One Life* (New York: Crown, 1971); Philip Friedman, *Their Brothers' Keepers* (New York: Crown, 1957); and Korbonski's *The Polish Underground State,* cited earlier.

75. Wandycz, *The United States and Poland,* pp. 242–43. The figure of 80,000 appears rather consistently in the literature.

76. Lucjan Dobroszycki, "Restoring Jewish Life in Post-War Poland," *Soviet Jewish Affairs* (1973), III, 65, 70.

77. Memo of conversation, November 9, 1945, in Matthews-Hickerson Files, box 17, DS/NA; interview with B. B. Kopecki. Irving Brant, a prominent American Jewish journalist who visited Poland in 1945, blamed the NSZ for the attacks on the Jews. ltr., Brant to Truman, January 14, 1946, in Truman Papers, PSF, box 186, HST/L.

78. Memo, Keith to Lane, July 11, 1946, in Lane Papers, box 25, folder 270, YU/L. Some of the top Jewish leaders in the Warsaw regime included Berman, Minc, Zambrowski, Olszewski, Grosz, and Radkiewicz. Some non-Jewish Polish leaders, like Gomulka, Cyrankiewicz, and Ochab, had Jewish wives. Significantly, there was a virtual Jewish monopoly over the security apparatus in Poland. See R.V. Burks, *The Dynamics of Communism in Eastern Europe.* (Princeton: Princeton University Press, 1961), p. 166. Cardinal Augustus Hlond, speaking for the Roman Catholic church in Poland, also took the position that Kielce was to a large degree "due to Jews who today occupy leading positions in Poland's Government and endeavor to introduce a governmental structure that a majority of the people do not desire." Hlond was criticized by the American and World Federations for Polish Jews. *New York Times,* July 12, 1946; July 13, 1946.

79. "The Jews in Poland since the Liberation," May 15, 1946, in OSS/DS Reports, MF Roll 9; memo, Jonas to Anglo-American Committee of Inquiry, December 31, 1945, in OSS/DS, Reports, MF Roll 3.

80. Memo, Keith to Lane, July 12, 1946, in Lane Papers, box 25, folder 470, YU/L.

81. Lane, *I Saw Poland Betrayed,* pp. 246–51; Korbonski, *Warsaw in Chains,* pp. 121–22.

82. *New York Times,* July 10, 1946, July 12, 1946.

83. Ibid., July 7, 1946; Korbonski, *Warsaw in Chains,* p. 123.

84. Lane, *I Saw Poland Betrayed,* p. 248.

85. Ibid.; *New York Times,* July 7, 1946.

86. Mikolajczyk, *The Rape of Poland,* p. 167; interview with Korbonski; Dziewanowski, *The Communist Party of Poland,* p. 202.

87. "Political Situation," Mikolajczyk Papers, box 40, HI; ltr., Lane to Elbrick, July 15, 1946, in Lane Papers, box 70, folder 1255, YU/L; Korbonski, *Warsaw in Chains.* pp. 122–23; Dobroszycki, "Restoring Jewish Life in Post-War Poland," p. 68.

88. Msg., Lane to Secretary of State, July 25, 1946; msg., Acheson to Lane, August 12, 1946; msg., Erhardt to Secretary of State, September 3, 1946; msg., Lane to Secretary of State, September 6, 1946, in U.S., Department of State, *Foreign Relations of the United States 1946.* Vol: V. *The British Commonwealth; Western and Central Europe* (Washington, D.C.: United States Government Printing Office, 1969), pp. 174, 178, 185–86, 186–87. Hereinafter cited as *FRUS,* V, 1946.

89. See issues of *Poland of Today* for the period 1946–1948.

CHAPTER IV

1. Memo of conversation (unsigned), July 15, 1946; memo of conversation (unsigned), July 16, 1946, in RG 59, box 6381, DS/NA.

2. Msg., Acheson to Byrnes, October 5, 1946, in *FRUS,* VI, 1946, 504–6; 549.

3. Memo, Keith to secretary of state, April 9, 1947, in RG 59, box 3426, DS/NA; msg., Lane to Byrnes, October 4, 1946, in *FRUS,* VI, 1946, 500–2.

4. Msg., Byrnes to Clayton, September 24, 1946, in U.S., Department of State, *Foreign Relations of the United States, 1946.* Vol. VII: *The Near East and Africa* (Washington: United States Government Printing Office, 1969), p. 223.

5. Msg., Byrnes to Acheson, October 4, 1946; msg., Acheson to Byrnes, October 5, 1946, in DS/NA.

6. Clark M. Clifford, "American Relations with the Soviet Union: A Report to the President by Special Counsel to the President," September 24, 1946, in HST/L.

7. Ibid.

8. Ltr., Lane to Keith, October 14, 1946, in Lane Papers, box 70, folder 1258, YU/L.

9. Memo, Lane to secretary of state, November 25, 1946, in *FRUS,* VI, 1946, 520–21. While in Paris for consultations with Byrnes and other State Department officials in October, Lane had received assurances that no further economic aid would be given to Poland until specific conditions were met. Ltr., Lane to Keith, October 17, 1946, in Lane Papers, box 25, folder 482, YU/L. Lane took the currency exchange matter so seriously that he threatened to resign as ambassador. Ltr., Lane to Elbrick, December 10, 1946, ibid., box 70, folder 1259. Lane's position on aid to Poland was so tough that he even recommended against "granting . . . further charitable assistance to Poland." Msg., Lane to Byrnes, October 8, 1946, in *FRUS,* VI, 1946, 506–8. By the summer of 1946, the Poles showed unconcealed contempt for Lane who, they said, made no effort to understand the situation in Poland. Memo, Hickerson to Byrnes, July 22, 1946, ibid., pp. 483–84; U.S., Department of State, *Bulletin,* August 11, 1946, p. 265.

10. Memo of conversation, December 16, 1946, in RG 59, box 6381, DS/NA.

11. Memo of conversation, December 18, 1946, in Matthews-Hickerson files, box 10, DS/NA.

12. Msg., Lane to Byrnes, December 22, 1946, in *FRUS,* VI, 1946, 546–48; msg., Lane to secretary of state, February 3, 1947; msg., Lane to secretary of state, February 17, 1947 in U.S., Department of State, *Foreign Relations of the United States, 1947.* Vol.

IV: *Eastern Europe: The Soviet Union* (Washington: United States Government Printing Office, 1972), pp. 414–16, 418–19. Hereinafter cited as *FRUS,* IV, 1947. Lane erroneously claimed that he had "always" felt the United States should be friendly with the PPS. Ltr., Lane to Elbrick, December 10, 1946, in Lane Papers, box 70, folder 1259, YU/L.

13. Cable, "Arthur Bliss Lane: Cold Warrior in Warsaw, 1945–47," p. 77.

14. Memo of conversation by Thompson, December 18, 1946, in RG 59, box 3, in DS/NA; memo of conversation, including draft agreement for claims commission (unsigned), December 18, 1946, *ibid.,* RG 59, box 6381; U.S., Department of State, *Bulletin,* January 5, 1947, p. 28. The Poles were especially angry with the British, who did not ratify a Polish-British agreement providing for return of some of Polish gold until Poland honored its commitment to hold free elections. *Dziennik Polski,* July, 1946; memo, British Embassy to Department of State, October 17, 1946, in *FRUS,* VI, 1946, 510–11.

15. See *FRUS,* VI, 1946, 528, n. 67.

16. U.S., Department of State, *Bulletin,* September 15, 1946, pp. 496–501.

17. Conover, "James F. Byrnes, Germany and the Cold War, 1946," p. 150.

18. U.S., Department of State, *Bulletin,* September 15, 1946, pp. 496–501.

19. Ltr., Lane to Keith, October 17, 1946, in Lane Papers, box 25, folder 482, YU/L.

20. Ministry for Foreign Affairs of the Polish People's Republic, *Documents on the Hostile Policy of the United States Government towards People's Poland* (Warsaw: 1953), p. 22.

21. Text of Gomulka's speech, September 8, 1946, in Embassy of Poland, *Poland of Today* (November, 1946), I, 11.

22. Lane, *I Saw Poland Betrayed,* pp. 260–61.

23. *Glos Ludu,* November 27, 1946; *Zycie Warszawy,* September 8, 1946.

24. Mikolajczyk, *The Rape of Poland,* p. 172.

25. Interview with Kopecki. In view of the Polish uproar over the speech by Byrnes, the State Department decided it would be prudent not to protest the nationalization of assets of Standard Oil of New Jersey in former German territories acquired by Poland. Memo by Thompson, October 30, 1946, in *FRUS,* VI, 1946, 512–14.

26. Lane, *I Saw Poland Betrayed,* p. 263.

27. *Gazeta Ludowa,* September 8, 1946; September 10, 1946; *Zycie Warszawy,* September 10, 1946.

28. Ibid., September 9, 1946.

29. Embassy of Poland, *Poland, Germany and European Peace: Official Documents, 1944–48* (London: Embassy of Poland, 1948), p. 112.

30. Msg., Lane to Byrnes, September 17, 1946, in *FRUS,* VI, 1946, 494–95; Lane, *I Saw Poland Betrayed,* pp. 154, 265. As a result of the speech, the Poles speeded up the process of repopulating the western lands with Polish settlers. Msg., Lane to Byrnes, October 3, 1946, in *FRUS,* VI, 1946, 500.

31. Borkowski, "Ksztaltowanie Sie Antymikolajczykowskiej Opozycji w Kierownictwie Polskiego Stronnictwa Ludowego, 1946–1947," pp. 107–8; Gora, *Polska Rzeczpospolita Ludowa, 1944–1947,* pp. 213–14.

32. "Political Situation," in Mikolajczyk Papers, box 40, HI.

33. Korbonski, *Politics of Socialist Agriculture,* pp. 124–25.

34. Resolutions of the Supreme Council of the PSL, October 6–7, 1946, in Mikolajczyk Papers, box 38, HI.

35. Memo, Mikolajczyk to Stalin, October 10, 1946, ibid., box 39.

36. Msg., Lane to secretary of state, August 1, 1946; msg., Acheson to Caffery, August 5, 1946, in *FRUS,* VI, 1946, 487–88, 488–89.

37. Memo of conversation, November 22, 1946, in Matthews-Hickerson Files, RG 59, box 3, DS/NA.

38. Korbonski, *Warsaw in Chains,* p. 179.

39. Memo, Mikolajczyk to the governments of the United States, Great Britain and the Soviet Union, December 18, 1946, in Lane Papers, box 25, folder 486, YU/L; ltr., Smith to Molotov, January 5, 1947; msg., Smith to secretary of state, January 15, 1947; ltr., Lane to Rzymowski, January 9, 1947; msg., Lane to secretary of state, January 14, 1947, in *FRUS,* IV, 1947, 402–04, including note 3, p. 402; 405–08. The State Department worried that Mikolajczyk's appeal would embarrass the United States "by making it appear that we were backing one particular party in [the] Pol[ish] elections rather than carrying out our obligation to insure free elections regardless of outcome," a rather curious position to take in the face of the known efforts by the Soviets to back the Polish communists. Msg., Acheson to Keith, November 18, 1946, ibid., VI, 1946, 516.

40. Korbonski, *Warsaw in Chains,* pp. 158, 179; msg., Lane to Byrnes, December 14, 1946, in *FRUS,* VI, 1946, 536–38. There had been talk about the possibility of a civil war in Poland since the spring. See Chapter II above.

41. Note on Polish elections by Mikolajczyk, in Mikolajczyk Papers, box 40, HI.

42. Msg., Acheson to Keith, November 18, 1946, in *FRUS,* VI, 1946, 516.

43. "R," "The Fate of Polish Socialism," pp. 131–32.

44. Mikolajczyk, *The Rape of Poland,* p. 171.

45. Ltr., Lane to Burke, August 30, 1946, in Lane Papers, box 70, YU/L.

46. H.W. Henderson, *The Great Polish Election Fraud* (Glasgow: 1947), n.p.

47. Quoted in Starr, *Poland, 1944–1962,* p. 49.

48. Mikolajczyk, *The Rape of Poland,* pp. 185–86.

49. A. Bregman, ed., *Faked Elections in Poland as Reported by Foreign Observers* (London: Polish Freedom Movement, n.d.), p. 25.

50. Lane, *I Saw Poland Betrayed,* pp. 278–79.

51. Quoted in Mikolajczyk, *The Rape of Poland,* p. 298.

52. Lane, *I Saw Poland Betrayed,* pp. 279–80; Mikolajczyk, *The Rape of Poland,* p. 189.

53. Bregman, *Faked Elections in Poland,* pp. 25–26.

54. Lane, *I Saw Poland Betrayed,* p. 278.

55. Bregman, *Faked Elections in Poland,* pp. 26–27; Mikolajczyk, *The Rape of Poland,* p. 194.

56. Mikolajczyk, *The Rape of Poland,* p. 211; msg., Lane to secretary of state, January 21, 1947, in *FRUS,* IV, 1947, 410–11.

57. Mikolajczyk, *The Rape of Poland,* p. 197.

58. Ibid., p. 185.

59. Korbonski, *Warsaw in Chains,* p. 191.

156 BITTER LEGACY

60. Bregman, *Faked Elections in Poland*, p. 36; Lane, *I Saw Poland Betrayed*, p. 285. After the Grocholski trial, Ambassador Lane became concerned about the personal safety of Mikolajczyk. He admonished the State Department, "As we took such an important role in urging Mikolajczyk join the Provisional Govt., I feel that we have far more than a humanitarian responsibility to endeavor to protect him from the fate of Mikailovitch." msg., Lane to secretary of state, January 18, 1947, in *FRUS*, IV, 1947, 408–10.

61. *Dziennik Ustaw*, 1946, 48, 274; msg., Keith to secretary of state, November 19, 1946, in Truman Papers, PSF, box 189, HST/L; Dziewanowski, *The Communist Party of Poland*, p. 203.

62. Korbonski, *Warsaw in Chains*, p. 193.

63. Bregman, *Faked Elections in Poland*, pp. 32–33; *New York Times*, January 20, 1947.

64. Bregman, *Faked Elections in Poland*, p. 32.

65. Ibid.

66. Mikolajczyk, *The Rape of Poland*, pp. 181, 199.

67. Ibid., Korbonski, *Warsaw in Chains*, p. 196.

68. Gora, *Polska Rzeczpospolita Ludowa, 1944–1974*, p. 219.

69. Dziewanowski, *The Communist Party of Poland*, p. 349, n. 48; statement by Mikolajczyk, undated, in Mikolajczyk Papers, box 42, HI. Jozef Swiatlo, an officer in the Polish security police who later defected to the West, admitted that he served on a special commission to falsify the results of the elections. Edward J. Rozek, *Allied Wartime Diplomacy: A Pattern in Poland* (New York: John Wiley and Sons, 1958), pp. 457–58.

70. "The New Polish Government," May 14, 1947, in OSS/DS Intelligence and Research Reports, Roll 9. The new cabinet consisted of the following members: Jozef Cyrankiewicz, president of the council of ministers; Wladyslaw Gomulka, first vice-president and minister of recovered territories; Antoni Korzycki, second vice-president; Zygmunt Modzelewski, minister of foreign affairs; Michal Rola-Zymierski, minister of national defense; Stanislaw Radkiewicz, minister of public security; Hilary Minc, minister of industry; Stanislaw Skrzeszewski, minister of education; Edward Osobka-Morawski, minister of public administration; Kazimierz Rusinek, minister of labor and social welfare; Henryk Swiatkowski, minister of justice; Ludwik Grosfeld, director of shipping and foreign trade; Konstanty Dabrowski, minister of finance; Michal Kaczorowski, minister of reconstruction; Jan Dab-Kociol, minister of agriculture and land reform; Jozef Putek, minister of posts and telegraph; Boleslaw Podedworny, minister of forests; Stefan Dybowski, minister of cultural affairs; Wlodzimierz Lechowicz, minister of commerce and supply; Jan Rabanowski, minister of communications; Feliks Widy-Wirski, director of ministry of information and propaganda; Tadeusz Michejda, minister of health; Wincenty Rzymowski, minister without portfolio; Wincenty Baranowski, minister without portfolio.

71. Ibid.,

72. Mikolajczyk, *The Rape of Poland*, pp. 204–5.

73. Quoted in Korbonski, *Warsaw in Chains*, pp. 214–17.

74. Ibid., p. 217.

75. Polish Information Service, *The Provisional Constitution of February 20, 1947* (New York: Polish Information Service, 1947).

76. "The New Polish Government."

77. Quoted in ibid.

78. Korbonski, *Warsaw in Chains,* p. 232.

79. U.S., Department of State, *Bulletin,* February 9, 1947; "The New Polish Government."

80. Glinka-Janczewski, "American Policy toward Poland under the Truman Administration," pp. 274–75.

81. *New York Times,* January 30, 1947.

82. "The New Polish Government."

83. Lockhart, "Meeting with Mikolajczyk, pp. 6–7.

84. Msg., Lane to secretary of state, January 23, 1947, in *FRUS,* IV, 1947, 411–14.

85. Lane, *I Saw Poland Betrayed,* p. 301.

CHAPTER V

1. Lukas, *The Strange Allies,* pp. 53–56; Lane, *I Saw Poland Betrayed,* pp. 131–32.

2. Ltr., Lane to Matthews, February 6, 1947, in Lane Papers, box 70, folder 1262, YU/L.

3. Ibid.

4. Memo of conversation, February 4, 1947, in *FRUS,* IV, 1947, 417–18.

5. Griffis, *Lying in State,* pp. 17–20, 144–45. His foreign experience had been limited to a wartime mission to Sweden to buy ball bearings in order to reduce Swedish exports of that critical item to Germany. Newsclip, *New York Journal American,* March 29, 1947, in Griffis Papers, box 2, HST/L.

6. Newsclip, *New York Herald Tribune,* March 31, 1947, ibid. Griffis's confirmation by the Senate was delayed because he had made a favorable statement about Hitler during the war. Griffis, *Lying in State,* pp. 159–60.

7. Msg., Griffis to secretary of state, August 8, 1947, in Griffis Papers, box 8, HST/L.

8. Ltr., by Griffis, March 11, 1948, ibid.; Griffis, *Lying in State,* pp. 167–68.

9. Ltr., by Griffis, August 7, 1947, in Griffis Papers, box 8, HST/L.

10. Ltr., by Griffis, October 20, 1947, ibid.

11. Ltr., Lane to Matthews, February 6, 1947, in Lane Papers, box 70, folder 1262, YU/L.

12. Newsclip, *New York Herald Tribune,* July 20, 1947, in Griffis Papers, box 2, HST/L; msg., Griffis to Marshall, October 10, 1947, in *FRUS,* IV, 1947, 455–56.

13. *Szpilki,* June 3, 1947.

14. Ltr., by Griffis, October 20, 1947. Griffis noted the constant talk of war in the Polish press, "the thesis always being that the United States will attack Russia." He estimated that 50 percent or more of the editorial and essay comment in the Polish press were attacks against the United States.

15. For representative articles, see "Yet Once Again: Poland," *Catholic World,*

CLXIV (February, 1947), 391–93; J. Lada, "Soviet Policy toward Poland," *Catholic World,* CLXV, (June, 1947), 271–72; Freda Bruce Lockhart, "The Polish Pantomime," *Nineteenth Century and After,* CXLI (February, 1947), 88–91; "Red Victory in Poland," *Scholastic,* L (February 24, 1947), 5–6; S. Wolf, "The Polish Elections and After," *Contemporary Review,* CLXXI (March, 1947), 145–49; Arthur Bliss Lane, "How Russia Rules Poland," *Life,* XXIII (July 14, 1947), 98ff.; Dorothy Thompson, "Poland Two Years after Yalta," *American Mercury,* LXIV (May, 1947), 534–41.

16. See Chapter VII below.

17. Polish American Congress, *The Story of the Polish American Congress,* p. 69; memo of conversation with enclosures, July 7, 1947, in RG 59, box 3426, in DS/NA.

18. Polish American Congress, "Voice of America," June 4, 1947.

19. Memo of conversation with enclosures, July 7, 1947, in RG 59, box 3426, in DS/NA.

20. Ltr., by Griffis, August 7, 1947.

21. Ltr., by Griffis, October 20, 1947.

22. Ltr., by Griffis, August 7, 1947.

23. Ltr., by Griffis, October 20, 1947.

24. Msg., Clayton to Lovett, July 29, 1947; msg., Griffis to secretary of state, in *FRUS,* IV, 1947, 435–38, 456; ltr., by Griffis, August 7, 1947, in Griffis Papers, box 8, HST/L.

25. Memo of conversation by Garner, September 30, 1947, in *FRUS,* IV, 1947, 454–55.

26. Memo of conversation by Bohlen, February 7, 1947, in Bohlen Papers, box 4, DS/NA; memo of conversation by Thompson, September 30, 1947, in *FRUS,* IV, 1947, 452–53.

27. Memo of conversation by Thompson, April 3, 1947; memo of conversation by Marshall, August 6, 1947; memo of conversation, October 29, 1947, in *FRUS,* IV, 1947, 421–23, 438–41, 457. On January 31, 1948, the unused portion of the $40 million Export-Import Bank credit, granted in 1946, was cancelled. Cable, "The United States and the Polish Question," p. 509.

28. S. Harrison Thomson and Ona K.D. Ringwood, "Problems of Polish Foreign Policy," *Foreign Policy Reports,* XXIII, (December 1, 1947), 236.

29. Speech by Cyrankiewicz to Sejm, June 19, 1947, quoted in *Poland of Today* (August, 1947), p. 1.

30. Embassy of Poland (London), *Poland, Germany and European Peace: Official Documents, 1944–48,* pp. 62–63.

31. Ltr., Griffis to Lovett, August 18, 1947, in *FRUS,* IV, 1947, 443.

32. Korbonski, *Warsaw in Chains,* p. 246.

33. For UNRRA activities in Poland, see Chapter VI below.

34. Memo of conversation, June 5, 1947, in RG 59, box 6381, DS/NA.

35. Memo of conversation, February 19, 1947, ibid.; memo by Keith, November 12, 1946, in Lane Papers, box 25, folder 483, YU/L.

36. Ltr., with enclosures, Pate to Lane, March 21, 1947, ibid., box 26, folder 495.

37. George Woodbridge, *UNRRA: The History of the United Nations Relief and Rehabilitation Administration* (3 vols.; New York: Columbia University Press, 1950), II, 219.

38. Msg., Keith to secretary of state, April 10, 1947, in RG 59, box 6381, DS/NA.

39. Msg., Keith to secretary of state, April 11, 1947, in RG 59, box 6381, DS/NA. Former president Herbert Hoover and former ambassador Lane also believed that Poland did not need additional relief from the United States. Ltr., Lane to Keith, March 19, 1947, in Lane Papers, box 26, folder 495, in YU/L.

40. U.S., *Congressional Record,* XCIII, 80th Cong., 1st Sess., 1947, Part 3, 3822, 4218–19, 4227–28.

41. Msg., Acheson to American Embassy (Warsaw), March 29, 1947; msg., Marshall to American Embassy (Warsaw), May 5, 1947, in RG 59, box 6381, in DS/NA.

42. Editorial note, *FRUS,* IV, 1947, 434–35; U.S. Department of State, *Bulletin,* August 3, 1947, 223–24.

43. Griffis, *Lying in State,* p. 202.

44. 61 *Stat.* 125; Thomas G. Paterson, *Soviet-American Confrontation: Postwar Reconstruction and the Origins of the Cold War* (Baltimore: Johns Hopkins University Press, 1973), pp. 96–97. After Poland had been excluded from the list of countries to receive relief from the United States, the Polish government ordered the airplane of the American air attaché out of Poland.

45. Msg., Griffis to secretary of state, August 2, 1947, in RG 59, box 6381, DS/NA.

46. Quoted in *Poland of Today* (September, 1947), pp. 1, 13.

47. Memo of conversation, August 5, 1947, in RG 59, box 6381, DS/NA.

48. Ibid.; msg., Griffis to secretary of state, August 5, 1947.

49. Memo of conversation by Thompson, July 23, 1947, in RG 59, box 6381, DS/NA.

50. Msg., Keith to secretary of state, May 17, 1947, ibid.; A.J. Wycislo, "American Catholic Relief for Poland," *Polish American Studies,* XIX (1962), 103. The State Department took the position that private agencies in the United States could best meet Poland's relief needs. Ltr., with memo, Read to Marshall, December 10, 1947; ltr., Austen to Read, December 15, 1947, in RG 59, box 6381, DS/NA.

51. Msg., Griffis to secretary of state, August 2, 1947, in RG 59, box 6381, DS/NA.

52. Minutes, council of ministers, April 9, 1947, in Truman Papers, PSF: Subject, box 166, HST/L.

53. U.S., Department of State, "Agreements Reached at the Cairo, Tehran, Yalta, and Potsdam Conferences," September, 1948, in ibid.

54. Ltr., Smith to Lane, February 1, 1947, in Lane Papers, box 25, folder 486, YU/L.

55. Ltr., Lane to Marshall, April 29, 1947; memo of conversation, May 9, 1947, in *FRUS,* IV, 1947, 425–29. The British were more realistic about the matter and were willing to accept the de facto Polish-German frontier. Memo, Bohlen to secretary of state, February 19, 1947, in Bohlen Papers, box 4, DS/NA.

56. Ltr., Lane to Marshall, May 10 1947, in Lane Papers, box 71, folder 1273, YU/L.

57. Ministry for Foreign Affairs of the Polish People's Republic, *Documents,* p. 24; *Tydzien,* May 2, 1947.

58. *Zycie Warszawy,* April 22, 1947.

59. Interview with A. Tarnowski, in mid-European Studies Center, *W Obronie Wolnosci i Niepodleglosci Rzeczypospolitej Polskiej. Dokumenty: Lipiec, 1947-Maj 1948* (London: Mid-European Studies Center, 1948), pp. 7–9.

60. Ltr., by Griffis, August 7, 1947, in Griffis Papers, box 8, HST/L.
61. Ministry for Foreign Affairs of the Polish People's Republic, *Documents,* pp. 26–30. In July 1947 the Poles had asked for restitution for the horses confiscated by the Germans during the wartime occupation of their country. The United States replied that the horses had been taken from the Germans by the Allies in April 1945 and became their property. The refusal to offer restitution to the Poles was just another issue dividing the two nations. Ibid., pp. 72–75.
62. Korbonski, *The Politics of Socialist Agriculture,* pp. 129–30.
63. Ibid., p. 130 and n. 119; editorial note, *FRUS,* IV, 1947, 445.
64. Ltr., by Griffis, March 11, 1948, in Griffis Papers, box 8, HST/L; Mikolajczyk, *The Rape of Poland,* p. 223.
65. Memo, Bohlen to Marshall, September 25, 1947, in Bohlen Papers, box 4, DS/NA.
66. Korbonski, *Warsaw in Chains,* pp. 249, 260–63.
67. Interview with Korbonski.
68. Korbonski, *Warsaw in Chains,* p. 249.
69. Memo by Andrews, November 17, 1947, in *FRUS,* IV, 1947, 460.
70. Address by Mikolajczyk to Royal Institute of International Affairs, November 13, 1947, in Mikolajczyk Papers, box 42, HI.
71. Memo by Andrews, November 17, 1947, in *FRUS,* IV, 1947, 460.
72. Griffis, *Lying in State,* p. 171.
73. Memo by Andrews, November 17, 1947, in *FRUS,* IV, 1947, 460–63; Griffis, *Lying in State,* pp. 172–74. The official American version of Mikolajczyk's escape makes reference to a male companion who joined Mikolajczyk in the truck that took them to Gdynia. But Paul Zaleski, Mikolajczyk's secretary, disputes that anyone accompanied the Polish leader. Zaleski wrote: "I was the last person who said good-by to Mikolajczyk in Warsaw. He told me that he was very sorry that he could not take me or anybody else . . . with him. As far as I know, he did not take anybody along with him." Zaleski said that he left Warsaw twenty-four hours after Mikolajczyk's departure. Ltr., Zaleski to author, May 4, 1981.
74. Griffis, *Lying in State,* p. 174. Zaleski and Korbonski have denied that Hulewicz was Mikolajczyk's wife. Ltr., Zaleski to author; ltr., Korbonski to author, May 18, 1981. Korbonski said: "Mrs. Mikolajczyk did not return to Poland in 1945 but stayed in England where she welcomed her husband after his successful escape in 1947." Ltr., Korbonski to author.
75. Memo by Andrews, November 17, 1947, in *FRUS,* IV, 1947, 464; msgs., (1947) in Griffis Papers, box 8, HST/L.
76. Korbonski, *Warsaw in Chains,* pp. 265–75.
77. Wandycz, *The United States and Poland,* p. 328.
78. *Gazeta Ludowa,* October 26, 1947; November 11, 1947.
79. Quoted in *New York Times,* October 29, 1947.
80. Ltr., by Griffis, March 11, 1948, in Griffis Papers, box 8, in HST/L.
81. *New York Times,* November 7, 1947; Ministry for Foreign Affairs of the Polish People's Republic, *Documents,* pp. 137–38.
82. For Mikolajczyk's version, see *The Rape of Poland,* pp. 244–50. For Griffis' account, see *Lying in State,* pp. 171–75.

83. Msg., Griffis to acting secretary of state, November 21, 1947, in *FRUS,* IV, 1947, 465–67.

84. "R," "The Fate of Polish Socialism," pp. 134–42. The PSL and SL formally merged in October, 1949, becoming the *Zjednoczone Stronnictwo Ludowe* (ZSL) (United Peasant party).

85. Msg., Griffis to secretary of state, November 15, 1947, in *FRUS,* IV, 1947, 459.

CHAPTER VI

1. Msg., Osobka-Morawski to Lehman, October 3, 1944; msg., Lehman to Osobka-Morawski, October 11, 1944; press release, October 30, 1944, in Hugh Jackson Papers, Herbert H. Lehman Papers, School of International Affairs, Columbia University. Hereinafter cited as HJP in HHLP/CU.

2. Press release, October 30, 1944, in HJP in HHLP/CU.

3. Lane, *I Saw Poland Betrayed,* p. 143.

4. Ibid.; memo of conversation by Underwood, October 1, 1945, in *FRUS,* V, 1945, 382–83.

5. George Woodbridge, *UNRRA,* II, 204–06, 211–12; "Polish Mission, 1945–47," in UNRRA Records, RG 17, United Nations Archives. Hereinafter cited as UN/A.

6. Woodbridge, *UNRRA,* II, 211–12; Lane, *I Saw Poland Betrayed,* p. 213.

7. Woodbridge, *UNRRA,* II, 205.

8. "Polish Mission, 1945–1947," Robert G.A. Jackson, oral history, Columbia University, pp. 175, 204.

9. Ltr., Lane to Lyon, September 16, 1946; ltr., Atherton to Lane, April 9, 1947, in Lane Papers, box 70, and box 26, respectively, YU/L.

10. Woodbridge, *UNRRA,* II, 208; Kowalski, *Polityka Zagraniczna RP,* pp. 208–10.

11. Ltr., Drury to Lehman, February 21, 1946; ltr., Drury to Lehman, March 2, 1946, in UNRRA records, box 75, 024, UN/A.

12. Msg., Lane to secretary of state, February 25, 1946, in *FRUS,* VI, 1946, 400–3.

13. Woodbridge, *UNRRA,* II, 208.

14. "U.S. Opinion on Russia in World Affairs," January 9, 1947, in RG 59, box 45, DS/NA; Cable, "The United States and the Polish Question," pp. 251–52.

15. Ibid., p. 224; ltr., Lane to Herter, September 26, 1945; ltr., Herter to Lane, October 6, 1945, in Lane Papers, boxes 69 and 23, respectively, YU/L; Lane, *I Saw Poland Betrayed,* p. 224; ltr., by Griffis, August 7, 1947; Dean Acheson, *Present at the Creation: My Years in the State Department* (New York: New American Library, 1970), p. 271; U.S., Department of State, *Bulletin,* May 26, 1946, p. 897; Paterson, *Soviet-American Confrontation,* pp. 92–93.

16. Ibid., pp. 22–23, 80; U.S., Department of State, *FRUS: Potsdam,* I, 784–85; *New York Times,* November 29, 1946; UNRRA, 8th Report to Congress on Operations of UNRRA, p. 40.

17. Msg., Acheson to Lane, September 14, 1945; msg., Lane to secretary of state, September 24, 1945, in U.S., Department of State, *Foreign Relations of the United States, 1946.* Vol. II: *Council of Foreign Ministers* (Washington: United States Government Printing Office, 1970), pp. 1029–30; 8th Report to Congress on Operations of UNRRA, p. 2; ltr., Lane to Durbrow, October 16, 1945, in Lane Papers, box 69, YU/L; msg., Lane to Byrnes, November 14, 1945, in *FRUS,* V, 1945, 414–17. Lane com-

plained that UNRRA trucks, carrying political slogans, were used to celebrate May Day in 1946. Lane, *I Saw Poland Betrayed,* p. 208. The Polish American press charged that the Soviets stole UNRRA goods intended for the Poles. *Narod Polski,* March 21, 1946.

18. Ltr., Drury to editors, *Life,* January 20, 1947, and enclosure (*"Life's* Reports: Poland Abuses UNRRA"); ltr., Harward to Drury, April 4, 1947, in UNRRA records, box 75,024, UN/A; Korbonski, *Warsaw in Chains,* p. 147.

19. Woodbridge, *UNRRA,* II, 220–21. The chief of the American Red Cross mission to Poland stated flatly: "Polish Government is concerned primarily with supplying various foods to people who support it and it has no serious interest to assist those who do not support it or whose support is not important to it such as invalids, tuberculars, and repatriates once they have arrived. Evidence is plentiful." Msg., Keith to secretary of state, April 16, 1947, in RG 59, box 6381, DS/NA.

20. Ltr., Drury to Beamish, December 5, 1946, in UNRRA records, box 75,024, UN/A; Woodbridge, *UNRRA,* II, 213–14; Lane, *I Saw Poland Betrayed,* pp. 185–86.

21. Ltr., Drury to editors, *Life,* January 20, 1947, and enclosure (*"Life's* Reports: Poland Abuses UNRRA); msg., Drury to LaGuardia, December 18, 1946, in UNRRA records, box 75,024, UN/A.

22. Ltr., Lane to LaGuardia, February 1, 1947; ltr., Fulbright to Lane, March 7, 1947, in Lane Papers, boxes 70 and 26 and folders 1262 and 493, respectively, YU/L.

23. Ibid.; ltr., Lane to Fulbright, March 12, 1947, in ibid., box 70, folder 1263, YU/L.

24. Alton, *Polish Postwar Economy,* pp. 268–69.

25. Woodbridge, *UNRRA,* II, 210, 214–17, 223–24. Polish Americans who wished to do so could send livestock to their relatives in Poland through UNRRA. Ltr., Russell to Fudalla, June 4, 1946, in RG 59, box 6381, DS/NA. Lane told Durbrow, "The UNRRA people told me that the Government program for UNRRA distribution is 70 percent divided between Katowice and Lodz (obviously because of the industrial workers there and the resultant political implications), 20 percent for the Warsaw district and 10 percent for the remainder of the country, but nary a pound for Krakow," Ltr., Lane to Durbrow, December 20, 1945, in Lane Papers, box 69, folder 1247, YU/L.

26. Jackson, oral history, pp. 204–5.

27. Woodbridge, *UNRRA,* II, 227.

28. Memo, with enclosure, Ramsey to secretary of state, October 26, 1948, in RG 59, box 3426, DS/NA; address by Rusinek, June 27, 1947, in Robert Jackson Papers, HHLP/CU; memo, by Sabin, April 22, 1947, in UNRRA records, box 75,022, UN/A. Mikolajczyk, *The Rape of Poland,* p. 216.

29. UNRRA, *Journal,* V (August 9, 1946), 37.

30. Paterson, *Soviet-American Confrontation,* p. 85; Brant, *The New Poland,* p. 18.

31. Paterson, *Soviet-American Confrontation,* p. 91.

32. For a contrary view, see ibid., pp. 85, 98.

33. "Summary of Foreign Voluntary Agencies," in UNRRA records, box 75,039, UN/A.

34. For a brief survey of the history of the *Rada* during the war years, see Lukas, *The Strange Allies,* pp. 108–9, 111, 115.

35. American Relief for Poland, *The Facts You Want To Know About: American Relief for Poland* (Chicago: American Relief for Poland, 1947), n.p.

36. Jedrzejewicz, *Polonia Amerykanska,* pp. 149–50.

37. *Narod Polski,* January 10, 1946, June 5, 1947; U.S., *Congressional Record,* 79th Cong., 2nd Sess., 1946, XCII, Parts 9–10, Appendices, 1193.

38. Msg., McCormack for Warsaw, November 10, 1945; ltr., Ringland to Stevens, November 20, 1945, in RG 59, box 6381, DS/NA; *Washington Post,* November 13, 1945; Brant, *The New Poland,* pp. 23–24.

39. American Relief for Poland, *The Facts You Want To Know About: American Relief for Poland;* "Summary of Foreign Voluntary Agencies;" Treasurer's report, American Relief for Poland, October 1, 1944 to July 31, 1946, in American Relief for Poland File, PI.

40. Msg., Griffis to secretary of state, April 17, 1948, in RG 59, box 6381, DS/NA.

41. Lane, *I Saw Poland Betrayed,* p. 147.

42. Ltr., with enclosure, Ryan to Kuppinger, March 26, 1946, in RG 59, box 6381, DS/NA; "Summary of Foreign Voluntary Agencies."

43. "Summary of Foreign Voluntary Agencies;" Wycislo, "American Catholic Relief for Poland," pp. 103–4.

44. Wycislo, "American Catholic Relief for Poland," p. 105.

45. Dobroszycki, "Restoring Jewish Life in Post-War Poland;" "Summary of Foreign Voluntary Agencies."

46. "Summary of Foreign Voluntary Agencies."

47. Paul Super, *Twenty-Five Years with the Poles* (New York: Super Memorial Fund, 1947), p. 360.

48. Lane, *I Saw Poland Betrayed,* p. 216.

49. Jerzy Zubrzycki, *Polish Immigrants in Britain: A Study of Adjustment* (The Hague: Martinus Nijhoff, 1956), pp. 51–53.

50. Wladyslaw Anders, *An Army in Exile: The Story of the Second Polish Corps* (London: Macmillan, 1949), p. 116.

51. Zubrzycki, *Polish Immigrants in Britain,* p. 53.

52. Woodbridge, *UNRRA,* III, 426.

53. Gora, *Polska Rzeczpospolita Ludowa,* p. 192. Estimates of Polish refugees in western Europe range from 1.7 million to 3.2 million. See "Poland: Exit the Emigres," *Newsweek,* XXVI (July 16, 1945), 50; and Wycislo, "American Catholic Relief for Poland," p. 103.

54. Rozek, *Allied Wartime Diplomacy,* p. 412.

55. Memo by Taylor, undated, in Myron Taylor Papers, box 3, HST/L.

56. Ltr., Stanton to Byrnes, August 24, 1945, in RG 59, box 6381, DS/NA.

57. Msg., Grew to Caffery, June 16, 1945, in *FRUS,* II, 1945, 1171; Kowalski, *Polityka Zagraniczna RP,* pp. 193–94.

58. Msg., Lane to secretary of state, August 25, 1945; msg., Lane to secretary of state, August 28, 1945 in U.S., Department of State, *Foreign Relations of the United States: Diplomatic Papers, 1945.* Vol. II: *General: Political and Economic Matters* (Washington, D.C.: United States Government Printing Office, 1967), pp. 1188–91, including note 85; p. 1190 and n. 89; p. 1191.

59. Ltr., and attachment, Byrnes to Vandenberg, November 7, 1945, in Vandenberg File, PI.

60. Jedrzejewicz, *Polonia Amerykanska,* pp. 146–48, 150.

61. Ltr., with attachment, Byrnes to Vandenberg, November 7, 1945.

62. Ltr., Vandenberg to Cytacki, November 3, 1945, in Vandenberg File, PI; quoted in Jedrzejewicz, *Polonia Amerykanska,* p. 148.

63. Ibid., pp. 148–49.

64. Rozmarek could also speak Spanish. Interview with Wanda Rozmarek, February 8, 1980.

65. Polish American Congress, *Story of the Polish American Congress,* pp. 66–67; Julius Epstein, *Operation Keelhaul: The Story of Forced Repatriation from 1944 to the Present* (Old Greenwich: Devin-Adair, 1973), p. 47; Wycislo, "American Catholic Relief for Poland," p. 103.

66. Some of the camps visited by the delegation included those located at Mannheim, Esslingen, Wiesbaden, Munich, Stuttgart, and Frankfurt.

67. Polish American Congress, *A Factual Report on the Plight of Displaced Persons in Germany* (Chicago: Polish American Congress, 1947), p. 1.

68. Polish American Congress, *Story of the Polish American Congress,* p. 88.

69. Polish American Congress, *A Factual Report on the Plight of Displaced Persons in Germany,* p. 2.

70. Statement by General McNarney, September 26, 1946, in UNRRA records, box 75,028, UN/A.

71. Transcript of lecture by Warren, June 28, 1946, in George Warren Papers, box 1, HST/L.

72. Statement by General McNarney.

73. Statement by Charles M. Drury, September 26, 1946, in UNRRA records, box 75,028, UN/A.

74. Polish American Congress, *A Factual Report on the Plight of Displaced Persons in Germany,* p. 6.

75. Ibid., p. 2.

76. Ibid., pp. 2–3.

77. Ibid., pp. 4–5.

78. Ibid., p. 5.

79. *Narod Polski,* November 7, 1946.

80. Polish American Congress, *Story of the Polish American Congress,* p. 94. The Yugoslavians and the Soviets tried but failed to push proposals through the United Nations that would have denied relief to refugees who refused to return to their countries. *New York Times,* November 29, 1946; January 27, 1947.

81. "Displaced Persons," comments by LaGuardia, in UNRRA records, box 75,043, UN/A.

82. Ltr., Januszewski to Vandenberg, April 5, 1946, in Vandenberg file, PI.

83. Memo of conversation, March 18, 1947, in Lane Papers, box 26, folder 495, YU/L.

84. Msg., Clayton to Hilldring, August 7, 1946, in *FRUS,* V, 1946, 176–77; Woodbridge, *UNRRA,* III, 156.

85. Msg., Acheson to Harrison, August 14, 1946; msg., Murphy to secretary of state, August 24, 1946, in *FRUS,* V, 1946, 179–81. Byrnes admitted that approximately 20,000 Poles were employed, as civilians, to guard German prisoners of war. He told the press, "The Army determined that it was better to put them to work as civilians

and relieve American soldiers than to have them there doing nothing and being fed." Memo of press and radio news conferences, February 8, [1946], in Byrnes Papers, folder 557, CU/L.

86. For efforts to form a Polish army in the Soviet Union and its subsequent evacuation, see Lukas, *The Strange Allies,* pp. 12–22.

87. Communiqué of the Potsdam Conference, in *FRUS: Potsdam,* II, 1508.

88. Msg., Lane to secretary of state, September 20, 1945; msg., Lane to secretary of state, December 19, 1945; msg., Lane to secretary of state, December 21, 1945 in *FRUS,* V, 1945, 372–74, 432–34. Possibly the Warsaw government took note of the example of Czechoslovakia where soldiers who returned from abroad became the focal point for the pro-West feelings of the population. "Poles: Refuge in Britain," *Newsweek,* XXVII (June 3, 1946), 42.

89. Ltr., Lane to Durbrow, March 11, 1946, in Lane Papers, box 69, folder 1251, YU/L; memo of conversation by Elbrick, December 24, 1946, in *FRUS,* VI, 1946, 551–52; U.S., War Department, Intelligence Review, "Repatriation of Polish Forces," April 11, 1946, in naval aide file, box 16, HST/L.

90. Memo of conversation by Durbrow, November 9, 1945, in *FRUS,* V, 1945, 404–9. Polish historians argue that the return of Polish veterans from abroad would have strengthened, not weakened, the prestige of the Warsaw government and that it was the West which deliberately raised obstacles to the repatriation of these men. Kowalski, *Polityka Zagraniczna RP,* pp. 184–85, 191.

91. Kowalski, *Polityka Zagraniczna RP,* p. 188; "General Anders' Polish Second Army Corps As A Source of International Misunderstanding," March 15, 1946, in OSS/DS Intelligence and Research Reports, Roll 9.

92. Nikolai Tolstoy, *The Secret Betrayal* (New York: Charles Scribner's Sons, 1977), pp. 340–41; minutes, council of foreign ministers, July 12, 1946, in *FRUS,* II, 1946, 930.

93. "General Anders' Polish Second Army Corps as a Source of International Misunderstanding."

94. Zubrzycki, *Polish Immigrants in Britain,* p. 58.

95. "Bitter-enders: Anders Refuses to go Home," *Newsweek,* XXVI (July 23, 1945), 45–46; "General Anders' Polish Second Army Corps as a Source of International Misunderstanding."

96. "Poland: Surplus Heroes," *Time,* XLVII (March 25, 1946), 36; U.S., War Department, Intelligence Review, "The Polish Resettlement Corps in Great Britain," in naval aide file, box 18, HST/L. When they learned that their units had to move north of a line extending between Edinburgh and Glasgow prior to disbandment, embittered junior officers of the Polish II Corps said: "We started the war in Russian Siberia; we will finish it in British Siberia." Edward Weintal, "Polish Army Awaits End in Its Own 'British Siberia,'" *Newsweek,* XXVII (January 28, 1946), 35. Anders became such a delicate political issue that the United States denied him a visa to enter the country in 1946 to speak to Polish American organizations.

97. Betts, *Central and South East Europe,* pp. 160–61.

98. This was a major criticism of Polonia by a spokesman for the Coordinating Committee of American-Polish Associations in the East. Report, September 29, 1945,

Skoniecki Papers. This is not to deny that some efforts were made earlier by Polish Americans either to prevent the disbandment of Polish units or to integrate them within the United States Army. For example, see ltr., Januszewski to Byrnes, February 21, 1946, in Komitet Narodowy Amerykanow Pochodzenia Polskiego, *Biuletyn Organizacyjny* (Luty-Marzec, 1946); msg., Adeski to Truman, March 25, 1946, in Truman Papers, official file, HST/L. For American attitudes concerning the admission of refugees into the United States, see "Fortnightly Survey of American Opinion on International Affairs," no. 59, September 19, 1946, in RG 59, box 11, DS/NA.

99. Polish American Congress, *Story of the Polish American Congress,* p. 96.

100. *Chicago Tribune,* June 14, 1947; statement by President Truman, June 16, 1950, in PSF file, HST/L.

101. Polish American Congress, *Story of the Polish American Congress,* p. 85; Polish American Congress, *A Factual Report on the Plight of Displaced Persons in Germany,* pp. 6–7.

102. Thaddeus T. Krysiewicz, "The Polish Immigration Committee in the United States: A Historical Study of the American Committee for the Relief of Polish Immigrants, 1947–1952" (unpublished master's thesis, Fordham University, 1953), pp. 4–35.

CHAPTER VII

1. Polish American Congress, *Story of the Polish American Congress,* p. 52; *Dziennik Zwiazkowy,* February 20, 1945; March 1, 1945; March 3, 1945.

2. Polish American Congress, *Bulletin,* March–April, 1945, p. 4.

3. Quoted from the *Sign* in Polish American Congress, *The Voice of America,* September 27, 1945, p. 2.

4. Polish American Congress, *Story of the Polish American Congress,* p. 70.

5. *Narod Polski,* December 13, 1945; December 27, 1945; June 27, 1946; July 18, 1946; August 7, 1947; *Zgoda,* October 13, 1946.

6. Polish American Congress, *Delegates Newsletter,* May, 1946, p. 1; Polish American Congress, *Story of the Polish American Congress,* pp. 76–77.

7. *Zgoda,* October 13, 1946.

8. Polish American Congress, *Story of the Polish American Congress,* p. 103.

9. Ibid., p. 66.

10. See Chapter I above.

11. Polish American Congress, *Story of the Polish American Congress,* p. 66; Polish American Congress, *Bulletin,* August–September, 1945, p. 2.

12. Ltr., Rozmarek to Truman, October 20, 1945, in Polish American Congress file, PI; Polish American Congress, *Story of the Polish American Congress,* p. 71.

13. *Detroit Free Press,* October 12, 1945.

14. Quoted in *Zgoda,* June 23, 1946.

15. Memo of Polish American Congress "On the Necessity of Rejecting the Yalta Pact to Save the Peace," November 22, 1946, in Rozmarek File, PI.

16. Memo by Rozmarek, November 24, 1946, in ibid.

17. Report, September 29, 1945, Skoniecki Papers; interview with Pelagia Lukaszewska.

18. Irons, "The Test Is Poland," p. 55.
19. Jedrzejewicz, *Polonia Amerykanska,* p. 157.
20. Ibid., pp. 172–74.
21. Ibid., p. 191.
22. Polish American Congress, *Story of the Polish American Congress,* p. 108.
23. Ibid., pp. 99–100. Throughout 1947, the Polish American Congress repeated its recommendations that the UN take up the Polish question. Ibid., pp. 105, 110.
24. *Narod Polski,* February 6, 1947; *Zgoda,* February 2, 1947; *Dziennik Zwiazkowy,* January 20, 1947.
25. Polish American Congress, *Story of the Polish American Congress,* p. 93.
26. Ibid., pp. 80, 88.
27. *Zgoda,* April 15, 1948.
28. Polish American Congress, *Delegates Newsletter,* May, 1946, p. 1.
29. *Narod Polski,* February 6, 1947; Polish American Congress, *Story of the Polish American Congress,* p. 103.
30. Polish American Congress, *Story of the Polish American Congress,* p. 107.
31. *Narod Polski,* April 3, 1947.
32. Jedrzejewicz, *Polonia Amerykanska,* pp. 189, 193.
33. Polish American Congress, *Story of the Polish American Congress,* p. 113.
34. *Dziennik Zwiazkowy,* September 10, 1946.
35. *Zgoda,* September 29, 1946; report, September 29, 1945, Skoniecki Papers.
36. Minutes, Fifth Annual Convention, KNAPP, November 16–17, 1946, p. 15, in PI.
37. *Dziennik Zwiazkowy,* September 10, 1946; September 11, 1946.
38. Polish American Congress, *In Defense of Poland's Western Boundary: An Economic Study* (Chicago: Polish American Congress, n.d.), n.p.; Polish American Congress, *Delegates Newsletter,* May, 1946, p. 1; *Narod Polski,* May 22, 1947; Jedrzejewicz, *Polonia Amerykanska,* p. 192.
39. Polish American Congress, *Delegates Newsletter,* May, 1946, p. 1.
40. Ltr., with attachment, Barry to Byrnes, January 23, 1946, in RG 59, box 6381, DS/NA.
41. Quoted in Cable, "The United States and the Polish Question," p. 264.
42. Lukas, *The Strange Allies,* pp. 53, 143–44.
43. Ltr., Krzycki to Truman, September 13, 1946; msg., Lane to secretary of state, December 21, 1946, in RG 59, box 6381, DS/NA.
44. Memo, by Rozmarek [undated], in Rozmarek file, PI.
45. Louis L. Gerson, *The Hyphenate in Recent American Politics and Diplomacy* (Lawrence: University of Kansas Press, 1964), pp. 173–76. Kowalski speaks of the support of the Council of Democratic Groups of Americans of Polish Descent for the Warsaw government in protesting the state department's withholding of credits to Poland in the spring of 1946. Kowalski, *Polityka Zagraniczna,* pp. 214–15.
46. Ltr., Januszewski to Vandenberg, January 12, 1946, in Vandenberg file, PI.
47. *Dziennik Zwiazkowy,* May 2, 1946.
48. Memo of conversation between Tarnowski and Vandenberg, January 29, 1946, in Vandenberg file, PI.
49. Athan G. Theoharis, *The Yalta Myths: An Issue in United States Politics,*

1945–55 (Columbia: University of Missouri Press, 1970), pp. 40, 55; Arthur H. Vandenberg, Jr., ed., *The Private Papers of Senator Vandenberg* (Boston: Houghton Mifflin, 1952), pp. 313–14.

50. Interview with Pelagia Lukaszewska.

51. *Chicago Tribune,* October 14, 1946; October 27, 1946; October 28, 1946.

52. Petrov, *A Study in Diplomacy,* p. 359.

53. Theoharis claims Rozmarek urged Polish Americans to vote Republican in 1946. Theoharis's documentation does not support the claim. See Athan Theoharis, "The Republican Party and Yalta: Partisan Exploitation of the Polish American Concern over the Conference, 1945–60," *Polish American Studies,* XXVIII (Spring, 1971), 8.

54. Irons, "The Test Is Poland," p. 59.

55. Interview with Pelagia Lukaszewska.

56. Peter Irons, "America's Cold War Crusade: Politics and Foreign Policy, 1942–48" (unpublished Ph.D. dissertation, Boston University, 1973), pp. 349–55.

57. See Table II, ibid., p. 355. The Polish Roman Catholic Union noted that the results of the 1946 election were not entirely advantageous for Polonia because the Polish American delegation in Congress was reduced from nine to seven members. *Narod Polski,* November 14, 1946.

58. Jedrzejewicz, *Polonia Amerykanska,* pp. 188, 201; ltr., Walkowicz to Mikolajczyk, November 22, 1947, in Mikolajczyk Papers, box 50, HI. The effort in some Polish American circles to discredit Mikolajczyk was followed closely by former Ambassador Lane. Ltr., Lane to Keith, January 10, 1948, in Lane Papers, box 72, YU/L.

59. *Dziennik Zwiazkowy,* December 2, 1947.

60. "Protokol Posiedzenia Przedstawicieli Kongresu Polonii Amerykanskiej i Prezydium Polskiego Stronnictwa Ludowego, odbytego dniu 15 grudnia 1947 w Chicago," in Mikolajczyk Papers, box 50, HI.

61. *New York Times,* December 18, 1947; *Dziennik Zwiazkowy,* December 17, 1947. Stefan Korbonski claimed authorship for much of the agreement. Interview with Korbonski.

62. *Zgoda,* January 15, 1948; *Dziennik Zwiazkowy,* December 17, 1947.

63. Jedrzejewicz, *Polonia Amerykanska,* pp. 205–9; report, September 29, 1945, Skoniecki Papers.

64. Ltr., Lane to Keith, April 29, 1948; ltr., Lane to Keith, June 24, 1948; ltr., Sapieha to Lane, September 6, 1948, in Lane Papers, boxes 32 and 73, YU/L; interview with Korbonski; memo of conversation by Elbrick, June 11, 1948, in U.S., Department of State, *Foreign Relations of the United States, 1948.* Vol. IV: *Eastern Europe: The Soviet Union* (Washington, D.C.: United States Government Printing Office, 1974), pp. 421–23. Hereinafter cited as *FRUS,* IV, 1948.

65. Memo of conversation by Stevens, March 8, 1948, in *FRUS,* IV, 1948, 404–6.

66. Samuel L. Sharp, *Poland: White Eagle on a Red Field* (Cambridge, Mass.: Harvard University Press 1953), p. 196.

67. Lane, *I Saw Poland Betrayed,* p. 305.

68. Radio broadcast, April 5, 1947, in Lane Papers, box 98, YU/L.

69. Polish American Congress, *The Story of the Polish American Congress,* pp. 111–12.

70. Ltr., Lane to Frary, February 5, 1948, in Lane Papers, box 72, YU/L.

71. Committee to Stop World Communism. *Once Again: It Is Later than You Think* (Chicago: Committee to Stop World Communism, n.d.).

72. See correspondence in Lane Papers, boxes 72 and 73, YU/L.

73. Ltr., Lesly to Lane, April 21, 1948; ltr., Lane to Plusdrak, May 21, 1948 in Lane Papers, boxes 31 and 73, respectively, YU/L.

CHAPTER VIII

1. Quoted in Merrill A. White, "Some Considerations of United States Foreign Policy toward Eastern Europe, 1941–1964," *Polish Review,* X (1965), 8.

Bibliography

UNPUBLISHED MANUSCRIPTS

American Relief for Poland file, Jozef Pilsudski Institute of America, New York, New York.

Charles E. Bohlen, Papers, Library of Congress and National Archives, Washington, D.C.

James F. Byrnes, Papers, The Robert Muldrow Cooper Library, Clemson University, Clemson, South Carolina.

Joseph E. Davies, Diary and Papers, Library of Congress, Washington, D.C.

Stanton Griffis, Papers, Harry S. Truman Library, Independence, Missouri.

Harry L. Hopkins, Papers, Franklin D. Roosevelt Library, Hyde Park, New York.

Hugh Jackson, Papers, Herbert H. Lehman Papers and Suite, School of International Affairs, Columbia University, New York, New York.

R.G.A. Jackson, Papers, Herbert H. Lehman Papers and Suite, School of International Affairs, Columbia University, New York, New York.

Arthur Bliss Lane, Papers, Sterling Library, Yale University, New Haven, Connecticut.

Stanislaw Mikolajczyk, Papers, Hoover Institution on War, Revolution, and Peace, Stanford, California.

Dillon S. Myer, Papers, Harry S. Truman Library, Independence, Missouri.

Philleo Nash, Papers, Harry S. Truman Library, Independence, Missouri.

Polish American Congress file, Jozef Pilsudski Institute of America, New York, New York.

Records of the Department of State, National Archives, Washington, D.C.

Records of the Joint Chiefs of Staff, National Archives, Washington, D.C.

Records of the Office of Strategic Services, National Archives, Washington, D.C.

Records of the United Nations Relief and Rehabilitation Administration, United Nations Archives, New York, New York.

Records of the War Refugee Board, Franklin D. Roosevelt Library, Hyde Park, New York.

Franklin D. Roosevelt, Papers, Franklin D. Roosevelt Library, Hyde Park, New York.

Samuel I. Rosenman, Papers, Harry S. Truman Library, Independence, Missouri.

Charles Rozmarek file, Jozef Pilsudski Institute of America, New York, New York.

A.A. Skoniecki, selected papers in author's files.

Edward R. Stettinius, Jr., Papers, University of Virginia Library, Charlottesville, Virginia.

Henry L. Stimson, Diary and Papers, Sterling Library, Yale University, New Haven, Connecticut.
Myron C. Taylor, Papers, Harry S. Truman Library, Independence, Missouri.
Harry S. Truman, Papers, Harry S. Truman Library, Independence, Missouri.
Arthur H. Vandenberg file, Jozef Pilsudski Institute of America, New York, New York.
George L. Warren, Papers, Harry S. Truman Library, Independence, Missouri.

INTERVIEWS, LETTERS, AND ORAL HISTORY

Interview, James Bochan, May 25, 1980, Cookeville, Tennessee.
Interview, Waclaw Jedrejewicz, June 24, 1980, New York, New York.
Interview B.B. Kopecki (pseud.), June 28, 1979, Warsaw, Poland.
Interview, Stefan Korbonski, June 20, 1980, Washington, D.C.
Interview, Pelagia Lukaszewska, August 1, 1980, North Miami Beach, Florida.
Interview (telephone), Wanda Rozmarek, February 8, 1980.
Interview (telephone), Paul Zaleski, June 18, 1980.
Letter, Stefan Korbonski to author, May 18, 1981.
Letter, Paul Zaleski to author, May 4, 1981.
Oral history, Sir Robert G.A. Jackson, Columbia University, New York, New York.

UNPUBLISHED STUDIES

Cable, John N. "The United States and the Polish Question, 1939–1948." Ph.D. diss., Vanderbilt University, 1972.
Conover, Denise O'Neal. "James F. Byrnes, Germany and the Cold War, 1946." Ph.D. diss., Washington State University, 1978.
Glinka-Janczewski, George H. "American Policy toward Poland under the Truman Administration." Ph.D. diss., Georgetown University, 1965.
Irons, Peter. "America's Cold War Crusade: Politics and Foreign Policy, 1942–1948." Ph.D. diss., Boston University, 1973.
Krysiewicz, Thaddeus T. "The Polish Immigration Committee in the United States: A Historical Study of the American Committee for the Relief of Polish Immigrants, 1947–1952." Master's thesis, Fordham University, 1953.

PUBLISHED DOCUMENTS

Beitzell, Robert. ed. *Tehran, Yalta, Potsdam: The Soviet Protocols.* Hattiesburg, Mississippi: Academic International Press, 1970.
Embassy of Poland. *Poland, Germany and European Peace: Official Documents, 1944–48.* London: Embassy of Poland, 1948.

172 BITTER LEGACY

Ministry for Foreign Affairs of the Polish People's Republic. *Documents on the Hostile Policy of the United States Government toward People's Poland.* Warsaw: 1953.

Poland. Central Board of Planning. *Polish National Economic Plan.* Warsaw: Central Board of Planning, 1946.

Poland. *Dziennik Ustaw.* 1945–1948.

Poland. *Rocznik Statystyczny.* 1947–1948.

Polish American Congress. *Polish American Congress, Inc., 1944–1948: Selected Documents.* Chicago: Polish American Congress, 1948.

Polish American Congress. *Story of the Polish American Congress in Press Clippings, 1944–1948.* Chicago: Alliance Printers and Publishers, 1948.

Polish Information Service. *The Provisional Constitution of February 20, 1947.* New York: Polish Information Service, 1947.

Polska i Wielka Brytania przed i po Konferencji Krmyskiej: Dokumenty. London: 1946.

Public Papers of the Presidents of the United States: Harry S. Truman, 1945–48. Washington, D.C.: United States Government Printing Office, 1961–1964.

United Nations Relief and Rehabilitation Administration, *8th Report to Congress on Operations of UNRRA.* Washington, D.C.: United States Government Printing Office, 1946.

United Nations Relief and Rehabilitation Administration. *Journal,* V (August 9, 1946).

U.S., *Congressional Record.* 1945–1948.

U.S., The Department of State. *Bulletin.* 1945–1948.

U.S., Department of State. *Foreign Relations of the United States: Diplomatic Papers. The Conference of Berlin (The Potsdam Conference), 1945.* Vols. I–II. Washington, D.C.: United States Government Printing Office, 1960.

U.S., Department of State. *Foreign Relations of the United States: Diplomatic papers, 1945.* Vol. II: *General: Political and Economic Matters.* Washington, D.C.: United States Government Printing Office, 1967.

U.S., Department of State. *Foreign Relations of the United States: Diplomatic Papers, 1945.* Vol. V: *Europe.* Washington, D.C.: United States Government Printing Office, 1967.

U.S., Department of State. *Foreign Relations of the United States, 1946.* Vol. II: *Council of Foreign Ministers.* Washington, D.C.: United States Government Printing Office, 1970.

U.S., Department of State. *Foreign Relations of the United States, 1946.* Vol. V: *The British Commonwealth; Western and Central Europe.* Washington, D.C.: United States Government Printing Office, 1969.

U.S., Department of State. *Foreign Relations of the United States, 1946.* Vol. VI: *Eastern Europe; The Soviet Union.* Washington, D.C.: United States Government Printing Office, 1969.

U.S., Department of State. *Foreign Relations of the United States, 1946.* Vol. VII: *The Near East and Africa.* Washington, D.C.: United States Government Printing Office, 1969.

U.S., Department of State. *Foreign Relations of the United States, 1947.* Vol. III: *The British Commonwealth; Europe.* Washington, D.C.: United States Government Printing Office, 1972.

U.S., Department of State. *Foreign Relations of the United States, 1947.* Vol. IV: *Eastern Europe; The Soviet Union.* Washington, D.C.: United States Government Printing Office, 1972.

U.S., Department of State. *Foreign Relations of the United States, 1948.* Vol. IV: *Eastern Europe; The Soviet Union.* Washington, D.C.: United States Government Printing Office, 1974.

U.S., *Statutes at Large,* LXI.

MEMOIRS, AUTOBIOGRAPHIES, AND RECOLLECTIONS

Acheson, Dean. *Present at the Creation: My Years in the State Department.* New York: New American Library, 1970.

Anders, W. *An Army in Exile: The Story of the Second Polish Corps.* London: Macmillan, 1949.

Bierut, Boleslaw. *O Partii.* Warsaw: Ksiazka i Wiedza, 1952.

Blum, John M., ed. *The Price of Vision: The Diary of Henry A. Wallace, 1942–1946.* Boston: Houghton Mifflin, 1973.

Bohlen, Charles E. *Witness to History, 1929–1969.* New York: Norton, 1973.

Brant, Irving. *The New Poland.* New York: Universe, 1946.

Bregman, A., ed. *Faked Elections in Poland as Reported by Foreign Observers.* London: Polish Freedom Movement. n.d.

Byrnes, James F. *All in One Lifetime.* New York: Harper, 1958.

Byrnes, James F. *Speaking Frankly.* New York: Harper, 1947.

Campbell, Thomas M., and Herring, George C. *The Diaries of Edward R. Stettinius, Jr.* New York: New Viewpoints, 1975.

Churchill, Winston S. *Triumph and Tragedy.* Boston: Houghton Mifflin, 1953.

Ciechanowski, Jan. *Defeat in Victory.* Garden City, N.Y.: Doubleday, 1947.

Deane, John R. *The Strange Alliance: The Story of American Efforts at Wartime Co-operation with Russia.* London: John Murray, 1947.

Dilks, David. ed. *The Diaries of Sir Alexander Cadogan, 1938–1945.* New York: G.P. Putnam's, 1972.

Dziewanowski, M.K., ed. *Poland To-Day as Seen by Foreign Observers.* 2nd ed.; London: Polish Freedom Movement, 1946.

Eden, Anthony. *The Memoirs of Anthony Eden, Earl of Avon: The Reckoning.* Boston: Houghton Mifflin, 1965.

Ferrell, Robert H., ed. *Off the Record: The Private Papers of Harry S. Truman.* New York: Harper and Row, 1980.

Gomulka, Wladyslaw. *Artykuly i Przemowienia.* 2 vols.; Warsaw: Ksiazka i Wiedza, 1962–1964.

Gomulka-Wieslaw, Wladyslaw. *W Walce o Demokracje Ludowa.* 2 vols.; Lodz: Spoldzielna Wydawnicza Ksiazka, 1947.

Grew, Joseph C. *Turbulent Era: A Diplomatic Record of Forty Years, 1904–45.* 2 vols.; Boston: Houghton Mifflin, 1952.

Griffis, Stanton. *Lying in State.* Garden City, N.Y.: Doubleday, 1952.

Harriman, W. Averell, and Abel, Elie. *Special Envoy to Churchill and Stalin, 1941–46.* New York: Random House, 1975.

Henderson, H.W. *The Great Polish Election Fraud.* Glasgow: 1947.

Korbonski, Stefan. *Warsaw in Chains.* New York: Macmillan, 1959.

Lane, Arthur Bliss. *I Saw Poland Betrayed: An American Ambassador Reports to the American People.* Indianapolis: Bobbs-Merrill, 1948.

Lerski, George J., comp. *Herbert Hoover and Poland: A Documentary History of a Friendship.* Stanford: Hoover Institution Press, 1977.

Mikolajczyk, Stanislaw. *The Rape of Poland: Pattern of Soviet Aggression.* New York: McGraw Hill, 1948.

Milosz, Czeslaw. *The Captive Mind.* New York: Vintage, 1955.

Nagorski, Zygmunt. *Ludzie Mego Czasu: Sylwetki.* Paris: Ksiegarnia Polska w Paryzu, 1964.

Polish American Congress. *A Factual Report on the Plight of Displaced Persons in Germany.* Chicago: Polish American Congress, 1947.

Redding, Jack. *Inside the Democratic Party.* Indianapolis: Bobbs-Merrill, 1958.

Smith, Walter Bedell. *My Three Years in Moscow.* Philadelphia: J.B. Lippincott, 1950.

Strong, Anna Louise. *I Saw the New Poland.* Boston: Little Brown, 1946.

Stypulkowski, Zbigniew. *Invitation to Moscow.* London: 1952.

Super, Paul. *Twenty-Five Years with the Poles.* New York: Paul Super Memorial Fund, 1947.

Truman, Harry S. *Memoirs by Harry S. Truman.* 2 vols.; Garden City, N.Y.: Doubleday, 1955–1956.

Truman, Margaret. *Harry S. Truman.* New York: William Morrow, 1973.

SECONDARY WORKS

Alton, Thad Paul. *Polish Postwar Economy.* Westport, Conn.: Greenwood, 1974.

American Relief for Poland. *The Facts You Want To Know About: American Relief for Poland.* Chicago: American Relief for Poland, 1946.

Arnold, Stanislaw, and Zychowski, Marian. *Zarys Historii Polski: Od Poczatkow Panstwa do Czasow Najnowszych.* N.C.: Wydawnictwo Polonia, 1962.

Barghoorn, Frederick C. *The Soviet Image of the United States: A Study in Distortion.* New York: Harcourt Brace, 1950.

Bernstein, Barton J., ed. *Politics and Policies of the Truman Administration.* Chicago: Quadrangle, 1970.

Bethell, Nicholas. *Gomulka: His Poland, His Communism.* New York: Holt, Rinehart and Winston, 1969.

Bethell, Nicholas. *The Last Secret: The Delivery to Stalin of Over Two Million Russians by Britain and the United States.* New York: Basic, 1974.

Betts, R.R., ed. *Central and South East Europe, 1945–1948.* Westport, Conn.: Greenwood Press, 1971.

Brzezinski, Zbigniew K. *The Soviet Bloc: Unity and Conflict.* Cambridge, Mass.: Harvard Univerity Press, 1960.

Burks, R.V. *The Dynamics of Communism in Eastern Europe.* Princeton: Princeton University Press, 1961.

Campbell, John C. *The United States in World Affairs, 1945–47.* New York: Harper, 1947.

Campbell, Thomas M. *Masquerade Peace: America's UN Policy, 1944–1945.* Tallahassee: Florida State University Press, 1973.

Committee to Stop World Communism. *Once Again It Is Later Than You Think.* Chicago: Committee to Stop World Communism, n.d.

Council of Polish Political Parties. *For the Freedom of Poland and Central-Eastern Europe: Documents, 1946–47.* London: 1947.

Davies, Raymond Arthur. *The Truth about Poland.* Toronto: 1946.

Davis, Lynn Etheridge. *The Cold War Begins: Soviet-American Conflict over Eastern Europe.* Princeton: Princeton University Press, 1974.

Deutscher, Isaac. *Stalin: A Political Biography.* New York: Vintage, 1960.

Divine, Robert A. *Foreign Policy and U.S. Presidential Elections, 1940–1948.* New York: New Viewpoints, 1974.

Divine, Robert A. *Since 1945: Politics and Diplomacy in Recent American History.* 2d ed.; New York: John Wiley and Sons, 1979.

Drzewieniecki, W.M. *The German-Polish Frontier.* Chicago: Polish Western Association of America, 1959.

Dziewanowski, M.K. *The Communist Party of Poland: An Outline of History.* Cambridge, Mass.: Harvard University Press, 1959.

Epstein, Julius. *Operation Keelhaul: The Story of Forced Repatriation from 1944 to the Present.* Old Greenwich, Conn.: Devin-Adair, 1973.

Feis, Herbert. *Between War and Peace: The Potsdam Conference.* Princeton: Princeton University Press, 1960.

Feis, Herbert. *From Trust to Terror: The Onset of the Cold War, 1945–1950.* New York: Norton, 1970.

Ferrell, Robert H., ed. *The American Secretaries of State and Their Diplomacy.* Vol. XIV: *James F. Byrnes* by George Curry. New York: Cooper Square, 1965.

Gaddis, John Lewis. *The United States and the Origins of the Cold War, 1941–1947.* New York: Columbia University Press, 1972.

Gerson, Louis L. *The Hyphenate in Recent American Politics and Diplomacy.* Lawrence: University of Kansas Press, 1964.

Gora, Wladyslaw. *Polska Rzeczpospolita Ludowa, 1944–1974.* Warszawa: Ksiazka i Wiedza, 1974.

Gumkowski, Janusz, and Leszczynski, Kazimierz. *Poland under Nazi Occupation.* Warsaw: Polonia Publishing House, 1961.

Halecki, L. *A History of Poland.* New York: Roy, 1943.

Halle, Louis. *The Cold War as History.* New York: Harper, 1967.

Hammond, Paul Y. *The Cold War Years: American Foreign Policy Since 1945.* New York: Harcourt, Brace and World, 1969.
Henderson, H.W. *Why Don't the Poles Go Home?* Glasgow: 1946.
Herz, Martin F. *Beginnings of the Cold War.* Bloomington: Indiana University Press, 1966.
Hiscocks, Richard. *Poland: Bridge for the Abyss?: An Interpretation of Developments in Post-War Poland.* London: Oxford University Press, 1963.
Jedrzejewicz, Waclaw. *Polonia Amerykanska w Polityce Polskiej: Historia Komitetu Narodowego Amerykanow Polskiego Pochodzenia.* New York: National Committee of Americans of Polish Descent, 1954.
Jozwiak, F. *P.P.R. w Walce o Wyzwolenie Narodowe i Spoleczne.* Warsaw: Ksiazka i Wiedza, 1952.
Kacewicz, George V. *Great Britain, The Soviet Union and the Polish Government-in-Exile, 1939–1945.* The Hague: Martinus Nijhoff, 1979.
Kertesz, Stephen D., ed. *The Fate of East Central Europe: Hopes and Failures of American Foreign Policy.* Notre Dame, Ind.: University of Notre Dame Press, 1956.
Kolko, Gabriel. *The Politics of War: the World and United States Foreign Policy, 1943–45.* New York: Random House, 1968.
Kolko, Joyce and Gabriel. *The Limits of Power: The World and United States Foreign Policy, 1945–54.* New York: Harper and Row, 1972.
Kolomyjczyk, Norbert. *PPR: 1944–1945.* Warsaw: Ksiazka i Wiedza, 1965.
Korbonski, Andrzej. *Politics of Socialist Agriculture in Poland 1945–1960.* New York: Columbia University Press, 1965.
Korbonski, Stefan. *The Polish Underground State: A Guide to the Underground, 1939–1945.* Boulder, Colo.: East European Quarterly, 1978.
Kovrig, Bennett. *The Myth of Liberation: East-Central Europe in U.S. Diplomacy and Politics Since 1941.* Baltimore: Johns Hopkins University Press, 1973.
Kowalski, W.T. *Polityka Zagraniczna RP.* Warsaw: Ksiazka i Wiedza, 1971.
Kowalski, W.T. *Walka Dyplomatyczna o Miejsce Polski w Europie, 1939–1945.* Warsaw: Ksiazka i Wiedza, 1970.
Kozlowska, Helena, ed. *W Dziesiata Rocznice Powstania Polskiej Partii Robotniczej: Materialy i Dokumenty, Stycien 1942-Grudzien 1948.* Warsaw: Ksiazka i Wiedza, 1952.
Kwiatkowski, Jan K. *Komunisci w Polsce: Rodowod, Taktyka, Ludzie.* Brussels: Polski Instytut Wydawniczy, 1946.
LaFeber, Walter. *America, Russia, and the Cold War, 1945–1966.* New York: John Wiley, 1967.
Lukacs, John. *A New History of the Cold War.* New York: Anchor, 1966.
Lukas, Richard C. *The Strange Allies: The United States and Poland, 1941–1945.* Knoxville: University of Tennessee Press, 1978.
Lundestad, Geir. *The American Non-Policy towards Eastern Europe, 1943–47: Universalism in an Area Not of Essential Interest to the United States.* Oslo: Universitetsforlaget, 1978.

Mastny, Vojtech. *Russia's Road to the Cold War: Diplomacy, Warfare and the Politics of Communism, 1941-1945.* New York: Columbia University Press, 1979.

McNeill, William H. *America, Britain and Russia: Their Cooperation and Conflict, 1941-1946.* London: Oxford University Press, 1953.

Mee, Charles L., Jr. *Meeting at Potsdam.* New York: Dell, 1975.

Mid-European Studies Center. *W Obronie Wolnosci i Niepodleglosci. Dokumenty: Lipiec, 1947-Maj, 1948.* London: 1948.

Minc, Hilary. *Poland's Economy: Present and Future.* New York: Polish Research Information Service, 1949.

Pastusiak, Longin. *Roosevelt a Sprawa Polska.* Warsaw: Ksiazka i Wiedza, 1980.

Paterson, Thomas G., ed. *Containment and the Cold War: American Foreign Policy Since 1945.* Reading, Mass: Addison-Wesley, 1973.

Paterson, Thomas G. *On Every Front: The Making of the Cold War.* New York: Norton, 1979.

Paterson, Thomas G. *Soviet-American Confrontation: Postwar Reconstruction and the Origins of the Cold War.* Baltimore: Johns Hopkins University Press, 1973.

Petrov, Vladimir. *A Study in Diplomacy: The Story of Arthur Bliss Lane.* Chicago: Henry Regnery, 1971.

Pobog - Malinowski, Wladyslaw. *Najnowsza Historia Polityczna Polski, 1864-1945.* Tom Trzeci: *Okres 1939-1945.* London: Gryf, 1960.

Polish American Congress. *Dziesiec Lat Walki i Krzywdy.* Chicago: Komisji Wspolpracy z Poloniami w Innych Krajach, Kongresu Polonii Amerykanskiej, 1949.

Polish American Congress. *In Defense of Poland's Western Boundary: An Economic Study.* Chicago: Polish American Congress, n.d.

Polonsky, Antony. *The Great Powers and the Polish Question, 1941-1945: A Documentary Study in Cold War Origins.* London: London School of Economics and Political Science, 1976.

Polska Akademia Nauk, Instytut Historii. *Polska Ludowa: Materialy i Studia.* Vol. I. Warsaw: Panstwowe Wydawnictwo Naukowe, 1962.

Pragier, Adam. *Czas Przeszly Dokonany.* London: B. Swiderski, 1966.

Price, Harry B. *The Marshall Plan and Its Meaning.* Ithaca: Cornell University Press, 1955.

Rose, Lisle. *Dubious Victory: The United States and the End of World War II.* Kent, Ohio: Kent State University Press, 1973.

Rozek, Edward J. *Allied Wartime Diplomacy: A Pattern in Poland.* New York: John Wiley, 1958.

Seton-Watson, Hugh. *The East European Revolution.* New York: Frederick A. Praeger, 1951.

Sharp, Samuel L. *Poland: White Eagle on a Red Field.* Cambridge, Mass.: Harvard University Press, 1953.

Starr, Richard F. *Poland, 1944-1962: The Sovietization of a Captive People.* Baton Rouge: Louisiana State University Press, 1962.

Terlecki, T. *Polska a Zachod: Proba Syntezy.* London: Naklad Stowarzyszenia Pisarzy Polskich, 1947.

Theoharis, Athan G. *The Yalta Myths: An Issue in U.S. Politics, 1945–1955.* Columbia: University of Missouri Press, 1970.

Tolstoy, Nikolai. *The Secret Betrayal.* New York: Charles Scribner's, 1977.

Ulam, Adam B. *Expansion and Coexistence: The History of Soviet Foreign Policy, 1917–67.* New York: Frederick A. Praeger, 1968.

Ulam, Adam B. *The Rivals: America and Russia since World War II.* New York: Penguin, 1976.

Ulam, Adam B. *Titoism and the Cominform.* Westport, Conn.: Greenwood, 1971.

Ullman, Walter. *The United States in Prague, 1945–1948.* Boulder, Colo.: East European Quarterly, 1978.

Wandycz, Piotr S. *The United States and Poland.* Cambridge, Mass.: Harvard University Press, 1980.

de Weydenthal, Jan B. *The Communists of Poland: An Historical Outline.* Stanford: Hoover Institution Press, 1978.

Wiewiora, Boleslaw. *Granica Polsko-Niemiecka w Swietle Prawa Miedzynarodowego.* Poznan: Instytut Zachodni, 1957.

Williams, William A. *The Tragedy of American Diplomacy.* New York: Dell, 1972.

Wiskemann, Elizabeth. *Germany's Eastern Neighbours: Problems Relating to the Oder-Neisse Line and the Czech Frontier Regions.* London: Oxford University Press, 1956.

Woodbridge, George. *UNRRA: The History of the United Nations Relief and Rehabilitation Administration.* 3 vols.; New York: Columbia University Press, 1950.

Yergin, Daniel. *Shattered Peace.* Boston: Houghton Mifflin, 1977.

Zabiello, Stanislaw. *O Rzad i Granice: Walka Dyplomatyczna o Sprawe Polska w II Wojnie Swiatowej.* Warszawa: Instytut Wydawniczy Pax, 1970.

Zachodnia Agencja Prasowa. *1939–1945: War Losses in Poland.* Poznan: Wydawnictwo Zachodnie, 1960.

de Zayas, Alfred M. *Nemesis at Potsdam: The Anglo-Americans and the Expulsion of the Germans.* London: Routledge and Kegan Paul, 1977.

Zhdanov, Andrei. *The International Situation.* Moscow: Foreign Languages Publishing House, 1947.

Zubrzycki, Jerzy. *Polish Immigrants in Britain: A Study of Adjustment.* The Hague: Martinus Nijhoff, 1956.

ARTICLES AND PERIODICALS

Adler, Les K., and Paterson, Thomas G. "Red Fascism: The Merger of Nazi Germany and Soviet Russia in the American Image of Totalitarianism, 1930–1950's," *American Historical Review,* LXXV (April, 1970), 1046–64.

Barghoorn, Frederick C. "The Soviet Union between War and Cold War,"

Annals of the American Academy of Political and Social Science, CCLXIII (May, 1949), 1–8.

"Bitter-enders: Anders Refuses To Go Home," *Newsweek,* XXVI (July 23, 1945), 45–46.

Black, C. E. "Soviet Policy in Eastern Europe," *Annals of the American Academy of Political and Social Science,* CCLXIII (May, 1949), 152–64.

Boyle, Peter G. "The British Foreign Office View of Soviet-American Relations, 1945–46," *Diplomatic History,* III (Summer, 1979), 307–20.

Cable, John N. "Arthur Bliss Lane: Cold Warrior in Warsaw, 1945–47," *Polish American Studies,* XXX (Autumn, 1973), 66–82.

Divine, Robert A. "The Cold War and the Election of 1948," *Journal of American History,* LIX (June, 1972), 90–110.

Dobroszycki, Lucjan. "Restoring Jewish Life in Post-War Poland," *Soviet Jewish Affairs,* III (1973), 58–72.

Garrett, Stephen. "Eastern European Ethnic Groups and American Foreign Policy," *Political Science Quarterly,* XCIII (Summer, 1978), 301–23.

Garson, Robert. "The Role of Eastern Europe in America's Containment Policy, 1945–48," *Journal of American Studies,* XIII (April, 1979), 73–92.

Irons, Peter H. "The Test is Poland: Polish Americans and the Origins of the Cold War," *Polish American Studies,* XXX (Autumn, 1973), 5–63.

Janczewski, George H. "The Significance of the Polish Vote in the American National Election Campaign of 1948," *Polish Review,* XIII (1968), 101–9.

Komitet Narodowy Amerykanow Pochodzenia Polskiego, *Biuletyn Organizacyjny.* 1945–48.

Lada, J. "Soviet Policy toward Poland," *Catholic World,* CLXV (June, 1947), 271–72.

Lane, Arthur Bliss, "How Russia Rules Poland," *Life,* XXIII (July 14, 1947), 98–100, 103–4, 106, 109–110, 112.

Landau, Z. "Poland and America: The Economic Connection, 1918–39," *Polish American Studies,* XXXII (Autumn, 1975), 38–50.

"Letter from Stalin," *Newsweek,* XXV (May 28, 1945), 56.

Lockhart, Freda Bruce. "Meeting with Mikolajczyk," *Nineteenth Century and After,* CXLIII (January, 1948), 1–11.

Lockhart, Freda Bruce. "The Polish Pantomime," *Nineteenth Century and After,* CXLI (February, 1947), 88–91.

Mark, Eduard. " 'Today Has Been a Historical One:' Harry S. Truman's Diary of the Potsdam Conference," *Diplomatic History,* IV (Summer, 1980), 317–26.

Mastny, Vojtech. "The Cassandra in the Foreign Commissariat: Maxim Litvinov and the Cold War," *Foreign Affairs,* LIV (January, 1976), 366–76.

Paterson, Thomas G. "Potsdam, the Atomic Bomb and the Cold War: A Discussion with James F. Byrnes," *Pacific Historical Review,* XLI (May, 1972), 225–30.

Paterson, Thomas G. "Presidential Foreign Policy, Public Opinion, and Congress: The Truman Years," *Diplomatic History,* III (Winter, 1979), 1–18.

"The Peace: Red Seeds of a Polish Civil War," *Newsweek,* XXVII (May 27, 1946), 36.

Pienkos, Donald E. "The Polish American Congress: An Appraisal," *Polish American Studies,* XXXVI (Autumn, 1979), 5–43.

"Poland: Exit the Emigres," *Newsweek,* XXVI (July 16, 1945), 50, 52.

"Poland: Report from Warsaw," *Time,* XLVII (May 13, 1946), 40, 45.

"Poland: Surplus Heroes," *Time,* XLVII (March 25, 1946), 36.

"Poland: The House on Szucha Avenue," *Time,* XLVIII (December, 9, 1946), 32–33.

"Poles: Refuge in Britain," *Newsweek,* XXVII (June 3, 1946), 42–43.

Polish American Congress. *Bulletin.* 1945.

Polish American Congress. *Delegates Newsletter.* 1946–48.

Polish Embassy in Washington. *Poland of Today.* 1946–48.

"R," "The Fate of Polish Socialism," *Foreign Affairs,* XXVIII (October, 1949), 125–42.

Theoharis, Athan G. "The Republican Party and Yalta: Partisan Exploitation of the Polish American Concern over the Conference, 1945–60," *Polish American Studies,* XXVIII (Spring, 1971), 5–19.

Thompson, Dorothy. "Poland Two Years after Yalta," *American Mercury,* LXIV (May, 1947), 534–41.

Thomson, S. Harrison. "The New Poland," *Foreign Policy Reports,* XXIII (December 1, 1947), 226–34.

Thomson, S. Harrison, and Ringwood, Ona K. D. "Problems of Polish Foreign Policy," *Foreign Policy Reports,* XXIII (December 1, 1947), 235–36.

Weintal, Edward. "Polish Army Awaits End in Its Own 'British Siberia,' " *Newsweek,* XXVII (January 28, 1946), 35.

White, Merrill A. "Some Considerations of United States Foreign Policy toward Eastern Europe, 1941–64," *Polish Review,* X (1965), 3–42.

Wolf, S. "The Polish Elections and After," *Contemporary Review,* CLXXI (March, 1947), 145–49.

Wycislo, A.J. "American Catholic Relief for Poland," *Polish American Studies,* XIX (1962), 100–7.

"Yet Once Again: Poland," *Catholic World,* CLXIV (February, 1947), 391–93.

Zlotowska, M. "I Came Back from Poland," *Harper's Magazine,* CXCIII (November, 1946), 428–29.

Zyzniewski, Stanley. "The Soviet Economic Impact on Poland," *American Slavic and East European Review,* XVIII (April, 1959), 205–25.

NEWSPAPERS

Chicago Tribune. 1945–1947.
Detroit Free Press. 1945–1947.
Dziennik Polski. 1946.
Dziennik Zwiazkowy. 1945–1948.

Gazeta Ludowa. 1945–1947.
Glos Ludu. 1945–1947.
Narod Polski. 1945–1948.
New York Times. 1945–1948.
Tydzien. 1947.
Zgoda. 1945–1948.
Zycie Warszawy. 1945–1947.

Index